W9-DGV-382

WITHDRAWN

Carlos Fuentes, Mexico, and Modernity

Maarten van Delden

Vanderbilt University Press

This publication is made from recycled paper and meets the minimum require-
ments of American National Standard for Information Sciences — Permanence of
Paper for Printed Library Materials. ∞

Library of Congress Cataloging-in-Publication Data

Van Delden, Maarten, 1958-
   Carlos Fuentes, Mexico and modernity / by Maarten van Delden. --
1st ed.
     p. cm.
   Includes bibliographical references (p.) and index.
   ISBN 0-8265-1295-X (alk. paper)
   1. Fuentes, Carlos--Criticism and interpretation. 2. Mexico--In
literature. I. Title.
PQ7297.F793Z933 1997
863--dc21   97-33812
                                        CIP

Manufactured in the United States of America

Contents

for Illa

Acknowledgments

For support and encouragement offered during the time I was working on this book, I am grateful to Walter Abish, Ernst van Alphen, David Damrosch, Leslie Fishbein, Harald Hendrix, Zoltan Kemeny, Luz Rodríguez Carranza, Enrico Mario Santí, and George Yúdice, as well as to my parents, Margreet van Deursen and Henk van Delden, and to my brother, Aarnout van Delden. A grant from the U.S.–Mexico Fund for Culture allowed me to make several especially productive trips to Mexico in 1996. In Mexico, Danubio Torres Fierro helped me locate some materials that were of great value to my research, and Alberto Ruy Sánchez gave generously of his time to discuss with me the intricacies of the Mexican intellectual world; I am indebted to them both. In New York, my research assistants Carrie Barker and Camilla Fojas provided me with crucial help in the final phases of this project. I also benefited from the generosity of Don Skemer, curator of manuscripts in the Manuscripts Division of the Department of Rare Books and Special Collections of the Princeton University Library, who gave me access to some of the Carlos Fuentes papers at Princeton while these papers were still being indexed. My deepest thanks, finally, are for my beloved wife and constant companion, Illa Cha. I dedicate this book to her.

A Note on Translations

Where no information is provided on the translation of a text from Spanish or French into English, the translation is my own.

Carlos Fuentes, Mexico, and Modernity

CHAPTER I

Carlos Fuentes in the 1950s

The 1950s were a period of expansion and modernization in Mexican literary and cultural life. The initiation of new publishing ventures, the creation of cultural supplements by Mexico City's newspapers and magazines, the establishment of fellowships to support writers, and the emergence of a new reading public offered new opportunities for Mexico's writers.[1] One of the writers to benefit from these developments was Carlos Fuentes. He published his first book, a collection of short stories entitled *Los días enmascarados* (1954), in "Los Presentes," a series founded by Juan José Arreola in 1950.[2] He established a close relationship with Fernando Benítez, the man credited with pioneering the formula of the cultural supplement in Mexico,[3] and he became a regular contributor to the publications run by Benítez, as well as to numerous others. Fuentes also received financial support through the writer's program funded by the Instituto Nacional de Bellas Artes, support that helped him write his first novel, *La región más transparente* (1958).

It has been argued that the opening of new spaces in the Mexican literary and cultural world resulted in the professionalization of the Mexican writer, a process that entailed, among other things, the achievement of a previously unknown degree of autonomy with respect to the state, which in postrevolutionary Mexico had exercised significant control over Mexican cultural life.[4] Fuentes is widely regarded as the consummate example of this development.[5] But the modernization of the Mexican cultural sphere was not only reflected in the Mexican writer's relative emancipation from the tutelage of the state. It also entailed the opening up of Mexican culture to the outside world.

A key role in breaking down the barriers separating Mexican culture from the rest of the world was played by Octavio Paz, who returned to Mexico in 1953, after nine years abroad. Paz himself describes these years as a period in which he, along with a small group of younger intellectuals, tried to change the literary and artistic life of Mexico by "opening windows, introducing movements, works, and names that were unknown in Mexico."[6] Among the Mexican writers who were his allies in this effort to make Mexican culture more cosmopolitan, Paz singles out Carlos Fuentes.

Fuentes first made his presence felt in the Mexican literary world with the publication of *Los días enmascarados*, but he also claimed an important position for himself as co-editor, with Emmanuel Carballo, of the *Revista Mexicana de Literatura* for a two-year period running from September 1955 to August 1957. The twelve issues Fuentes and Carballo put out document a sustained attempt to develop and defend a cosmopolitan view of Mexican culture. Thus, the first issue of the *Revista* includes an essay by Carlos Blanco Aguinaga on Juan Rulfo's *Pedro Páramo*, in which Rulfo's work is placed in the context of the inward turn in literature pioneered by European writers like James Joyce, Marcel Proust, and Franz Kafka.[7] It also includes an essay by Jorge Portilla attacking what he calls the McCarthyism of certain nationalist critics in Mexico who wished to purge from the Mexican literary community writers they regarded as insufficiently Mexican, among them Paz, Arreola, Rulfo, and Fuentes.[8] This issue closes—as do subsequent issues—with a miscellaneous section of unsigned pieces under the heading "Talón de Aquiles." These pieces, written by Fuentes, include in the first issue an attack on literary and cultural nationalism, backed up by a lengthy quotation from Jorge Luis Borges's "El escritor argentino y la tradición,"[9] a comment on the Colombian literary journal *Mito*, which had recently published an article praising

Borges for recognizing the fact that Latin Americans have a capacity for the universal,[10] and a complaint concerning the difficulty of overcoming the retrograde nationalism that dominates Mexican cultural life, a complaint that concludes with a quotation from Octavio Paz to the effect that Mexican nationalism in the arts is essentially a consequence of European exoticism.[11]

The orientation established in the first issue of the *Revista* was continued in subsequent issues. A few examples will prove the point. Rafael Gutiérrez Girardot discusses Alfonso Reyes's vision of Latin America's incorporation into "Universal History and Western culture."[12] Emmanuel Carballo contributes an essay in which he claims that "Nationalism in literature is like original sin: one is born with it. . . . It is not necessary for us to defend it."[13] Jaime Torres Bodet argues that the local color of a work has nothing to do with its national character, for somebody who writes a commentary on Aristotle may be just as Mexican as somebody who discusses the poetry of Sor Juana Inés de la Cruz.[14] Fuentes, finally, engages in a somewhat recondite but highly symptomatic debate with a critic named José Luis González on the question of why Ben Jonson set *Volpone* in Italy rather than his native England. González argues that Jonson's purpose in writing *Volpone* was to denounce the corruption of the society in which he lived, and that he was forced to set the work in a foreign country to avoid possible reprisals from the ruling classes of his own country; Fuentes counters that Jonson had the freedom to choose whatever setting he pleased for his work because he was part of a supranational cultural community and not the "slave of a literary colony" where it was forbidden to treat the general human themes of corruption and avarice within certain precise geographical boundaries.[15] Whereas González aims to prove that Jonson's engagement was first and foremost with national issues, Fuentes reads Jonson as a writer interested in themes that were not tied to a particular time or place.

Fuentes was the right person for the role of scourge of Mexico's literary and cultural nationalists. The best accounts of the early part of Fuentes's career all stress the cosmopolitan quality of

his persona. In 1966, Luis Harss began one of the first serious critical evaluations of Fuentes's work with a brief overview of modern
Mexican literature, an overview that concluded with the assertion
(borrowed from Paz) that "to be a Mexican of the twentieth century
is to be contemporaries of all mankind."[16] Harss went on to say that
if there was one person well equipped to accomplish this aspiration
toward universality in Mexican literature, that person was Carlos
Fuentes. Because of his father's work as a diplomat, Fuentes had
grown up in various major cities of the Western Hemisphere —
Santiago, Buenos Aires, Montevideo, Rio de Janeiro,
Washington — and had acquired a broad international education.
José Donoso confirms this impression of Fuentes in his *Historia personal del "boom."* When Donoso first met Fuentes in Chile in 1962 he
was already an admirer of his literary work. He soon discovered
that Fuentes was as impressive in person as he was on the page:
"He spoke perfect English. He had read every novel . . . and seen
every painting and every movie in all the capitals of the world."[17] If
Fuentes proved to be, in Donoso's eyes, one of the "precipitating
factors of the *boom*,"[18] it was in large part because of his cosmopolitan culture and international connections. But the most vivid personal impression of the young Fuentes is without a doubt Elena
Poniatowska's 1985 portrait of the writer. Poniatowska recalls
among other things that the publication of *La región más transparente*
signaled the appearance of a new public figure: "Along with the
hardcover book, there emerges a sophisticated and cosmopolitan
young man, eager to prove that he owns the world."[19] Poniatowska
goes on to show how Fuentes's international success allowed him to
develop his cosmopolitan persona. By the 1960s Fuentes had
acquired a whole new cast of friends, people like Norman Mailer,
William Styron, Arthur Miller, Alberto Moravia, Geraldine
Chaplin, and Shirley MacLaine. Fuentes's international success also
appears to have influenced his conception of his audience:
Poniatowska records that Fuentes once told her that he thinks of
his audience as "a spiritual family consisting of writers scattered all
over the world who are united by bonds that transcend languages

and frontiers."[20] The writer emerges here as a figure who must break free of his cultural roots in order to become part of an elite, supranational community.

But when Fuentes gathers with his fellow writers from all over the world, what exactly does he contribute to the conversation? The answer to this question brings to light the reverse side of Fuentes's cosmopolitanism. For in spite of Fuentes's Borgesian emphasis in his debate with José Luis González on the right of the Latin American writer to handle a broad range of themes unrestricted by national borders, in practice his homeland Mexico has been Fuentes's principal subject as a writer. Indeed, Harss, Donoso, and Poniatowska all confirm this. Harss describes the central theme of *La región más transparente* as the "desperate search for the 'true face' of Mexico," and even complains that the novel's Mexicanist concerns are compulsive and anachronistic.[21] Poniatowska shares Harss's view of the nature of *La región*'s central preoccupation, though not his negative evaluation of the novel. She believes Fuentes's most important accomplishment in his first novel was his discovery of an entire dimension of Mexican reality ignored until then in Mexican literature: "Fuentes puts Mexico in our heads. . . . For the first time literature has something to do with real life."[22] Evidence that Fuentes's cosmopolitanism did not mean that he had escaped into some ethereal zone where all sense of one's specific cultural location ceases to matter can also be found in Donoso's portrait of Fuentes. Donoso discusses his friend's excellent connections in some of the most influential cultural circles in the West, but also his passionate commitment to the cause of his continent. He recalls that Fuentes was burning with enthusiasm for the Cuban Revolution when he first visited Chile in 1962. Fuentes told Donoso that all Latin Americans should look to Cuba. And in a memorable debate with Frank Tannenbaum, a professor of Latin American history at Columbia University, Fuentes eloquently denounced the interventionist policies of the United States in Latin America.[23]

Even in the case of the *Revista Mexicana de Literatura* it is clear that although the journal's principal goal was to attack the nationalist attitudes that had dominated Mexican cultural life since the Revolution, this did not mean that the journal was not interested in the question of national culture. In one entry in the "Talón de Aquiles" section of the journal, Fuentes discusses the need to stimulate a cultural dialogue between Europe and Mexico, but although he takes as his point of departure the view that the vitality of a culture depends to some degree on the range of its contacts with other cultures, he also states that the moment at which he is writing is a particularly propitious one for the type of exchange he wishes to see, in the first place because the experience of the Revolution, which Fuentes likens to a baptism, has given Mexico a new degree of self-awareness. In other words, Mexico is now ready to enter the arena of international cultural exchange because thanks to the Revolution the country now has an identity it can call its own. Fuentes sees this process of self-discovery reflected in recent literary developments: "We have writers who have begun, finally, to offer literary depictions of Mexico with a sense of human depth to them."[24] The idea that the writer's task is to explore the world that surrounds him also emerges in another "Talón de Aquiles" entry, in which Fuentes observes that "The most visible development in Mexican life of the last thirty years is the emergence . . . of an urban middle class and a wealthy and hedonistic bourgeoisie," and then complains that "we will search in vain for a novel that reflects this fact."[25] It is clear that Fuentes is describing here the project for *La región más transparente*.

From the start of his career Fuentes has projected a double profile as a writer and intellectual with a simultaneously national and cosmopolitan orientation.[26] The relationship between these two poles in Fuentes's literary and political identity has varied over the course of his career, but the polarity itself has continued to define his work. In the years of the *Revista Mexicana de Literatura*, Fuentes devoted himself principally to calling for an opening up of Mexican culture to the outside world. No doubt the strength of a narrow nationalist position in Mexican culture led Fuentes to emphasize his cosmopolitanism. By the end of the decade, however, in the heat of the ideological battles swirling around the Cuban Revolution,

Fuentes was beginning to present himself as in the first place an advocate of Latin American political causes, rather than as a connoisseur of Western cultural trends, though it is clear that Fuentes never regarded the two poles as incompatible with each other.

In the 1990s, Fuentes continues to position himself in relation to the same underlying set of problems, even if the manner in which these problems are conceptualized has changed. Fuentes has assumed a prominent role as an interpreter and advocate of Hispanic culture to the outside world.[27] At the same time he has staked out a position as a fiery spokesman for Mexican and Latin American independence.[28] But he also writes constantly about the need to break down the frontiers that separate different nations from each other. And he has developed a vision of contemporary culture as essentially global and multicultural in nature.[29]

The study I undertake in this book of Fuentes's fiction and nonfiction from the 1950s to the 1990s is structured around the ongoing tension in his work between nationalism and cosmopolitanism. This tension, in turn, stands in a complex relationship to the problem of modernity. For each pole of the opposition simultaneously reflects and resists certain key traits of the modern era. For a Mexican writer, to assume a cosmopolitan perspective implies a desire to keep up with developments in countries regarded as more advanced, that is, more modern. At the same time, we will see that many of the innovative literary, cultural, and philosophical currents Fuentes appropriated from abroad in fact articulated powerful critiques of important aspects of the modern world. The case of nationalism presents a similar ambiguity. On the one hand, nationalism may be regarded as an integral element of modernity, for it embodies the characteristically modern ideals of autonomy and self-determination;[30] on the other hand, it amounts to a reaction against modernity, for it provides a model of social integration to compensate for the widespread erosion in the modern era of traditional communal ties.[31] The oscillations in Fuentes's work between nationalist and cosmopolitan perspectives can be attributed, then, to the fact that he constantly deliberates between different methods of either achieving or opposing modernity. In assuming a cosmopolitan outlook, Fuentes shows that he shares in the quintessentially modern desire for innovation. But his openness to international developments in the arts also means that he absorbs the antagonism of aesthetic modernity toward certain key processes of social, economic and political modernization. In speaking as a nationalist, Fuentes recognizes the role that the idea of the nation plays in the constitution of modernity, in particular in fulfilling the promise of emancipation of which modernity is the bearer. Yet a sense of national identity is commonly rooted in pre-modern practices (whether real or invented), and it often serves as an instrument with which to resist the leveling and homogenizing effects of modernity.

In the chapters that follow, I explore Fuentes's literary and political career in relation to this fundamental ambivalence with regard to modernity. The ambivalence can be explained in a variety of ways. Certainly, Fuentes's position as a Mexican writer with a desire for international recognition has something to do with it. But it can also be attributed to the sheer complexity and diversity of modernity itself, a phenomenon that crosses the boundaries separating literature, philosophy, society, economics, and politics. Tensions and contradictions inevitably arise when a single concept moves between so many different spheres. I have chosen however, not to try to unify the notion of modernity as I use it in this work. Using a single, fixed definition of modernity as a point of departure might make for a simpler approach to Fuentes's work, but it would also limit our sense of its range. Each chapter in this book, then, will approach the question of Fuentes's relationship to modernity from a somewhat different angle. Such an approach does greater justice to the variety of manifestations of modernity, as well as to the richness and complexity of Fuentes's work.

CHAPTER II

Myth, Contingency, and Revolution

Alienation

In the modern era, traditional communal structures loosen their hold on the individual, a process experienced as both liberating and threatening. The modern individual revels in a sense of expanded opportunity, yet at the same time anguishes over the disappearance of shared meanings. This sense of alienation produces the critical and self-repudiating side of modernity, reflected in, among other things, the tendency of modern artists to project alternative scenarios of communal integration.[1] This is precisely the pattern we find in Fuentes's first novel, *La región más transparente*. For *La región* oscillates between two different perspectives on the nature of the self and its relations to history and the community. On the one hand, the novel outlines a view of the self that derives primarily from existentialist ideas found in the works of André Gide, Jean-Paul Sartre, and Albert Camus.[2] In this view, the self is discontinuous, contingent, wholly unaffected by any kind of sociocultural conditioning, permanently separated from a stable and enduring core of meaning—and it is precisely for this reason that it possesses an absolute freedom to mold itself into constantly new shapes.[3] On the other hand, the novel proposes a vision in which the self ceases to be a separate, distinct entity and instead merges entirely with the communal past, specifically with Mexico's Aztec heritage. This past is viewed as the origin and ground of an unalterable, culturally determined identity to which the self is inextricably attached. The rejection of Western individualism, and the search for a source of regeneration in an archaic past, links Fuentes to D. H. Lawrence, who in *The Plumed Serpent* (1926) had portrayed Mexico as the ideal site for a revival of primitive energies.[4] In *La región*, Fuentes explores the clash between these two views of selfhood and community on various textual levels, yet in the end he is unable—or unwilling—to opt in favor of one position or the other. Instead, he offers in the novel's closing section a utopian vision of revolution as a way of canceling the conflict between alienation and integration.

Meanings of a Meaningless Act

Toward the end of *La región*, Manuel Zamacona, the novel's intellectual spokesman, is senselessly murdered by a man he has never seen before.[5] Afterward, the killer coolly states that he did not like the way Zamacona had looked at him. The incident is reminiscent of the motif of the *acte gratuit* as it appears in the works of Gide, Sartre, and Camus. Fuentes himself suggests a link with the existentialist tradition in a 1966 interview with Emir Rodríguez Monegal. In speaking of how the social and cultural realities of Mexico have managed to anticipate certain artistic and philosophical currents in Europe and the United States, Fuentes observes, "It is very obvious that in Mexico one finds a kind of existentialism *avant la lettre*. Mexico is a country of the instant. The future is totally improbable, dangerous: you can get killed in a bar, as you turn the corner of a street, for making an ugly face, for eating a taco. You live in the present because the future is improbable."[6] Fuentes's comment suggests that the scene of Zamacona's death in fact illustrates the existentialist quality of Mexican life.[7]

However, the existentialist act in *La región* is presented in a manner radically different from similar incidents in the works of Fuentes's French precursors. Lafcadio Wluiki's gratuitous murder of a complete stranger—whom he pushes out of a moving train—in Gide's *Les caves du Vatican* (1914) and Meursault's unmotivated killing of an Arab in Camus's *L'étranger* (1942) are by no means identical actions, but what they have in common is that in each case the perpetrator is at the center of the narrative. The events are related from Lafcadio's and Meursault's points of view. In Fuentes the perspective is completely inverted: the protagonist becomes the victim and the killer remains a shadowy, indistinct figure on the margins of the narrative.

The symmetry of this inversion is reinforced by a number of other details connected with Lafcadio's *acte gratuit* in *Les caves du Vatican*. Even before he thrusts his victim out of the train, Lafcadio has been planning to leave Europe for what he calls "a new world,"[8] the islands of Java and Borneo. And as he begins to play with the idea of committing this unusual crime, he reminds himself that, in any case, the next day he will be "off to the islands,"[9] and so will never be found out. In this way, the two projects, the gratuitous murder and the voyage to a faraway place, become linked. Both are strategies for asserting one's freedom, for rejecting the old, oppressive ways of Europe. "'Let all that can be, be!' That's my view of the Creation," Lafcadio exclaims at one point, and throughout the novel he remains intent on demonstrating his love for what he calls "what might be."[10] The desire to transgress all limits, to expand the realm of the possible, is expressed both in geographical terms, in the plan to flee to the East Indies, and in ethical terms, in the unmotivated murder of a stranger. Both projects are ways of affirming that one is bound by nothing. Or, as Camus put it in *L'homme révolté* (1951): "The defense of absolute liberty achieves its crowning expression in the theory of the *acte gratuit*."[11]

In *La región*, Natasha, an aging singer from St. Petersburg, alerts us to a difference between Mexico and Europe that speaks directly to this question of freedom and the transgression of limits: "At least we Europeans always have that left: the possibility of *s'enfuir*, of searching for a *là-bas*, for an El Dorado on some other continent than our own. But you? Not you, *mon vieux*, you don't have your *là-bas*, you're already there, you're already at the limit. And there you have to make a choice, *vero*?" (179/138). In Gide, the idea of the limit depends on a more fundamental conceptual division of the world into a center (Europe) and a periphery (the non-European parts of the globe). From the perspective of the center, the existence of the periphery guarantees the possibility of freedom and escape. From the periphery itself, however, things look very different. If one's existence is perceived as already being at the limit, then the possibility of further displacement disappears. This results in the undoing of the very concept of the limit, and in the collapse of the chain of analogies whereby a writer such as Gide links the notion of the limit to the ideas of the escape to a new world, the *acte gratuit*, and freedom. This emerges very clearly in the case of Zamacona's death. Fuentes does not use the incident to demonstrate the absolute nature of individual freedom. Instead, with the focus now on the victim, the scene evokes the old Latin American theme of a violent and hostile environment from which there is no escape. And even if we were to extract from this episode a different kind of existentialist motif—such as the notion of the absurd—such elements would exist in a state of tension with the larger narrative pattern into which the episode is absorbed. For Zamacona is only one of a number of the novel's characters who suffer a violent death on Mexico's Independence Day, and this juxtaposition of death and celebration is clearly designed to recall the ancient Aztec belief that human sacrifices are necessary to ensure the continuity of life. The series of deaths at the end of the novel hints at the persistence of these mythical patterns beneath the surface of modern Mexico and at the fragility of the individual in the face of such forces.

Fuentes's second novel, *Las buenas conciencias* (1959),[12] also includes a scene modeled on the existentialist motif of the *acte gratuit*, even if the victim of the crime is a cat rather than a person. In fact, the scene in which Jaime Ceballos, the protagonist of the novel, uses a rock to smash the skull of a cat that has come to rub its back against his knee, follows the existentialist pattern more closely than the scene of Zamacona's death, inasmuch as it restores the equation of protagonist and killer. Yet here too there are elements that require a different interpretation from the standard existentialist one.

The main character in *Las buenas conciencias* is the same Jaime Ceballos who appears toward the end of *La región* as the young and ambitious lawyer from the provinces making his rather pale and awkward first appearance in Mexico City's social world, accompanied by his glamorous fiancée, Betina Régules. He returns in the New Year's Eve party scene in *La muerte de Artemio Cruz* (1962), evidently having shed his youthful nervousness, for we see him making a bold play for the aging Artemio's attention and favors, and we are given to understand that Jaime is in some ways a younger version of Artemio. *Las buenas conciencias* focuses on the years of Jaime's adolescence in the provincial town of Guanajuato. A mixture of religious and literary influences (readings in the Bible, in Stendhal, Nietzsche, and Dostoyevsky) produces in Jaime a state of spiritual exaltation and an attitude of rebellion vis-à-vis his high bourgeois background.

His indignation is aimed in the first place at the hypocrisy of the lives led by his elders. Everything in the world of the Guanajuato bourgeoisie revolves around appearances. Ironically enough, the original patriarch of the Ceballos family, a poor immigrant from Spain who arrives in Guanajuato around 1852, is a draper whose professional motto is "a good piece of cloth sells itself" (16/4). The subsequent development of the family business casts some doubt on Higinio Ceballos's conception of value as something clear and self-evident, as something that does not need to advertise itself. For Fuentes shows that factors other than hard work and reliable craftsmanship are responsible for the Ceballos family's rapid rise to wealth. "Ceballos e Hijos" does not simply sell pieces of cloth; it is also in the business of marketing fashion. Higinio's wife Margarita has a special gift for remaining *au courant* with what is happening in "the great centers of fashion" (18/6), a skill that allows her to act as a pacesetter for the other women of her class in Guanajuato. Her son Pepe, in the meantime, makes a point of *not* assuming that the family's wares will simply sell themselves. His contribution to the business consists of market research: he takes advantage of the social events he attends to determine what the ladies and gentlemen of the town need for their wardrobes (19/7). The Ceballos family owes its prosperity at least in part to its ability both to shape and to comply with changes in consumer taste, changes that undermine the

very notion that commodities possess fixed values. Yet this is exactly the notion to which the bourgeoisie clings, anxious as it is to forget the contingent nature of its economic success and social status.
This fear of change also helps explain the final ironic twist in
Fuentes's chronicle of the relationship between fashion and social
status in the Ceballos family: Jorge and Asunción Balcárcel
(Jaime's aunt and uncle as well as his foster parents) have such an
exacerbated and rigid sense of their respectability that they ostenta-
tiously spurn the vagaries of fashion, always wearing the same style
of clothing (138/106), even though it is to the business of fashion
that Asunción Balcárcel owes her social rank.

It is against this ambiguous world—simultaneously fixed and
fluid—that Jaime rebels. On one level, Jaime's murder of the cat
condenses in a single and sudden act his struggle to free himself
from the normative expectations of his society. He tells himself that
to him it is permitted to commit this crime: it is the "prize of freedom" (185/143) he has earned for himself through the extremism of
his behavior (earlier in the novel he had flagellated himself with a
whip covered with thorns). But if on the one hand Jaime's killing of
the cat appears to constitute a bid for a state of absolute freedom,
on the other hand his crime is absorbed into a very different narrative pattern that links a series of acts of cruelty and cowardice.
Jaime's inability to free himself from the narrow, repressive values
of his class is most apparent in the scene in which he refuses to
acknowledge his mother, a woman of lower-class background who
was evicted from her home and dispossessed of her child by her
snobbish in-laws, the Balcárcels. In a strange way, then, the rejection of external norms that expresses itself through the murder of
the cat can be read not only as an existentialist gesture, but also as a
conformist one. After all, the novel ends with Jaime returning to
the embrace of his family, and one gets a distinct sense that the *acte
gratuit* acts as a catalyst in this process. The killing of the cat initially appears to demonstrate a freedom from all conventional constraints, yet in the end has the effect of sealing Jaime's decision to
cease his struggle against the expectations of his family and his
class. Yet, in a final paradoxical twist, Fuentes shows how Jaime's

integration into the established order does not mean that Jaime will from now on adopt a posture of unquestioning obedience. In fact, Jaime's return to the family involves at the same time an overcoming of the two father-figures in his life: his actual father, Rodolfo Ceballos, who dies at the end of the novel, and to whom Jaime refuses to grant a final token of filial love, and his foster father, Jorge Balcárcel, who loses his authority over Jaime after Jaime encounters him in a brothel. The novel concludes on this ambiguous note: what appears to be a rebellion may actually be the opposite, while a gesture of subservience may conceal a deeper rebellion.[13]

If we return now to the scene of Zamacona's death in *La región*, we will see that it, too, possesses a fundamentally ambiguous structure. Earlier, I demonstrated how Fuentes inverts the ostensibly existentialist elements in this scene: Zamacona's death illustrates not the power of the individual but the power of ancient mythological rhythms. Such a reading is at odds with the interpretation Fuentes himself offers in the interview with Rodríguez Monegal, for he proposes there that we should regard the scene as evidence of the instantaneousness of Mexican life, of its fundamentally existentialist quality. In fact, Fuentes never wholly eliminates either of these two possible readings. Two details in the scene of Zamacona's death will indicate how Fuentes holds together the two alternative interpretations. First, when Zamacona gets out from his car and approaches the *cantina* he recites to himself a line from Nerval: "et c'est toujours la seule — ou c'est le seul moment" (390/309). Nerval's idea that each moment in time is unique anticipates the existentialist conception of time, in which every instant is a new creation, disconnected from past and future.[14] This notion of temporality is a focal point of Sartre's well-known analysis of Camus's *L'étranger*. Sartre describes Meursault as a man for whom "only the concrete present matters."[15] He links this vision of time to Camus's absurdist world-view in which God is dead and death is everything: "The fact that death awaits us at the end of the road makes the future go up in smoke. Our life has no tomorrow; it is a succession of moments in the present."[16] Fuentes's use of the quotation from Nerval seems designed to allude to such ideas about time, and thus to prepare us for the sudden, inexplicable flare-up of violence that leaves Zamacona dead.[17]

But if this leads to a view of Zamacona's death as an absurd, meaningless event, another feature of this episode suggests a quite different point of view: the emphasis on the eyes and on the act of seeing. Zamacona's killer, as I observed earlier, justifies his deed by saying that he did not like the way Zamacona had looked at him. Furthermore, the only mention of the murderer's appearance is of his eyes: "One of the men turned to face Manuel Zamacona; spinning off the wood bar like a top, his marble eyes round and submerged, he fired his pistol two, three, five times at Zamacona's body" (390/309). The killer's submerged and marblelike eyes link him to the realm of the invisible, subsisting beneath the surface of Fuentes's Mexico. Invisibility is generally associated in *La región* with Mexico's pre-Hispanic past, a connection captured most vividly in the figure of Hortensia Chacón, the blind woman who leads the powerful self-made banker Federico Robles back to his indigenous roots. Hortensia represents the beneficent side of the dark world abiding beneath the country's semblance of progress and modernity, whereas the killer represents the violent, menacing side of this world: figuratively blind where Hortensia is literally so, this anonymous figure wishes to punish Zamacona for the look in his eyes, that is, for his location within the visible world of modern Mexico. Wanting to blind him as much as to kill him, he demonstrates the enduring power of Mexico's past.

There can be little doubt that the manner in which Zamacona dies reveals the persistence of an atavistic violence lurking beneath the country's surface life. The question that remains unanswered, however, is whether this violence remains integrated with ancient cosmological rhythms, or whether it has lost its connection with ritual and has been expelled into a world of existential absurdity. This ambiguity is sustained in the development of the novel's plot after Zamacona's death.[18]

It is difficult to ignore the connection between Ixca Cienfuegos's search, at his mother's behest, for a sacrificial victim with which to propitiate the gods, and the series of deaths that occur toward the end of the novel. But we can never be sure that the sacrifices really are sacrifices, nor that they are responsible for a renewal of the life-cycle. Ixca's mother, Teódula Moctezuma, for her part, does not question the significance of these events. After Norma Larragoiti dies in the fire that burns down her house, she tells Ixca that she believes the sacrifice has now been fulfilled, and that the normal course of life will be resumed. At the same moment, as if to confirm Teódula's vision of life's rebirth, the sun begins to rise.

Fuentes does not always represent this idea of cyclical return with such solemnity. Part Two of the novel concludes with the destruction or downfall of many of the central characters. Part Three resumes three years later with the description of the youthful romance between Jaime Ceballos and Betina Régules. But Jaime and Betina have such stale and conventional natures that we inevitably sense an element of parody in this vision of life's regener-ation. The effect is reinforced when the scene shifts once again to a party hosted by Bobó Gutiérrez, whom we observe greeting his guests with the exact same words he had used approximately three years earlier, near the beginning of the novel: "My darlings! Enter and apprehend the eternal verities" (28/11; 439/350). Bobó's eternal verities are clearly a mockery. We recognize here not return and renewal, but paralysis and decay.

Fuentes leaves his readers suspended between a world ruled by profound mythological rhythms, and an alternative, modern world of drift and contingency. He never fully decides which of these two pictures is finally truer to the reality of Mexico.[19] This same conflict shapes the meditation on identity and authenticity that receives novelistic form through the contrasting careers of Ixca Cienfuegos and Rodrigo Pola. Although two other characters, Federico Robles and Manuel Zamacona, are also central to the development of this theme, I shall focus on Ixca and Rodrigo because their confronta-tion after Bobó's last party effectively brings the plot of the novel to a close, thus suggesting the importance of these two figures to Fuentes's articulation of the problem of subjectivity.

Versions of the Self

Rodrigo Pola is an emblematic modern personality—a type toward the definition of which the existentialists made a key contribution. Rodrigo's connection with this tradition of the modern self is clear from the first words he speaks in the novel. Into a discussion about the social function of art, he interjects the following observation: "We don't all have to be part of the stinking crowd or, on the other hand, an *homme révolté*" (41/22). Although Rodrigo appears to reject the opposition he posits here, these words in fact encapsulate the defining axis of his personality, a conflict between conformity and rebellion. The allusion to Camus is clearly meant to recall the existentialist emphasis on subjectivity, on the need for individuals to create their own values without reference to a realm of a priori truths, or to society's received notions. Initially, Rodrigo's actions are guided by a similar search for authentic self-definition.

As he grows up, Rodrigo—who wants to be a writer—has to struggle against the oppressive demands of his mother Rosenda, who, having lost her husband during the Mexican Revolution, cannot bear the thought of her son also escaping from her grip. The conflict between Rodrigo and his mother revolves around the question of who creates the self and thus has power over it. Rosenda wishes the moment in which she gave birth to her son to be prolonged forever. She wants always to be the mother, with the child owing its existence to her alone. Rodrigo speaks with horror of "that desire to suck me dry, to trap me between her thighs and to be forever . . . giving birth to me without rest, in an interminable childbirth of nights and days and years" (145/109). To this idea of the enduring power derived from the act of giving birth to a child, Rodrigo opposes a notion of figurative birth in which the self engenders itself: "I felt I was . . . the son not so much of my parents as of my own, brief, yes, but for me unique, irreplaceable experience" (151/114). In this, he appears to be heeding the existentialist exhortation to free oneself from all forms of external conditioning.

It is worth recalling, however, that there were different phases within French existentialism. The earlier work of Sartre and Camus tended to emphasize the absolute nature of individual freedom, and favored the themes of anxiety, absurdity, and superfluousness, whereas their later work sought to establish a more affirmative view of existentialist philosophy. In *L'existentialisme est un humanisme* (1946) Sartre argues that existentialism provides the philosophical basis for an attitude of engagement with the world and commitment to one's fellow human beings.[20] Camus's *L'homme révolté* interprets the act of rebellion against an intolerable situation not as an individualistic gesture, but as a sign of the fundamental truth of human solidarity. Rebellion, according to Camus, is always potentially an act of self-sacrifice, and so implies the existence of values that transcend the individual. Camus himself regarded the shift in his work from a concern with the absurd to a concern with rebellion as the sign of a new focus on the group instead of the individual: "In the experience of the absurd, suffering is individual. From the moment of rebellion, it becomes collective, an experience we all share."[21]

Rodrigo, by opposing *l'homme révolté* to the man of the crowd, evokes the more strictly individualistic side of existentialist thought. But in the course of the novel, Rodrigo's efforts to assert his own uniqueness become increasingly fruitless. This failure implies a critique of the early version of existentialism, with its one-sided emphasis on self-creation and self-renewal as the path to authentic selfhood, and its neglect of the social dimension of human life. Rodrigo's pursuit of a total freedom from all external constraints leads first to feelings of alienation and inauthenticity, and eventually to a complete turnaround, an unconditional surrender to society's norms of success.

In one episode, we see Rodrigo making faces at himself in the mirror, rapidly shifting expressions, "until he felt that his face and its reflection were two distinct entities, as far removed from each other as the real moon which nobody knows and its reflection in a pond" (242/189). This scene recalls a similar moment in *La nausée* where Roquentin studies his reflection in a mirror and is struck by the incomprehensible, alien appearance of his own face.[22] Fuentes's adaptation of this motif suggests a similar perspective on the impossibility of discovering a stable, continuous identity, and the consequent susceptibility of the self to being constantly remolded into new shapes. For a moment, Rodrigo seems to recoil from his performance; he sits down to write, to leave what he calls "a single true record" (242/189). Ironically enough, the text he produces articulates a theory of the self as a mask, a form of play. Everything becomes arbitrary and gratuitous. The self is cast loose from any serious attachment, even from that most fundamental attachment to the body itself. Thus, Rodrigo is at one point led to assert that it is a matter of indifference whether one's face is, in actual fact, ugly or beautiful; the act of self-creation can apply even to one's physical appearance. The material world, even in its most primary manifestation, is fully subject to the individual will: "The problem is to know how to imagine one's own face. It doesn't matter whether one's face is, in actual fact, frightening or beautiful. You either imagine your face to be interesting, strong, clear-cut or you imagine it to be ridiculous, foolish and ugly" (242–43/190).

If the theory of the mask is initially designed to free the self from all forms of predetermination, then Rodrigo's radical application of this principle appears to produce the opposite result. Rodrigo himself eventually recognizes that the histrionic self-display into which he has fallen effectively obliterates the possibility of achieving genuine freedom; he admits that he has become a captive of his own game: "One becomes the slave of one's own game, the movement itself conquers and condemns the person who initiated it, and then only the movement matters; one is swung this way and that, more object than agent" (249/194).

A few pages later, the description of a thunderstorm serves to dramatize the extent of Rodrigo's estrangement from the world:"The storm enveloped him in an implacable, liquid drumming. Up above, the skies exchanged thunderclaps and flashes of somber light: all the myths and symbols rooted in the appearance of nature came together in the powerful sky, the assembler of an occult force. The firmament resounded with a sadness removed from all circumstance: not gratuitous, but self-sufficient" (258/201). Fuentes's conception of the natural world, as it emerges from this passage, has important implications for his view of the status of the perceiving subject. The storm's concentrated, implacable power, its relation to the deep, continuous rhythms of nature, and its aura of timelessness are at the farthest possible remove from the inconsequentiality and arbitrariness that define Rodrigo's relations to himself and to the world. The implications of this contrast for Fuentes's larger view of the self can be sensed most clearly through a comparison with certain passages in Sartre's *La nausée* that deal with the same issues.

Fuentes's use of the pathetic fallacy encourages a view of the realms of the human and the non-human as deeply interrelated. The reference to the sky's occult powers may appear to lift the natural world to a position that transcends the human, but it also implies that nature is pregnant with meanings that are of great consequence to human life. The use of the verb "to envelop" suggests that in this world it is impossible to think of human beings as separate from the universe in which they live. Roquentin, in *La nausée*, recognizes this human inclination to search for connections between ourselves and the physical world, to treat it, for example, as a text waiting for its meaning to be unveiled. At one point he describes a priest walking along the seaside as he reads from his breviary: "Now and then, he raises his head and looks approvingly upon the sea; the sea is also a breviary, it speaks of God." But Roquentin furiously rejects this attempt at humanization: "The *true* sea is cold and black, and full of animals; it crawls about under this thin green film which has been made to deceive people."[23] In *La nausée* the world of objects and natural processes does not envelop the human world in a transcendent, protective manner; instead, it is conceived as a realm of brute, unredeemable fact from which a lucid consciousness will recoil in horror.

If Rodrigo is a failed existentialist, part of the explanation lies in the way Fuentes has stacked the deck against him. In a world where natural phenomena exude such a compelling and inscrutable sense of purpose and power, individuals can hardly presume to play God with their own existence.[24] Fuentes has created a character with existentialist features, but has placed him in a setting entirely different from the kind that would have been envisioned by the existentialists themselves. As a result, the existentialist project is invalidated.

Ixca Cienfuegos represents, on the level of character, the same mythical forces which Fuentes evokes through his description of the thunderstorm. Ixca, whose first name derives from the Nahuatl word for "bake" or "cook," and whose last name alludes to the original time in Aztec mythology when fires lit up the universe, is a shadowy yet central presence in the novel. One character compares him to God, because of his seeming omnipresence (41/22). Ixca is engaged in a more secretive and solitary version of the quest of Cipriano and Ramón in Lawrence's *The Plumed Serpent* to bring about a religious revival in Mexico. Ixca's search for a sacrificial victim is part of an attempt to reintegrate Mexican society into a sacred, cosmic order, and thus to overcome the kind of self-division and self-estrangement suffered by a typically modern character such as Rodrigo. The contrast between the two men emerges clearly in the description of an early evening walk they take along the Paseo de la Reforma: "Rodrigo watched the dust accumulating on his yellow shoes. He was conscious of every nervous movement he made. And Cienfuegos looked as if he weren't walking at all, as if the soft summer breeze were pushing him along, as if he didn't have those legs, those hands which bothered Rodrigo so much" (132/97).

Whereas Rodrigo is severely afflicted with the modern disease of self-consciousness, Ixca is entirely at ease with himself. He is in possession of an unfissured consciousness that exists in a state of harmony with the natural world. Ixca does not search for an increasingly intense awareness of his own separateness from others. He is deeply at odds with the idea of a unique, individual personality waiting to be liberated from external oppression. Fuentes shows him in an intense, sometimes conflictive relationship with his mother, in which he submits to her wishes rather than rebel, as Rodrigo does. Rather than self-regard, he advocates self-forgetfulness, which he views as the "key to happiness" (30/12). One should aim not to "liberate oneself," but to "subdue others" (30/12). Ixca's vision ultimately evolves out of his belief in the absolute nature of the nation's origins, and the priority of these origins over the claims of contemporary individuals. Mexico, he claims, "is something fixed forever, incapable of evolution. An immovable rock that tolerates everything. All kinds of slime can grow on that rock, but the rock itself doesn't change, it is the same forever" (138/102). At one point, Ixca urges Rodrigo to choose between the two Mexicos, the ancient and the modern: "Over here you will be anonymous, a brother to everyone in solitude. Over there you will have your name, and in the crowd nobody will touch you, and you will not touch anybody" (76–77/51). The possession of a name becomes an emblem of the barren, atomistic individualism that rules over the contemporary world. In the mythical world Ixca believes in, the individual is absorbed into a larger order of communal belonging.

Neither Rodrigo nor Ixca offers a satisfying solution to the problem of authenticity.[25] Rodrigo's inner restlessness seems so gratuitous and self-indulgent that it comes as no surprise to see him eventually give up his rebellion against the world. If each new mask is the result of an arbitrary choice, then why not choose the mask that will bring success and prosperity? By the end of the novel, Rodrigo has become a successful writer of screenplays for the movie industry, a hack who has cynically mastered a simple formula for success.

But if Rodrigo's cult of individuality ultimately proves fruitless and self-defeating, Ixca's violent attack on the notion of a personal life does not seem much more appealing. His behavior becomes increasingly menacing, at times literally poisonous. We may note, for example, the terror he inspires in little Jorgito Morales when he meets him outside the Cathedral and offers to buy him some candy. In order to escape from Ixca's grip, Jorgito bites his hand, drawing blood. But the next time we see him, over a hundred pages later, the boy is dead. Because it is never clear that the regeneration Ixca is after actually takes place, we are left simply with the image of a man who goes around causing havoc in the lives of others. If Rodrigo's emptiness is that of a life lived without reference to the transcendent, then Ixca displays the perhaps more sinister emptiness of someone who has voided himself of all human emotions: "in reality Ixca sustained himself above an immense void, a void into which neither pity, nor love, nor even the hatred of others was allowed to enter" (316/249).

The final confrontation between Ixca and Rodrigo, three years after the main events of the novel, brings the novel's plot to a close, and seems designed to show that although their respective destinies are diametrically opposed, they are equally stunted and unfulfilled. Rodrigo scales the heights of social success, but Ixca disappears from Mexico City altogether, living in obscurity with Rosa Morales, the cleaning lady, and her remaining children. On the surface, Rodrigo has been transformed into a new person, yet he is haunted by the past: "Do you think that because I'm over here I'm no longer over there? . . . Do you think that a new life destroys and cancels the old?" (446/355). Ixca, on the other hand, while having apparently reconciled himself to the demands of the mythical past, now finds himself abandoned in the present, divided from the very past he thought he was embracing. He describes his condition in the same plaintive tones as Rodrigo: "Do you think I remember my own face? My life begins every day . . . and I never have any recollection of what happened before" (452/361).

Wendy Faris has drawn attention to Fuentes's fondness for the rhetorical figure of the chiasmus,[26] which he employs at the level both of individual sentences and of plot structures. The paths followed by Rodrigo and Ixca trace a chiastic design. If at the beginning of the novel Rodrigo represents the present-oriented pole, and Ixca the past-oriented, then the final confrontation between the two men constitutes a complete reversal of this relationship. By the end of the novel, Rodrigo can no longer escape the past, while Ixca lives his life as though it were starting anew at every instant.

The result of this chiastic pattern is to lead the novel into an impasse. The plot of *La región* offers no clear resolution to the problems of authenticity and national identity which the novel articulates. Fuentes rejects the existentialist project of liberating the self from the past, of investing life with value simply through the agency of free individual choice, but he also rejects the attempt to provoke a return to the cultural origins of Mexico. Both these approaches to the problems of subjectivity and community are shown to be fruitless, even self-canceling.

Revolution

The novel, however, does not end with the conversation between Rodrigo and Ixca. After the two friends separate, the text undergoes a series of unusual transformations. Ixca gradually sheds his corporeality, and little by little absorbs the different facets of the surrounding city, until eventually he and the city become a single entity. In a subsequent transformation, Ixca becomes the characters of the novel itself, so that finally Ixca, the city, and the book become metaphors for each other, in an operation that may be understood as an attempt to lift the novel onto a plane distinct from ordinary narrativity. In a final transition, Ixca disappears into his own voice, but the voice that speaks in the novel's concluding chapter is no longer tied to a particular space or time; it is a voice that aims to give a total and instantaneous vision of Mexico, as well as of the novel Fuentes has written about it. The final chapter is a mélange of densely metaphorical descriptions of the Mexican people, scenes from Mexican history, and echoes of the main narrative of the novel itself. The title of the chapter, "La región más transparente del aire," suggests an attempt to recapitulate and condense the novel, to project, within the space of a few pages, a *mise en abîme* of the text as a whole. What this implies is that in some ways this final section of *La región* gives the reader the key to Fuentes's vision.

The guiding conception behind this remarkable novelistic flight is the attempt to escape from linear time, to propose and embody an alternative vision of temporality in which, as Fuentes writes, "everything lives at the same time" (454/363). Among writers of the present century, Fuentes clearly does not stand alone in his fascination with the break with linear time. For Octavio Paz, for example, the idea of a zone of pure time, beyond chronology, provides the very basis for his definition of poetry: "The poem is mediation: thanks to the poem, original time, father of all times, incarnates in an instant. Succession becomes pure present, a spring that nourishes itself and transmutes man."[27] In the area of the novel, one of the most influential codifications of the modernist aesthetic, Joseph Frank's 1945 essay "Spatial Form in Modern Literature," centers precisely on this attempt to create forms that are not dependent on linear, chronological methods of organization.[28] Frank's essay, particularly his discussion of the basic features of spatial form and the type of content it conveys, clarifies Fuentes's relationship to modernist writing.[29] It also contributes to an understanding of the function of the novel's final chapter, in which the techniques of spatial form are most emphatically deployed, and appear to constitute an effort to escape from the impasse with which the plot of the novel concludes.

According to Frank, in the works of poets such as T. S. Eliot and Ezra Pound and of novelists such as James Joyce, Marcel Proust, and Djuna Barnes, the normal temporal unfolding of the text is repeatedly interrupted, with the result that the unity of these works is no longer located in a continuous narrative progression, but in the reflexive references and cross-references relating different points in the text to one another. The reader, in reconstructing these patterns, must ignore the aspects of temporal flow and external reference that are fundamental to more conventional works of literature. The reconstructed patterns must be perceived simultaneously, as a configuration in space. Frank goes on to argue that the most important consequence of the deployment of spatial form in literature is the erasure of a sense of historical depth. Moments in time become locked together in a timeless unity that evokes the world of myth rather than history.

Clearly, numerous objections could be made to the concept of spatial form, in particular to the term itself, which may seem inappropriately metaphorical.[30] My interest here, however, is not in the accuracy of the term itself, but in the narrative techniques that the term was designed to describe and in the revolt against linear, progressive time implied by the use of these techniques. Fuentes's attempt, in *La región*, to disrupt the straightforward temporal flow of the novel is not restricted to the final chapter. To the extent that the novel as a whole constitutes an attempt—along the lines of Joyce's *Ulysses* (1922) and John Dos Passos's *Manhattan Transfer* (1925)— to re-create the life of a city within its pages, the rejection of a sequential organization of the text appears entirely fitting. What Frank would call the "spatializing" technique of the juxtaposition of unrelated textual fragments corresponds to the essentially spatial entity being represented. A typical instance of this technique occurs near the beginning of Fuentes's novel, where the narrator, in a decidedly small-scale imitation of the "Wandering Rocks" chapter of *Ulysses*, traces the simultaneous activities in different parts of the city of various characters on the morning after one of Bobó's parties (62–64/39–41). The revolt against linear time is also apparent in those moments in the text when past and present are conflated within the mind of an individual character. This device is used most strikingly in the case of Federico Robles, who, as a firm believer in economic progress and a builder of postrevolutionary Mexico, represents the attachment to the singularity of chronological time in one of its most powerful forms. Although he rejects the past, Robles nevertheless, at Ixca's urging, undertakes the perilous journey inward and is eventually led to an almost Proustian apprehension of pure time freed from the habitual constraints of consecutiveness. In one scene, Robles bites Hortensia's hair while making love to her, an act that suddenly evokes an image from the day he fought at the battle of Celaya during the Mexican Revolution, and bit the reins of his horse as he rode into the fray. The merging of past and present is underscored by the paratactic arrangement of the following two sentences: "The blood-drenched plain of Celaya. The damp and open body of Hortensia" (287/223). Robles's vision is particularly significant inasmuch as it seems to be at least partly responsible for his decision to abandon his public role as a powerful financier in the nation's capital and return to his obscure roots in the country. His decision constitutes an explicit rejection of the rigorously linear time of economic progress.

The important question is whether, as Frank would argue, the disruption of a continuous temporal progression within a narrative necessarily implies a return to the timeless world of myth. It seems doubtful, if only because it is not clear why a break with the linear organization of the text should automatically propel us into the realm of myth. The question, then, is what purpose Fuentes's use of these techniques serves. In answering, I want to focus in particular on the relationship between the main body of the narrative and the poetic finale with which it concludes. One of the most remarkable features of *La región* is that although most of the devices Frank enumerates in his article on spatial form are in evidence throughout the novel, they are most spectacularly exploited at the end, in a manner without real equivalent in the texts Frank discusses. This does not mean, however, that the reader is now truly transported into the realm of myth. I would suggest instead that the final section of the novel ought to be read as an attempt to lift the text onto a completely different level, in the hope of offering a resolution to the ambiguities with which the plot concludes. Because these ambiguities center on the opposition between the mythical and the existential views of life, it seems unlikely that such a resolution would take the form of a more determined affirmation of the mythical, a move that would simply eliminate one of the poles of the opposition.

We can begin measuring Fuentes's distance from the mythical approach by looking at the principal features of Frank's definition of myth. Frank quotes Mircea Eliade, who identifies myth as a realm of "eternal repetition," where time becomes "cosmic, cyclical and infinite."[31] Frank discovers a similar emphasis on repetition and uniformity in the works of modernists such as Joyce, Eliot, and Pound, whose techniques of juxtaposition and allusion he believes underline the fundamental sameness of the human condition through the ages. Octavio Paz, in his discussion of the poetic technique of *simultaneísmo* (which we may regard as another term for spatial form) in *Los hijos del limo* (1974), reaches a similar conclusion: he argues that Pound and Eliot developed their experimental poetic in order to "reconquer the tradition of the Divine Comedy, that is, the Western tradition."[32] Both projects, the return to myth and the recapture of tradition, are driven by a search for cultural coherence and identity.

Fuentes has frequently discussed the notion that different temporal planes may have a simultaneous existence, but he has a very different understanding of the implications of this fact. When he discusses "the simultaneity of Mexican times,"[33] which he opposes to the linearity of European time, he does not mean that the juxtaposition of these different temporal levels would reveal an underlying continuity between the various phases of Mexican history. Nor is this the effect he pursues at the end of *La región*. The torrent of images, names, and historical episodes he unleashes here evokes a tumultuous, unrestrained multiplicity. In "Kierkegaard en la Zona Rosa," Fuentes describes Mexican time not in terms of continuity and coherence, but as an unceasing process of metamorphosis.[34] In the same essay, Fuentes argues that the simultaneous existence in present-day Mexican culture of all the distinct historical periods through which the country has passed results from a decision of the land and its people to maintain alive all of time, for the simple reason that "no time has yet reached its fulfillment."[35] Fuentes's Mexican past, in other words, is profoundly different from the past to which the Anglo-American modernists wished to return. It offers not the fullness of an established tradition, but a variety of unfinished projects.

Fuentes attacks the proponents of modernization in Mexico, with their cult of the present and of progress, for having suppressed this feature of Mexican time. To return to the cultural and historical multiplicity of Mexico constitutes an act of liberation, a rebellion against the enslaving prejudices of modernity. Fuentes believes that such a rebellion in fact took place during the Mexican Revolution: "Only the Revolution—and that is why, in spite of everything it deserves a capital R—made all the pasts of Mexico present. It did so instantaneously, as if it knew that there would be no time to spare for this fiesta of incarnations."[36] Manuel Zamacona offers the same reading of the Mexican Revolution in *La región*, declaring at one point that "the Revolution reveals to us the totality of the history of Mexico" (281), a statement that exactly replicates statements Fuentes has made elsewhere in his own name. It is an idea that can be traced to Octavio Paz, who in *El laberinto de la soledad* describes the Mexican Revolution as "a movement that aimed to reconquer our past, to assimilate it and bring it to life in the present."[37] At the end of *La región*, Fuentes tries to reproduce on the aesthetic level this revolutionary resuscitation of Mexico's many-sided past. The vision of the simultaneous coexistence of all times overturns the linear approach to time represented by Rodrigo Pola, and by the new Mexican bourgeoisie's deification of progress. But the sense of ferment implied by this vision of time as *fiesta* also subverts the obsession with the unity and singularity of origins expressed in the figure of Ixca Cienfuegos. Fuentes's alternative is his concept of revolutionary time, a vision of simultaneity that promises freedom and possibility, but does not dispense with a strong sense of the shaping powers of the past. This paradoxical fusion of freedom and necessity, of futurity and pastness, of diversity and totality, is made possible by an ambiguity in the word "revolution," which generally refers to a clean break with the past, a drastic change in the social order, but, in an older version of the word, which Fuentes clearly wants his readers to recall, indicates a process of cyclical return.[38] In the imaginative space Fuentes creates at the end of *La región*, these two meanings are held together in an ultimately utopian gesture.

More Revolutions

A utopian vision of revolution has been a constant element in Fuentes's work.[39] In the 1980s and '90s, Fuentes has continued to discuss revolutions, in Mexico and elsewhere in Latin America, in exactly the same terms he used in the early days of his career. In the commencement speech he gave at Harvard in 1983, Fuentes declares that the Mexican Revolution brought to light "the totality of our history and the possibility of a culture."[40] He goes on to connect the Mexican experience with that of other countries now passing through revolutionary phases:"Paz himself, Diego Rivera and Carlos Chávez, Mariano Azuela and José Clemente Orozco, Juan Rulfo and Rufino Tamayo: we all work and exist because of the revolutionary experience of our country. How can we stand by as this experience is denied, through ignorance and arrogance, to other people, our brothers, in Central America and the Caribbean."[41] In a review of John Mason Hart's *Revolutionary Mexico*, Fuentes takes issue with Hart's claim that the Revolution was essentially "a war of national liberation against the U.S.," and argues instead for a reading of the Revolution as the expression of "a nation searching for itself."

Fuentes believes that this pursuit of "self-knowledge," this creation, through revolution, of "a cultural event" would have happened "with or without the United States."[42] (13). In *The Buried Mirror*, the companion text to the TV documentary Fuentes wrote to mark the quincentenary of Columbus's first voyage to the New World, the Mexican Revolution emerges as an event of profound self-discovery:

> In Mexico, for the first time a Spanish American nation saw itself as it really was, without disguises. . . . This was most apparent when Zapata's troops entered Mexico City in 1914, occupied the palaces of the aristocracy, and saw themselves reflected in the mirror of other people for the first time. Their faces were no longer masks, but the faces of women who had left their villages to follow the men; the scarred, menacing faces of guerilla fighters having breakfast at the posh Sanborn's Restaurant; the faces of children born between battles, far from their villages. They were all citizens of the revolution and of a new nation.[43]

Fuentes also embodied these same ideas about the Mexican Revolution in fictional form in these years. There is a scene in *Gringo viejo* (1985) in which the soldiers in the rebel army of Pancho Villa occupy the mansion of a wealthy family that has fled the country. When the soldiers enter the ballroom, with its huge mirrors, they are astonished at the sight of their own reflections; for the first time in their lives they are seeing their own bodies in their entirety. Fuentes is telling us that the Revolution has finally allowed these men and women to discover who they really are. A similar notion is articulated in the novel's broad opposition between Mexico before and Mexico during the Revolution. Before the Revolution the country was merely an aggregate of static and isolated communities. The Revolution sets the country in motion; the Mexican people leave their villages and towns and finally begin to discover the common purpose that binds the nation as a whole together. The Mexican Revolution, in this view, constitutes an explosive moment of self-recognition in the nation's history.

Fuentes's 1987 novel *Cristóbal Nonato*,[44] however, reveals a distinct shift in perspective: revolutions, both past and present, are depicted in a markedly less exalted light.[45] It is true, of course, that from the very start of his career, Fuentes has developed an alternative, darker view of the Mexican Revolution, a view that he has normally articulated through the motif of treachery. In *La región*, Rodrigo Pola's father Gervasio is the vehicle for this theme: he is shown betraying his comrades in arms as they attempt to flee from the enemy. In *La muerte de Artemio Cruz*, in turn, the idea that the Mexican Revolution was betrayed is at the heart of the novel's very conception. But the notion of betrayal as Fuentes applies it to the Mexican Revolution and its aftermath implies that something worthy was betrayed. The dystopian perspective, far from negating its utopian opposite, fortifies it, and presents it in a more dramatic light. What seems to be new in *Cristóbal Nonato* is the presentation of the Mexican Revolution as something faintly ridiculous. The spirit of the Mexican Revolution is recreated in a mocking, though affectionate, manner in the figure of General Rigoberto Palomar, who owes his high military rank to a somewhat unusual feat: at the age of eighteen he was elevated in one stroke from trumpeter to general for having recovered the arm General Alvaro Obregón lost during the battle of Celaya. In the novel's present, at the age of ninety-one, General Palomar is the last survivor of the Revolution, in which he maintains an irrational faith that is premised on two contradictory assumptions: "1) The Revolution was not over; and 2) the Revolution had triumphed and carried out all its promises" (77/67). Fuentes takes this discrediting of the concept of revolution even further in his depiction of the revolutionary spirit of the late twentieth century. The embodiment of this spirit is Matamoros Moreno, whose leadership of the revolutionary forces of Mexico is both absurd, in that it grows out of the resentments of a frustrated writer, and somewhat sinister, in that his being nicknamed "Ayatollah" links him to a reactionary religious fanaticism. In this way, the belief in the possible emergence of a new, more benign, order is severely attenuated.

A final element in Fuentes's revised view of the nature of revolution consists of his rethinking of the relationship between the erotic and the political. Wendy Faris has observed that, in much of Fuentes's work, "love and revolution are allied, the physical upheaval and implied freedom of eroticism often serving as analogues for social liberation, both moving us toward some kind of utopia."[46] In *Cristóbal Nonato*, however, the personal and the political are no longer so easily reconciled; the relationship between these two dimensions of existence turns out to be fraught with difficulties. When young Ángel Palomar abandons his wife in the middle of her pregnancy in order to pursue an infatuation with the vain and superficial daughter of one of Mexico's richest men, he manages to convince himself that he is doing so in order to keep alive his iconoclastic and rebellious spirit. He is, in other words, chasing Penny López for the right ideological reasons. But Ángel is not entirely convinced by his own attempt at self-justification; he continues to be perplexed by "the contradiction between his ideas and his practices," and he is finally unable to find the correct adjustment between his sex life and his politics: "His renascent sexuality, was it progressive or reactionary? Should his political activity lead him to monogamy or to the harem?" The only possible conclusion is that these two realms are in some sense incommensurable: "a good screw explodes all ideologies" (354/327). In this way, revolution, deprived of a clear basis in personal experience, becomes a far more complex, baffling and even improbable event.

The Revolution emerges as a confusing, even unknowable chapter in the nation's history in another text from the late 1980s. "El prisionero de Las Lomas" is set in modern-day Mexico, but the key point of reference for the actions of the protagonist is a famous incident in which a captain in the revolutionary army refused to obey his commanding officer's orders to execute a group of innocent laborers at a hacienda in the state of Morelos. But as the narrative proceeds, the story of what truly happened that morning at Santa Eulalia becomes increasingly unclear, until finally the protagonist is forced to accept the laconic, humorous wisdom of an old man who actually witnessed the events in question, but who has come to the conclusion that "they told so many different stories about what happened at Santa Eulalia, you might as well believe them all; it was the only way of not making a mistake."[47] The Mexican Revolution no longer brings to life the many dimensions of the nation's culture in a total act of self-recognition. Now, it decomposes into a series of mutually incompatible narratives, which forever impede the possibility of recovering the past. Instead of being a foundation, the Mexican Revolution is an enigma.

Yet it would be wrong to maintain that the very idea of revolution has been entirely discredited in Fuentes's recent work. José Francisco Conde Ortega argues that Fuentes has assumed a fundamentally critical posture in regard to the Mexican Revolution throughout his career. Conde Ortega himself subscribes to a deeply skeptical and disenchanted view of the Mexican Revolution: he maintains that the Revolution "began to lose vitality almost from the very moment it exploded."[48] In Conde Ortega's eyes, Fuentes shares this negative appraisal of the Mexican Revolution: "Carlos Fuentes also takes as his point of departure the failure of the Revolution."[49] It seems to me, however, that Conde Ortega is reinterpreting Fuentes's career in light of the concerns of the early 1990s, a moment in time when the crisis of the political system that emerged in Mexico out of the Revolution, as well as the collapse of the Communist regimes of the Soviet Union and Eastern Europe, led to widespread skepticism about the very idea of revolution. Yet Fuentes's response to the Zapatista uprising in Chiapas in early 1994 reveals a far more complex set of attitudes on Fuentes's part than Conde Ortega recognizes. On the one hand, Fuentes insists, in an open letter to the Zapatista leader *subcomandante* Marcos, that the resort to violence was unnecessary: "I will continue to insist that legal means be employed until they are exhausted, and when they are exhausted, that new political means be explored."[50] On the other hand, Fuentes acknowledges a debt of gratitude to the Zapatistas for having brought about a kind of resurrection of an entire forgotten zone of Mexican reality: "we are indebted to you . . . for having reminded us of all that we had forgotten."[51] Given that

Fuentes has consistently interpreted the Mexican Revolution as a return to the manifold and suppressed dimensions of Mexican history, his comments to Marcos indicate that he concurs with the Zapatistas' conception of themselves as heirs to the Mexican Revolution. Furthermore, Fuentes accounts for the fact that the uprising took place in the state of Chiapas by recalling that the Mexican Revolution never reached this part of Mexico. The implication is that the original revolutionary project still awaits its fulfillment in Chiapas. It is in this ambivalence—the rejection of violence, along with the recognition of the legitimacy of the aspirations embodied first in the Mexican Revolution of 1910–1917 and now in the Chiapas uprising—that Fuentes's current conception of revolution may be located.

CHAPTER III

Between Identity and Alternativity

Two Versions of Modernity

If, as Octavio Paz claims, the history of Latin America is the history of different attempts to achieve modernity,[1] then perhaps the history of Latin American intellectual life is the history of different attempts to define modernity. The debate on modernity in Latin America has been consistently characterized by a profound ambivalence on the part of its protagonists, an ambivalence one recognizes in the work of writers ranging from Sarmiento, whose propaganda for the cause of European civilization conceals a real sympathy for the cause of American barbarism,[2] to Paz himself, whose criticism of the devastation wrought by modernity has been matched in intensity only by his insistence that in order to survive and flourish Latin America must join the modern world.[3] Carlos Fuentes is no exception to this pattern, for he has put forward in his work, side by side, two entirely different views of modernity.

A good place to examine Fuentes's positions on the question of modernity is his 1990 collection of essays, *Valiente mundo nuevo*. From one perspective, Fuentes associates modernity with the Enlightenment, in particular with the Enlightenment belief in reason and progress.[4] But the belief in reason implies the belief in a uniform, universal human nature, while the belief in progress involves the belief in a single, invariant *telos* to the historical process. Such convictions account for one of modernity's salient features: the utopian desire to remake the world according to certain uniform, established categories. Yet the project of modernity, with its abstract, homogeneous thrust, inevitably clashes with the concrete, heterogeneous realities of the world's many cultures. The neglect of cultural diversity is, in fact, the most damning feature of modernity in Fuentes's eyes. It is a feature he is particularly alert to, for as a non-European it is easy for him to see how the supposed universality of modernity masks the interests of "the intellectual middle classes of the Europe of the Enlightenment and the Revolution" (44). Moreover, as a Mexican, that is, as a member of a multicultural society, Fuentes is highly sensitive to the need for social and political models—as well as conceptions of human nature—that show respect for cultural diversity.

Yet in the very same book Fuentes develops an entirely different perspective according to which the values of diversity and multiplicity, far from vanishing under modernity, flourish as never before. At several points in *Valiente mundo nuevo*, Fuentes recapitulates the argument he had put forward in his 1976 essay *Cervantes o la crítica de la lectura* concerning the transition from the closed, hierarchical world of the Middle Ages to the open, decentered world of the Renaissance. He returns in *Valiente mundo nuevo* to one of his principal sources for this argument, Umberto Eco's *Opera Aperta*, describing it as a "a brilliant study of the transition from the 'univocal' world of the Middle Ages to the 'pluridimensional' world of the Renaissance" (226). Fuentes also reiterates the view—developed at greater length in *Cervantes*—that the great figures of European Renaissance culture are the founders of the modern world. Cervantes, with his acceptance of "the diversity and mutability of the universe," Shakespeare, with his evocation of a new world of "questions, doubts and irrational fears," and Erasmus, with his plea for "the abandonment of all absolutes, whether of faith or of reason," establish an alternative tradition within modernity (53–55). This tradition resists "what Jean-François Lyotard calls 'the metanarratives of emancipation' of Enlightenment modernity" and instead promises a "multiplication of *multinarratives*" (25). Although

Fuentes never considers the matter directly, his book presents what is in effect a struggle between two different aspects of modernity.

Fuentes clearly wants to be regarded as a novelist in the tradition of Cervantes. The desire to steer critical interpretations of his work in a particular direction has been a constant feature of Fuentes's work. The publication of *La nueva novela hispanoamericana* in 1969 helped establish a view of Fuentes as a supremely innovative novelist, a novelist, also, with a powerful interest in the then fashionable topic of language. The essays collected in *Valiente mundo nuevo* and *Geografía de la novela* (1993), as well as statements Fuentes has made about his work in interviews, have helped shape a new critical consensus in which Fuentes figures as the great novelist of hybridity and heterogeneity, of multiplicity and open-endedness.[5] In this view, Fuentes appears as Mikhail Bakhtin's best student, and multiculturalism's most famous ambassador. There is much to be said for such a reading. In the broad cosmopolitan approach to literature advocated by Fuentes and his collaborators in the pages of the *Revista Mexicana de Literatura* in the mid-1950s, one can see a prefiguration of Fuentes's current enthusiasm for the cause of cultural diversity. In Fuentes's political writings, moreover, one sees a preference for antidogmatic positions from the very start of his career. In addition, Fuentes's political history has not been marked by the dramatic disavowals and abrupt changes of course we have seen in the careers of other Latin American writers of his generation. Yet the new consensus obscures certain features particularly of Fuentes's early work. For, if we follow Fuentes himself (who, in turn, derives his position from Lyotard) and view the belief in the grand narratives of emancipation and enlightenment as the key distinguishing feature of modernity, then it is clear that the very large body of work in the area of political journalism Fuentes produced from, roughly, the late 1950s to the mid-1960s can be located firmly within the very paradigm of modernity Fuentes currently seems to reject. Furthermore, Fuentes's major work of fiction from this period, *La muerte de Artemio Cruz* (1962), is marked, underneath the appearance of rupture and fragmentation, by a strong reliance on notions of unity and identity and by a strain of utopianism that links the novel to a now supposedly superseded modernity.

To Havana and Back

In the late 1950s and early 1960s, Fuentes regularly contributed articles on political topics to a variety of Mexican publications, such as *Novedades*, *Política*, *Siempre!* and "La Cultura en México," the cultural supplement of *Siempre!* These articles reveal a strong element of utopianism in Fuentes's political views, a utopianism that takes the form of a fervent belief in the concept of revolution, and receives its most significant inspiration from the example of the Cuban Revolution.

Fuentes's political position clearly became more radical under the impact of the Cuban Revolution.[6] In the mid-1950s, in the days of the *Revista Mexicana de Literatura*, Fuentes favored a Third Way that rejected both Soviet communism and U.S. capitalism.[7] It is also significant that Fuentes was sympathetic in these years to Albert Camus's critique of totalitarianism,[8] and that he regularly derided the cultural politics of socialist realism.[9] By the early 1960s, however, Fuentes had developed a far more sympathetic reading of the Soviet system. Soviet support for the Cuban Revolution surely had something to do with this, as did the process of de-Stalinization that the USSR was undergoing. Yet in Fuentes's case, de-Stalinization also encouraged a more favorable view of Stalin himself. In "Carne y cartón de Stalín," a piece published in *Política* in November 1961, Fuentes begins by claiming that under Stalin the Soviet Union had embarked on "a gigantic effort to rationalize fundamental social and economic relations."[10] This process of rationalization has produced for the first time in the country's history a diversified (and hence, modern) society. Fuentes suggests that this achievement can be attributed to factors such as education and industrialization, but also to "the iron-fisted planning imposed by Stalin."[11] Thus, Fuentes reads Stalinism as a grim necessity that ultimately served the interests of the country's progress and modernization.

Fuentes's view of the Cuban Revolution is considerably more lyrical, but it relies on the same narrative of progress that subtends his interpretation of the Russian Revolution and its aftermath. It is striking, for example, how frequently Fuentes traces an arc that links the Cuban Revolution to a variety of other revolutionary struggles around the world. Fuentes repeatedly states that the Mexican Revolution ought to be viewed as a precursor of the Cuban Revolution. In "El argumento de América Latina: Palabras a los norteamericanos," an article Fuentes published in *Siempre!* after the U.S. embassy denied him a visa to travel to the United States to debate Richard Goodwin of the State Department, he argues that the experiences of Mexico and Cuba teach the exact same lesson: that only a revolution can bring about genuine change.[12] In another *Política* article, he describes the Mexican Revolution as the precursor not just of the Cuban Revolution, but of the rise of the Third World as a whole: "Mexico is the solitary precursor of a movement that . . . now encompasses three quarters of the world."[13] The Spanish Civil War, too, occupies an important place within this broad historical narrative. In "EEUU: Notas para un análisis," Fuentes writes: "After the assassination in Spain of the ideal internationalism of the first few decades of the twentieth century, we are now witnessing the emergence of a concrete internationalism: that of the underdeveloped nations."[14] But the Cuban Revolution is not just part of the history of the Spanish-speaking world, or of the underdeveloped nations; it is also part of what Fuentes describes as a universal historical process. In an article he wrote for a special issue of "La Cultura en México" designed to mark the ninth anniversary of the assault on the Moncada barracks, an assault widely regarded as the start of the Cuban Revolution, Fuentes declares that "All authentic Revolutions are universal."[15] He goes on to evoke a grand parade of world-class revolutionaries—Spartacus and Christ, Saint-Just and Bolívar, Lenin and Gandhi, Zapata and Castro—all of whom express and incarnate the aspiration of people everywhere to pass from non-being to being. The existence of this common aspiration means that revolutions "are not the history of a handful of men in a specific place and at a specific time: they are the history of all mankind in an embrace that reaches across centuries and frontiers."[16] This permanent, universal quality of the revolutionary impulse means, of course, that further revolutions are continuously announcing themselves. In the early 1960s, Peru seemed to Fuentes to be especially ripe for a revolution. In "Latinoamérica:

Tierra nuestra," a report on a trip Fuentes made to several Latin American countries in early 1962, he asserts that "in Peru an explosion is brewing that will be very similar to the Mexican explosion of 1910."[17] In "América Latina surge a la escena," he repeats the same point: "One need only visit Peru to realize that a bloody, popular explosion is inevitable there, and that the Peruvian Revolution will be headed, above all, by *caudillos* of the people, by equivalents of our Villa and Zapata."[18] In "Doctrina Estrada para Perú," Fuentes writes that the Peruvian people are beginning to expect everything from "that magic word: Revolution."[19]

Fuentes claims, too, that "even without the example of Cuba, the emergence of revolutionary movements in Latin America would have been inevitable."[20] Yet there can be little doubt that Fuentes's own euphoria about the concept of revolution in these years was closely tied to the events in Cuba. Fuentes made several visits to Cuba in the early years of the Revolution; the reports he wrote on these trips testify to the extraordinary exaltation he experienced there. Although Fuentes did discuss certain concrete, practical issues, such as agrarian reform or the trials and executions conducted by the revolutionary regime immediately after it seized power, his articles on Cuba stress the emotional and spiritual dimension of the Revolution. In a piece he published in *Novedades* barely a month after the Revolution's triumph, Fuentes claims that "a profound and uplifting revolutionary emotion is felt in Cuba."[21] Later that year Fuentes attended a mass rally held in Havana to celebrate the 26th of July, and in a long article published in *Novedades* he offers a more extended account of the revolutionary emotion: "What great revolution is not, above all, a triumph of love, of fraternity? Men recognize themselves, and recognize their brothers; the dark cloth that separates us from each other is slashed by the revolution and we are all, as on the first day, sons of one earth and brothers of one flesh. It is impossible to wear a mask: these eyes are my eyes, this voice is my voice. To be everybody at once: this is the miracle of the Revolution."[22] Fuentes sees the Revolution as a supremely unifying event; it brings about a sudden return to a pristine state of universal fraternity. This vision of a society free of all strife and conflict is, in effect, a vision of a society outside of history. The Cuban Revolution has the freshness of the first day; it also has the fullness of the end of time. This explains why history is literally erased before Fuentes's eyes as he watches a military parade presided over by Fidel Castro and Lázaro Cárdenas, the ex-president of Mexico. The solemn spectacle of the marching cavalry transports Fuentes into the past: "We are reminded of the entrance of Emiliano Zapata into Mexico City, of the passing of the *agraristas* along the Avenida 5 de mayo. This morning, in Havana, Zapata leads all of Cuba, all of Spanish America: it is as if nobody had died in Chinameca. This is the revolution without betrayal, without factions, without the possibility of defeat."[23]

The Cuban Revolution heals all the wounds of Latin American history. It both resuscitates the past (Zapata rides again) and cancels it (Zapata never died). As the culmination and fulfillment of Latin America's struggles, the Cuban Revolution appears in Fuentes's eyes as a complete and rounded event, without fissures and discontinuities. Hence, Fuentes's repeated emphasis on the fact that the Revolution enjoys the total support of the Cuban people. Hence, also, the notion that there is no distance between the people and the commander of the Revolution: "Fidel speaks the language of the people: every peasant has a complete understanding of his words."[24] Hence, finally, the view of the Revolution as a completely *visible* event, an event in which the totality of a people manifests itself. At the end of his report on the mass rally of July 26, 1959, Fuentes writes: "Before my eyes the people in their totality pass, but not just of Cuba, of Mexico, of all of Spanish America."[25]

To regard history as wholly visible in this way implies that history is following an intelligible and even inevitable pattern. This sense of the transparency of the historical process also informs Fuentes's views on the relations between the United States and Latin America. Perhaps the most telling piece in this regard is "La hora de la definición: con el fascismo o con el pueblo," which appeared in *Política* shortly after the Bay of Pigs invasion in April 1961. Fuentes describes the conflict between the United States and its Latin American neighbors in extremely sharp terms. His picture of the United States owes a great deal to the work of the American sociologist C. Wright Mills, whom Fuentes had met in Cuba in the early days of the Revolution, and to whom he dedicated *La muerte de Artemio Cruz*. According to Fuentes "Everybody is now aware of one key, long disguised fact: in the US a centralized structure holds power, an aggressive, political, military and corporate elite, with shared interests and unified aims,"[26] an analysis that comes straight out of Mills's best-known work, *The Power Elite* (1956). Fuentes points out that there are no significant differences between the two large political parties in the United States: both are equally committed to the preservation of a global system of domination headed by the Pentagon and the White House, and both act in the interests of the country's two hundred largest corporations. Fuentes concludes that the United States is a fascist power: "Kennedy and Nixon threaten us with force just like Hitler and Mussolini threatened Czechoslovakia, Ethiopia, Austria and Albania."[27] As Fuentes turns to survey the forces aligned against the United States—with a special focus on Mexico—he sees reason for hope:

> For the first time in twenty years, the people have organized themselves, and have expressed their unanimous will. . . . The people of Mexico stand by Cuba and oppose the aggressive fascism of the US. The people of Mexico stand by Latin America and oppose Kennedy's policy of threats. But, above all, the people of Mexico stand by themselves, they have discovered themselves, and they have discovered their own power to organize, to express their will and to demand that the government respect it.[28]

In this passage the Mexican people constitute an impressive counter to the United States, yet at the same time the two entities are mirror images of each other. The integrated, centralized power structure of the United States stands in opposition to the unanimous, self-aware general will of the Mexican people. Neither of the two sides suffers from any internal divisions. Each is a cohesive, unified entity.

If the enemy is totally and irredeemably evil, then the only possible future that can be projected for him is annihilation. In Fuentes, this stance is reinforced by an appeal to the Marxist science of history, according to which societies move through a series of determinate stages that lead inevitably to the utopia of a classless society. That Fuentes's reading of history is shaped by this Marxist assumption is clear from a comment he makes on the Cuban situation in "De Bandung a Belgrado," a report on the Conference of Non-Aligned Nations held in Belgrade in September 1961. He explains why it was impossible for the United States to lead Cuba down the path of bourgeois democracy: "Cuba . . . had already passed through the stage of bourgeois democracy under North American guidance."[29] The Cuban Revolution, insofar as it was a worker's revolution, was following a specific historical logic. The country could not regress to a historical phase that had already been superseded. Developments in the capitalist world were, in the meantime, subject to a similar historical inevitability: "The Western nations, before abandoning the center of the stage of history, now embark, stripped of all disguises, upon the final phase of imperialism: *fascism*."[30]

In practice, however, it proved difficult for Fuentes to sustain such a univocal reading of the political conflicts triggered by the Cuban Revolution. Fuentes's publications were direct responses to specific situations, and as those situations evolved, his arguments and rhetoric evolved as well. To begin with, the facts of Mexican politics, as well as Fuentes's evident desire not to break off his dialogue with the Mexican political establishment, and especially with President Adolfo López Mateos, led him in due course to construct a more moderate position for himself. It may have been clear to Fuentes in the wake of the Bay of Pigs invasion that the Mexican people were solidly behind Cuba. Yet the Mexican government's position on Cuba was considerably more ambiguous, as was clear from the events at the Conference of the Organization of American States (OAS) held at Punta del Este, Uruguay, in early 1962. Seizing on the fact that Fidel Castro had declared openly that he was a Marxist-Leninist, the United States mounted an aggressive campaign to exclude Cuba from the OAS. Mexico merely abstained from the vote of exclusion, which carried by a margin of fourteen to one, with a total of six abstentions. But Mexico also took the initiative in constructing a consensus statement according to which the adherence of any member state to Marxism-Leninism was "incompatible with the principles and objectives of the inter-American system."[31] Fuentes initially interpreted the events at Punta del Este with the help of the same grid he had applied to the Bay of Pigs invasion. In a piece significantly entitled "Coexistencia o fascismo," he declares that Punta del Este signals the end of the OAS and the birth of a military fascist bloc in the Western Hemisphere. For Mexico the options are clear: "It must either take concrete political steps in favor of peaceful coexistence, which means leaving the OAS, or it must accept the new fascist order."[32]

The Mexican government chose to follow a more ambiguous path. Sensing perhaps that he was painting himself into a corner with his all-or-nothing view of the conflict between the United States and Latin America, Fuentes began to adopt a more conciliatory stance on the subject. Immediately after Punta del Este, Fuentes declared that a failure to leave the OAS was for Mexico tantamount to accepting the fascist U.S. plan for Latin America. Yet a few months later, with Mexico still a member of the OAS, Fuentes warmly applauded what he himself conceded were only marginal moves in the right direction on the part of the Mexican government. A joint declaration that came out of a meeting between President López Mateos and President Goulart of Brazil was praised by Fuentes for offering a tacit opening to the left.[33] This was a rather modest basis for hope—especially when compared with the apocalyptic tenor of Fuentes's earlier pronouncements on the international situation. Yet Fuentes stressed the importance of trying to prod the Mexican president in the right direction, rather than wait passively for what he calls a "presidential miracle"—the sudden transformation of the Mexican political scene by the rise to power of someone who is "one of us."[34] A similar sense of the value of slow, incremental gains in politics informs Fuentes's analysis of John F. Kennedy's visit to Mexico later the same year. While

Fuentes's friends over at *Política* ran a flaming editorial in which they compared John and Jacqueline Kennedy to Maximilian and Carlota,[35] Fuentes wrote a piece for *Siempre!* in which he emphasized the benefits Mexico had obtained from the meeting between López Mateos and Kennedy: "In exchange for Mexico's unconditional support for the Alliance for Progress, Kennedy gave his blessing to the political, economic and social policies of the current Mexican regime."[36] Fuentes insisted that this was an important concession given the belief in business circles that there were socialist aspects to the Mexican model. In March 1963, in an article in which Fuentes offered an overall assessment of López Mateos's foreign policy, he even expressed support and sympathy for the Mexican government's actions with regard to Cuba. After all, Fuentes wrote, Mexico was placed under enormous pressure by the United States, yet López Mateos refused to break off diplomatic relations with Cuba.[37]

Parallel to the more moderate reading of Mexico's goals and accomplishments in its relations with the always threatening neighbor to the north, we may observe a more conciliatory view of the United States itself. Clearly, the confrontation between the United States and Cuba in the early 1960s—in particular the Bay of Pigs invasion—elicited from Fuentes the most extreme type of analysis. In 1959, just after the overthrow of Batista, and before the United States had definitively embarked on its hostile course vis-à-vis the Cuban Revolution, Fuentes had published a piece in *Universidad de México* in which he viewed relations between Latin America and the United States in a far less confrontational light. In fact, Fuentes envisions in "América Latina y EEUU: Notas para un panorama" the creation of an alliance between revolutionary movements in Spanish America and what he calls "the broad democratic sectors of US society."[38] Such an alliance is not just a possibility, but a necessity: "A Spanish American revolution must appeal to those nuclei of democratic opinion in the US that are in a position to support our liberation movements."[39] Even in 1961, both before and after the Bay of Pigs invasion, Fuentes mentioned an aspect of U.S. society—the free press—which he believed compared favorably with the situation in Mexico, and moreover appeared to disprove the thesis that the United States was in the grip of a "power elite" and headed toward fascism.[40] The recognition that there existed in the United States a certain space for dissent became even stronger a few years later with the rise of the antiwar movement. In "Vietnam," a piece that appeared in "La Cultura en México" in July 1966, Fuentes sees in Senator Fulbright's opposition to the U.S. role in the South East Asian conflict an indication of "the true greatness of the US: that of permanent dissent."[41] Fuentes greets the social, cultural and political upheavals in the United States with enthusiasm, and he envisions the same kind of alliance between the United States and Latin America of which he had spoken in 1959: "Will we Latin Americans end up making our revolutions *with* the North American rebels?"[42]

Once Fuentes moved away from the polarized rhetoric that characterized some of his writings of the early 1960s, he himself became a victim of the polarization of Latin American intellectual debate in these years. In June 1966, Fuentes attended a meeting of the PEN Club in New York. Another prominent Latin American guest at the meeting was Pablo Neruda. In Cuba, the presence of leading Latin American leftist intellectuals at a literary event in the United States was not well received. A large group of Cuban intellectuals signed an open letter to Pablo Neruda in which the Chilean poet was bitterly denounced for his trip. The Cubans argued that the State Department's decision to award entry visas to certain Latin American leftists could only spring from a desire to draw them into a plot to cover up American crimes.[43] In a subsequent roundtable discussion between Roberto Fernández Retamar, Lisandro Otero, Edmundo Desnoes and Ambrosio Fornet, the same point was made in a more vivid fashion: the United States allows Latin American leftists into the country, several of the participants claimed, only so as to be better able to castrate them.[44] In the open letter to Neruda, the Cubans concluded with a call to arms: "We must declare a state of alert throughout the continent: an alert against the new imperialist penetration in the area of culture."[45]

Although Neruda was their prime target, the Cubans also vented their rage on Fuentes. Shortly after the PEN Club meeting, Fuentes published a piece in the Spanish edition of *Life* in which he described the meeting as an attempt to bury the Cold War in literature.[46] The Cubans insisted that it was unacceptable to speak of the end of the Cold War in any area at a time when the United States was savagely attacking Vietnam and preparing a new attack on Cuba. In the roundtable discussion, Desnoes argued that in writing for *Life* Fuentes had become complicit in the politics of a magazine that "has systematically attacked the Cuban Revolution, defended the US intervention in Santo Domingo, and backed up the worst goons in Latin America."[47]

Fuentes's relationship with the Cuban Revolution did not remain unaffected by the attack of the Cuban intellectuals. In a letter he wrote to Fernando Benítez in February 1967, Fuentes stated that he was prepared to go to Cuba "to demonstrate my permanent solidarity with the Cuban Revolution,"[48] but the trip was never made. In the "Cronología personal" Fuentes wrote in 1995 (in the third person) for Julio Ortega's *Retrato de Carlos Fuentes*, he describes the methods used by the Cuban intellectuals in their attack on Neruda and him as Stalinist, and states that from this moment on he did not return to Cuba.[49] Yet the difference between Fuentes's two assessments (in 1967 and 1995) of the imbroglio with the Cubans reveals a significant shift in Fuentes's position. On both occasions, Fuentes emphatically deplores what he regards as the misguided response of the Cubans to the presence of Neruda and himself at the New York PEN meeting. In 1967, however, Fuentes's primary concern is to emphasize his solidarity with the Cuban Revolution. By 1995 the value of solidarity takes a back seat to the value of pluralism. In retrospect, the fact that the Cubans misjudged the strength of his support for the Cuban Revolution seems less important than the fact that they failed to adhere to certain norms of tolerance and open-mindedness in their public debate with him. In 1967, Fuentes underlines his ongoing identification with the Cuban Revolution; in 1995, he stresses the failure of the Cuban intellectuals to break out of their narrow dogmas.

Modes of Redemption

La muerte de Artemio Cruz is both a paradigmatic modernist text, with its nonlinear narrative and interiorist focus, and a culminating instance of the novel of the Mexican Revolution, with its broad historical and political concerns.[50] By situating his novel at the intersection of these two literary modes, Fuentes to a certain extent enriches them both: his use of modernist techniques grants greater interest and complexity to a subject-matter often treated in a straightforward, documentary fashion, whereas his historical and political concerns help Fuentes transcend the often narrowly subjectivist nature of modernist fiction.[51] Yet there is also a loss in Fuentes's translation of a modernist aesthetic into a Mexican context. For if an interest in the topics of time and consciousness is one of the elements that links *Artemio Cruz* to the modernist tradition, then it must be noted that Fuentes's need to provide his novel with a clear political message—that the Mexican Revolution was betrayed by the greed and selfishness of its protagonists—in fact places clear limits on his exploration of these topics. In the classic modernist novel of such writers as Marcel Proust, Virginia Woolf, and William Faulkner, consciousness is experienced as fragmented in large part because of the inherently destructive nature of time. Thus, Georg Lukács speaks in *The Theory of the Novel* of how "the sluggish, yet constant progress of time . . . gradually robs subjectivity of all its possessions and imperceptibly forces alien contents into it."[52] Of course, there is also a social context to this experience: for Lukács the volatility of consciousness is a direct consequence of the disorientedness and meaninglessness of modern society itself. In *Artemio Cruz*, however, the specific features of the protagonist's career and character make it much more difficult to read the novel as a broad meditation on the topic of time. Fuentes unfolds a series of devices with which to illustrate the splintered condition of Artemio Cruz's consciousness—the shifts between first-, second-, and third-person narrative, the winding interior monologues, the theme of the double—yet this fragmented self belongs to a character who, as Gerald Martin points out, is explicitly judged and condemned in the novel.[53] The result is that the reader holds Artemio at a distance, for we regard his disintegrated consciousness not as an aspect of modern subjectivity itself, but rather as a form of punishment for Artemio's opportunism, his lack of an ethical core.[54]

Many critics read *Artemio Cruz* as a powerful study of the split condition of the self.[55] But what must be emphasized is that the process of psychic fragmentation Artemio undergoes is meaningful only against the backdrop of an alternative image of an unfissured self. Artemio's plight has a certain element of contingency to it: his destabilized subjectivity is the result of the personal choices he has made in the course of his life, but things could clearly have been otherwise. It is this "otherwise" that is captured in the evocation of various ephemeral moments of plenitude Artemio has experienced. These moments constitute the norm against which the fundamentally fractured quality of Artemio's consciousness appears as a deviation. The insistent presence in *Artemio Cruz* of an ideal of transparency—in the constitution of the self and in the self's relations with the world—helps us see the links between the novel and Fuentes's journalistic writings of the late 1950s and early 1960s. In his political commentaries, Fuentes makes constant use of unified categories—such as the notion of "the people"—and appeals repeatedly to a utopian vision of a disalienated society—for which Cuba under the new revolutionary regime provides the model. On the surface, *Artemio Cruz*, with its ambiguous protagonist and jagged narrative line, appears to resist the ideal of transparency that animates Fuentes's political journalism. Yet *Artemio Cruz* is, in fact, informed by the same utopian impulse as Fuentes's political writings, the same desire for the restoration of a state of social and political wholeness.[56]

A brief examination of a number of literary essays Fuentes first published in the late 1950s and early 1960s can help bring this aspect of Fuentes's aesthetics to light. In these essays—on Jane Austen, Herman Melville, and William Faulkner—Fuentes puts forward a broad interpretation of the history of the novel, an interpretation that helps us see where Fuentes locates his own work.[57] Fuentes divides the genre of the novel into two broad categories:

the classic and the modern. The former is the bourgeois realist novel, with its linear organization and its preference for unproblematic description. It is what Fuentes labels "the novel of recognition," a type of novel which confirms rather than subverts the order of the real. The prime example of this type of work is offered by Jane Austen: "In Jane Austen's novels the readers immediately recognized themselves: they saw themselves as they wanted to be seen" (29). Austen's novels serve to consecrate the new class in power—they provide the bourgeoisie with a portrait of itself, but above all they instill in it a good conscience about itself. Thus, the novelistic tradition Austen helped to establish presupposes a seamless relationship between text and reality, as well as between text and reader.

Fuentes rejects the Jane Austen type of novel, for it is far too cautious and conventional for his tastes. He clearly prefers what he sometimes calls the novel of radical modernity, and at other times the novel of tragic vision, a type of work of which the writings of Faulkner are a prime expression. For Fuentes, tragic vision, a quality he believes the modern world sorely lacks, is intimately related to the consciousness of something he calls "separation." In the essay on Austen, he defines "separation" as the opposite of "recognition," and suggests that William Blake, "in the midst of the victorious rise of the bourgeoisie" (28), offered the first powerful intuition of its meaning. Blake explored the reverse side of the safe and familiar world depicted by the bourgeois novelists. In the tradition of "poetic radicalism" (70) he inaugurated, identity is not held within a stable circumference, but rather discovers its own profound otherness. Faulkner belongs to this tradition precisely because his characters are not fixed and predictable figures, but rather "extreme, deep and secret possibilities" (70). In his discussion of Faulkner, Fuentes relates this discovery of the abyss within the self to man's paradoxical and tragic relationship to nature. Man, dependent upon nature for his survival, must use it, but in doing so he also violates it. He introduces evil into the natural order; he divides the earth, but as a result also divides himself, for the need to exploit nature signals the impossibility of living in harmony with nature. This, says Fuentes, explains why Faulkner gave the name Yoknapatawpha County to the imaginary world of his novels, for Yoknapatawpha means "the divided earth" in Chickasaw (64).

This tragic vision is embodied in Faulkner, but also in Dostoyevsky and Kafka, and in Poe and Melville, in an aesthetics of estrangement. These novelists all reject the familiar, and seek the unknown. They are in opposition to a world dominated by what Fuentes calls "a double rationality, of the reconciliation of man and God in Christianity, and of man and reason in history" (70–71). Against what we would now call the grand narratives of Christianity and the Enlightenment, Fuentes proposes a giddy vision of unremitting conflict, contradiction, and incompleteness. Against the novel of recognition, he proposes the novel of separation. Yet, interestingly enough, at several points in Fuentes's argument, the opposition between the two types of novel is erased.

Toward the end of his essay on Austen, Fuentes suddenly reverses direction, suggesting that, in light of certain traits inherent to the genre of the novel, Austen's work, almost in spite of itself, possesses a subversive dimension. Octavio Paz's definition of the novel as the "epic of a society in conflict with itself," and so as "an implicit judgement of that same society,"[58] leads Fuentes to the conclusion that even Austen's work—true as it must remain to the fundamental impulses of the genre—leaves "a space for doubt, for reflection, for the reader's alarmed consciousness" (31). Yet in the same way as Fuentes ends by discovering an unsuspected sense of openness in Austen's novels, his reading of Faulkner—and of the tragic vision in the modern novel—finally emphasizes a paradoxical sense of closure. Although the notion of "separation," as Fuentes uses it in *Casa con dos puertas*, appears on one level to denote the irremediably exilic nature of human existence itself, on a different level the term seems to allude to what is merely a stage in the development of human consciousness, or of human society. When Fuentes suggests that what Blake called "separation," Marx would later call "alienation" (28), the implication is that "separation," a condition denied and suppressed by the bourgeois realist aesthetics of "recognition," is discovered, but also overcome, in the Romantic visionary tradition embodied by Blake. Indeed, in the work of Blake and his successors (Fuentes mentions Brontë, Novalis, Hölderlin, Büchner, Marx, Nietzsche, Dostoyevsky, and Kafka) the aesthetics of estrangement serves ultimately to lead to a higher form of recognition—a kind of "other-recognition" to which Jane Austen remained immune (32). In his discussion of Faulkner, Fuentes describes an analogous process, though here he places it in a Christian framework: "Where formerly there was only being and contemplation, men introduce sin, and hence redemption; violation, and hence love; responsibility, and hence grace; grief, and hence happiness" (64). In this narrative, separation is merely a prelude to redemption. When, elsewhere in the same essay, Fuentes argues that in the work of James Joyce, William Faulkner, Hermann Broch, and Malcolm Lowry, the novel becomes poetry, he states his utopian vision, now shorn of its Christian connotations, with even greater force, for Fuentes draws his definition of poetry from surrealism: "For the surrealists, poetry and revolution were one and the same thing: both, in a fusion of identities, were to destroy all forms of alienation and reveal the complete reality of mankind, the vital correspondences between fact and dream, reality and desire, nature and the individual: between all the separated halves" (60).

Whether couched in a Christian or in a surrealist vocabulary, the promise of redemption constitutes one of the informing principles of Fuentes's aesthetics. This is clear not only in Fuentes's literary essays, but also in *Artemio Cruz*, where the protagonist is measured specifically in terms of his distance from the ideals of fusion and integration so vividly evoked in *Casa con dos puertas*. One of the key words used in the novel to capture Artemio's condition is the word "separation." On one level, the word captures the tragic truth about Artemio's life, a truth which his social self, oriented toward status and recognition, would prefer not to admit. From this perspective, Artemio's willingness to face this truth, at least in the inner recess of his self, grants a degree of depth and dignity to his character. Yet "separation" also emerges as the cost of Artemio's success, and therefore as the mode in which the novel expresses its condemnation of him.

"Separation" defines Artemio's relationship to his wife Catalina, who never forgives Artemio for having failed to save the life of her brother Gonzalo, with whom Artemio had shared a prison cell during the Revolution, nor for the ruthless way in which Artemio seized her along with her father's wealth after the Revolution. Near the beginning of the novel the narrator describes Catalina and Artemio listening to each other's movements through a door that separates their rooms. "Who will live in that separation?" he wonders (34/28). When, in an episode set in 1941, the narrator alternates between descriptions of Artemio conducting his business from his office, and Catalina and their daughter Laura going shopping, the point of the very modernist device is to show how husband and wife live in separate orbits. This dreadful sense of separation haunts Artemio's relations with all the women in his life: Regina meets a violent death during the Revolution, Laura slips away when Artemio—worried about appearances—refuses to divorce his wife, and Lila is only interested in Artemio's money. But Artemio's unhappy romances are a symptom, not a cause. Artemio is like Captain Ahab, of whom Fuentes writes in his essay on Melville that "rooted in the freedom of his own self, he ends by transgressing the freedom of his fellow human beings" (47). Artemio has a similarly immoderate conception of his own freedom: "Perhaps her hand speaks to you of an excess of freedom that defeats freedom. Freedom that raises an endless tower that does not reach heaven but splits the abyss, cleaves the earth. You will name it: separation" (85–86). But Artemio's pathologies also have a specifically Mexican genealogy. After all, Artemio corresponds very closely to the figure of the *chingón* so vividly described by Octavio Paz in *El laberinto de la soledad*. The *chingón* is the active, aggressive male who imposes his will on the passive, inert female.[59] According to Paz, Mexicans venerate the *chingón*; the result is to turn society into a battlefield, where all that counts is the ability to lord it over one's fellow human beings.[60] In a passage from *Artemio Cruz* that is clearly indebted to Paz, Fuentes describes the poisonous effects of such values: "the *chingada* who poisons love, dissolves friendship, smashes tenderness, the *chingada* who divides, who separates, who destroys, who poisons" (146/138). The irony in *Artemio Cruz* is, of course, that the *chingón* becomes the victim of his own violence. Artemio owes his social and financial success to his determination to climb to the top, and to his willingness to sacrifice others for the sake of his personal advancement, but his fate is to be haunted by feelings of inner division and incompleteness. The *chingón* masks a fragmented self; his willful separation from his fellow human beings results in a separation from himself. And so, Artemio's life, as he experiences it in retrospect, becomes a kind of protracted death. Near the end of the novel, with his life hanging by a thread, Artemio is rushed to the hospital for an operation. "I'm separated . . . I'm dying" (270/262) he thinks to himself. When, on the next page, Artemio reflects that "living is another separation" (271/263), the phrase does not so much undermine the earlier identification of separation with death as suggest that Artemio's life has, in fact, amounted to a kind of death-in-life. The idea of the identity of life and death is, of course, implied in the very title of the novel: *La muerte de Artemio Cruz* is, after all, the story of the *life* of Artemio Cruz.

Artemio is a social climber, but he is also a seeker after some form of redemption. However, given that the supreme form of redemption in the novel is achieved in the act of revolution, it is clear that Artemio is doomed to fail in his search. On his deathbed, Artemio remembers the Revolution: "Those faces you saw in Sonora and Chihuahua, faces you saw sleepy one day, hanging on for dear life, and the next furious, hurling themselves into that struggle devoid of reason or palliatives, into that embrace of men separated by other men" (276/268). But it is also at this moment that Artemio realizes that he has lived his entire life fearing a new revolution: "You feared it each of your days of power. You will fear that the amorous impulse will burst again" (276/268). Revolution as the highest form of eroticism: this conception also informs the role of Artemio's son Lorenzo in the novel. Lorenzo is the hero his father failed to be, for he dies fighting for his ideals, whereas Artemio let others die so that he could survive, but he is also his father's heir, for he explains his decision to join the Republican forces in the Spanish Civil War by telling his father that he is merely following in his footsteps.[61] In this way, Lorenzo reveals Artemio's ambivalence: Artemio both identifies with the revolutionary ideal of fraternity, yet fears the threat this ideal poses to his social and economic position.

The chapter that narrates the day of Lorenzo's death in Spain is the only chapter in the novel in which the protagonist is somebody other than Artemio. Yet the narrator says to Artemio that the day of Lorenzo's death is "one day that is more yours than any other day" (228/219). It is Artemio's day not only because he experiences the death of his son as the death of a part of himself, but also because Lorenzo's experiences cast a sharp light on Artemio's own trajectory. In this section, the image of the unfissured self, which helps the reader place Artemio's experience of psychic fragmentation in the proper perspective, obtains its clearest expression. The state of wholeness achieved by Lorenzo is linked in the first place to his ability to bring the private and public dimensions of his experience into conjunction with each other. The story of Lorenzo suggests that private fulfillment is only available to the individual who participates in some significant collective venture. Artemio ruthlessly disregards the claims of others in the course of his social ascent, and is punished, as it were, in the form of a series of stunted relationships with the women in his life, whereas Lorenzo dedicates himself to a noble cause and is, in effect, rewarded with a fulfilling, though brief, love affair with a Spanish woman named Dolores. Through the depiction of the amorous encounter between Lorenzo and Dolores, Fuentes creates an imaginary space in which love and politics, the private and the public, are fused into a harmonious whole. Lorenzo's and Dolores's lovemaking is preceded, and, in fact, enabled, by a joint act of courage that constitutes a clear political gesture. Fleeing for France along with a number of their companions, they are faced with a bridge that offers them their only means of escape, but that may well have been mined by the enemy. One member of the group, a man named Miguel, is ready to admit defeat. It is at this moment that Dolores takes Lorenzo's hand into her own. Slowly, hand in hand, they cross the bridge, risking their lives to prove to their comrades that it is safe. Their bravery is an expression of political hope; it refutes the temptation of despair reflected in Miguel's words. On the night following their daring walk across the bridge, Lorenzo and Dolores consummate their love. The two stages of the narrative are closely intertwined with each other: the burgeoning love between a man and a woman inspires them to an act of public heroism; their act of public heroism deepens their mutual attraction and prepares the way for the sexual consummation of their love. The fact that Lorenzo dies shortly afterward in a Fascist air attack is more than anything else a confirmation of the unity of love and politics, for the implication is that the kind of personal fulfillment Lorenzo and Dolores discover through each other is finally doomed in a world without social justice.

Doris Sommer has described *Artemio Cruz* as the most programmatic of the attacks by the writers associated with the Boom on the "romanticized history" of what she calls Latin America's "foundational fictions."[62] These fictions, ranging from José Mármol's *Amalia* (1851) to Rómulo Gallegos's *Doña Bárbara* (1929), fused romance with nation-building through the depiction of erotic unions that constituted idealized projections of the coming together of a people otherwise divided by race, class, region, or party line. Fuentes subverts this tradition by describing a nation-builder—for that is what Artemio is—whose "foundational love affairs . . . are revealed as rapes, or as power plays that need to traffic in women."[63] I think Sommer overstates the extent to which Fuentes in *Artemio Cruz* departs from his precursors, for the story of Lorenzo reveals how Fuentes continues to rely on romance as a way of imagining a political community. Thus, the encounter between Lorenzo and Dolores represents the rapprochement between Mexico and Spain—and so, in a broader sense, between Mexico and its Hispanic heritage—that resulted from the Mexican government's support for the Republic during the Spanish Civil War. The fact that the political community Fuentes imagines in *Artemio Cruz* with the help of Lorenzo and Dolores is not a *national* community does not diminish the novel's links with the tradition described by Sommer. It merely reflects the more internationalist orientation of political mobilization in the period in which Fuentes wrote *Artemio Cruz*, a tendency reflected in the first place in the impact of the Cuban Revolution throughout Latin America. Indeed, the Cuban Revolution is a strong presence in Fuentes's novel, for if the Lorenzo episode harks back to the Mexican Revolution, it also looks forward to the Cuban Revolution. Fuentes sketches a narrative in *Artemio Cruz* in which the revolutionary ideal, betrayed in Mexico, and defeated in Spain, now experiences a new dawn in Cuba. It is of crucial significance that Fuentes wrote part of *Artemio Cruz* in Cuba in the year after the Revolution, and that he wants his readers to know this, as we can see from the dates and place names that appear at the close of the text. In this sense, Roberto Fernández Retamar was right when he stated that *Artemio Cruz* was written "from the Cuban Revolution."[64] It is also for this reason that Gerald Martin need not be troubled—as he claims to be—by what he describes as "Fuentes's unfavourable comparison of the Mexican Revolution with the Spanish Civil War, as exemplified through his treatment of Cruz's son Lorenzo, who, unlike his father before him, dies heroically in the Iberian conflict, as if Mexico is inherently incapable of the 'true' ideals which are put into practice elsewhere."[65] Martin overlooks the passages in *Artemio Cruz* that present the revolutionary spirit in Mexico as a perennial threat to the status quo; what is more, he fails to see that the Mexican Revolution and the Spanish Civil War are presented in *Artemio Cruz* as stages in a historical development that culminates for now in the Cuban Revolution. It is wrong, therefore, to compare the Mexican Revolution and the Spanish Civil War as if they were discrete episodes, rather than part of a larger narrative that encompasses them both.

Lorenzo is perhaps the most important person in Artemio's life, for it is through his son that Artemio hopes to achieve a form of redemption from his own injured life. On his deathbed, Artemio repeatedly evokes a scene in which he goes horseback riding with Lorenzo. The scene is not fully described until we are well into the novel, yet Artemio condenses his recollection of it into two sentences, "That morning I waited for him with joy. We crossed the river on horseback," which he murmurs to himself over and over again in the novel's present-tense scenes, evidently delighting in the fact that his wife cannot decipher the meaning of his words. Filled with a private, enigmatic significance, the words gradually come to symbolize Artemio's true self, or, at least, the self he would have wanted to be. In the image of Artemio and his son riding across a river on their horses are compressed all of the old man's longings for a fulfilled, joyous existence.[66] The image is especially resonant because it foreshadows Lorenzo's walk across the bridge with Dolores. At the same time, as we will see later, it harks back to Artemio's childhood. Thus, the scene reveals Lorenzo's mediative role in the novel: he shows the path to the future, but he is also a bridge to the past. But we need to ask at this point what kind of weight is attached to the image of *crossing*. Why is the hope for redemption in this novel figured in precisely this fashion?

In a review, published in 1962, of Luis Buñuel's *The Exterminating Angel*, Fuentes wonders why human beings are so reluctant to *cross the threshold* that separates them from happiness. It is worth quoting at some length from this passage, inasmuch as it shows very clearly how the idea of crossing (a barrier, a divide) acquires in Fuentes's imagination at this point in time the significance of a profoundly transformative experience, an experience that opens the way to a utopian remaking of the world:

> Buñuel's question—the question of humanism—is clear and all-encompassing. Why do we not cross the threshold? . . . Why, if man is finally master of the possibility of overcoming, once and for all, poverty, sickness and ignorance, why does he not cross the threshold? Why, if he can see the gates of a terrestrial paradise, does he not pass through these gates, preferring to remain in the inferno of the past? Why, if he needs to take but one step in order to enter a humane world, the world of the future promised by science and technology, does he remain a prisoner of an old, inhumane, alienated existence? Why does man not cross the threshold?[67]

The various crossings described or imagined in *Artemio Cruz* do not immediately introduce the individuals who engage in them into a perfect world, but they clearly articulate the *hope* for a better life. It is surely also significant that Artemio's own last name is inscribed in the verb *cruzar* (to cross), as if to suggest that in the act of crossing he becomes his name, and therefore is finally most truly himself. In this act of self-realization, moreover, Artemio also manages to cancel the original, negative meaning of his name. For Artemio takes his last name from his mother, Isabel Cruz; in fact, as a child, he is known simply as "Cruz." But "Cruz" probably derives from the mark illiterate people use as a signature, so that more than a name it is a sign of Artemio's anonymity. He lives his childhood "without a real first or last name" (306/297–98), bearing only the mark of his missing identity. But when the *cruz* of Artemio's obscure origins becomes the *cruzamos* of his bond with his son, the name sheds its blankness, and instead reveals a rounded, completed self.

This interplay between emptiness and fullness also emerges from the way Artemio's last name links him to Christ. On the whole, of course, Artemio is a mock Christ-figure. To the extent that Artemio has built his career upon the sacrifices of others, his life is a parodic version of the life of Christ, who sacrificed himself for the sake of humanity. Yet the crossing of the river, viewed as a sign of Artemio's bond with his son, who, unlike his father, does sacrifice himself for a higher cause, reveals how Artemio's name, as well as his life, contains at least the shadow of a redemptive significance.[68]

The scene in which Artemio and Lorenzo go horseback riding takes place at the hacienda of Cocuya, near Veracruz, the very place, that is, where Artemio was born and grew up. The scene— reiterated in fragmentary form throughout the novel—expresses then a desire to return to the past. Yet this past turns out to be so violent and turbulent that we can see that Artemio wishes to restore what he has lost, but perhaps also to overcome what was done to him. Artemio, it turns out, is the product of the rape of his mother Isabel Cruz, a mulatto woman who lives on the Cocuya estate, by Atanasio Menchaca, the master of the property. Ireneo Menchaca, Atanasio's father, had built up a fortune thanks to his alliance with

General Antonio López de Santa Anna, a man who held the office of president of Mexico eleven times between 1833 and 1854, and who, as Fuentes writes in *The Buried Mirror*, came to represent "the prototype of the comic-opera Latin American dictator."[69] When, in 1867, in the last days of Maximilian's empire, Santa Anna makes a final attempt to seize power, Ireneo joins his old comrade, only to be dragged down in Santa Anna's defeat, meeting the end of "a life of chance and spins of the wheel of fortune, like that of the nation itself" (293/285). Having thrown in their lot with the losers in Mexico's protracted post-Independence political struggles, the Menchacas must now watch their properties being seized, just as the Menchacas themselves had once taken the land away from its rightful owners. For a while, the will to conquer survives in Atanasio, who is remembered many years later by his ninety-three-year-old mother "galloping over the fertile land, his whip in his hand, always ready to impose his decisive will, to satisfy his voracious appetites with the young peasant women, to defend his property, using his band of imported Negroes" (292/284). But Atanasio is killed in an ambush, and the Menchaca family must face utter ruin. Ireneo's widow Ludivinia (like a character out of Faulkner) locks herself in her room to brood upon the past, while her sole surviving son, the cowardly and dissolute Pedro, takes to the bottle. Against this background of decay and collapse, Artemio grows up. Yet in describing the peaceful rhythms of Artemio's childhood life, the novel presents us with its most extended and eloquent vision of a paradisical existence.

Artemio's mother is chased off the property by Atanasio, so Artemio is raised by his maternal uncle Lunero. Even as the hacienda falls further and further into ruin, Artemio's childhood transpires in a realm that appears to exist outside of time. He lives with Lunero in a shack by a river (the same river Artemio and Lorenzo will ride across on their horses many years later). In this close, intimate world, an idyllic existence unfolds. Artemio seems to merge entirely with the world around him. His body is shaped in interaction with the natural elements: his chest made strong from swimming against the current, his hair combed by the river, his arms the color of green fruit (283/275). He and his uncle go about their daily tasks without speaking: "They weren't there to talk or smile but to eat and sleep together and together to go out every daybreak, always silent, always weighed down by the tropical humidity, and together to do the work necessary to go on passing the days" (281/273). The feeling of togetherness between Artemio and Lunero is so deep that speech is unnecessary. Their existence is ruled by elemental rhythms that obviate language. In this world there is no division between self and other, a division that language attempts to bridge, but of which it is also the record. Nor is there any division between the inner self and its externalization through its activities, for the narrator makes it clear that labor is not an extrinsic aspect of the life of Artemio and Lunero. Rather, the performance of their daily tasks is an integral part of the natural flow of time.

But Artemio's harmonious life by the river is not designed to last. Lunero learns that the new master of the land needs more laborers on his tobacco plantation, and that the master's agent will come to take him away the next day. Artemio, hoping to avert the impending disaster, seizes a shotgun from the house, but in a moment of confusion he shoots and kills his uncle Pedro instead of the agent. Artemio's attempt to preserve the world of his childhood is doomed to fail: "And the shotgun weighed heavy, with a power that prolonged the boy's silent rage: rage because now he knew that life had enemies and that it was not any longer the uninterrupted flow of river and work: rage because now he would know separation" (305/296).

In returning to the hacienda at Cocuya many years later, Artemio evidently hopes to recreate his childhood world, and thereby to overcome the consciousness of separation that has haunted him ever since he was expelled from his childhood paradise. But it is significant that he hopes to accomplish this goal through his son Lorenzo: "For him alone will you have bought this land, rebuilt the hacienda, left him on it, the child-master, responsible for the harvests, open to the life of horses and hunting, swimming and fishing" (225/217). It is as if Artemio could only return to the past by means of the inheritance he grants his son. But the desire for permanence and continuity expressed in Artemio's dreams for his son is finally frustrated, in large part because Artemio's dreams are still so profoundly implicated in his family's turbulent and violent history.

Artemio's childhood world, apparently so peaceful and harmonious, is in reality already a divided realm. By the river, life unfolds in an uninterrupted flow. But immediately adjacent to this timeless enclosure stands the ruined mansion of the Menchaca family, symbol of historical decay and mutability, and, more in particular, of the abrupt, unpredictable cycles of nineteenth-century Mexican history. Clearly, Artemio's nostalgia is for the life he had with Lunero. The world Artemio tries to recreate with his son Lorenzo is in the first place one of intense proximity to nature. It is important to recall, moreover, that Artemio's mother was run off the Cocuya estate by Atanasio and that Artemio himself only barely escaped his father's murderous clutches: "Yes, Master Atanasio died at just the right time; he would have had the boy killed; Lunero saved him" (285/277). Artemio returns to Cocuya bearing his mother's name; on some level, he has come to reclaim his mother's rights to the land from which she was banished. In this way, it can be read as an act that is continuous with Artemio's killing of his uncle Pedro, an act of symbolical parricide with which Artemio revenges himself for the filicide his father was only just prevented from perpetrating. Cocuya represents, for the mature Artemio, a refuge from the male world of struggle and combat in which he has made a name for himself. Yet, in the end, he fails to free himself from the legacy of the Menchacas.

We may note that Artemio returns to Cocuya not in order to rebuild the hut in which he lived with his uncle Lunero, but in order to restore the mansion from which he had always been excluded. He may wish to avenge himself on his father, but he also wants to occupy his father's position. The rousing rides on horseback across the estate with his son Lorenzo represent a return to nature, but they also echo the conquering ways of Atanasio, who is repeatedly pictured on horseback, and so indirectly associated with the Spanish conquistadors. Furthermore, the bonding that takes place between Artemio and Lorenzo comes at the cost of excluding the boy's mother. In this way, it is almost as if Artemio were repeating his father's refusal to acknowledge the mother of his child.

The impossibility of returning to the undissociated realm of childhood illustrates how, for Artemio, such a world exists only in the realm of illusion. He can only live there by willfully ignoring the actual historical world. In this way, *Artemio Cruz* resembles Alejo Carpentier's *Los pasos perdidos* (1953). Carpentier's novel also recreates a place (Santa Mónica de los Venados) where the rift between nature and culture appears to have been healed. After witnessing the execution of a criminal (an episode structurally parallel to the episode in which Artemio shoots his uncle), the narrator, however, leaves Santa Mónica, and eventually must acknowledge that the utopia in which he had come to believe does not in fact exist. Yet *Artemio Cruz* cannot be read according to the same deconstructionist formula that has now become the standard reading of *Los pasos perdidos*.[70] The reconciliation of self and other, or of nature and culture, may remain out of reach for Artemio, but it is only so because of the nature of the choices he has made in his life, and, as we have now also seen, because of the burden of history which he bears. But the story of Lorenzo indicates that other choices can be made, while the references to Cuba suggest that the burden of history can be overcome. To place *Artemio Cruz* in the proper perspective, I turn now to *La campaña* (1990), a novel both more cheerful and less utopian than *Artemio Cruz*, a novel, furthermore, that illustrates the shift in Fuentes's work from a reliance on conceptions of identity to an interest in notions of alternativity. But first, I will show how this shift affected Fuentes's political commentaries in the 1980s.

Toward Alternativity

We will not find, when we turn to examine Fuentes's political journalism from the 1980s, an extremely pronounced contrast with his political journalism of the early 1960s. What is significant, however, is this: the Cuban Revolution and the subsequent U.S. attempt to derail the Revolution generated in Fuentes an intensely utopian and totalizing type of rhetoric; in the 1980s, confronted with an equally sordid episode in U.S. foreign policy—the contra war in Nicaragua—Fuentes's opposition was still firm, but it was couched in a far more open and complex vocabulary. A brief look at how Fuentes deals in his publications of the mid- to late 1980s with three of the issues he had touched on in his political journalism from the early 1960s—the definition of U.S. society, the nature of the forces lined up against U.S. imperialism, and the question of the historical process—will reveal in what sense his position changed.

In observing the United States in the 1980s, Fuentes sees a nation of paradoxes. In his prologue to the English translation of José E. Rodó's *Ariel*, Fuentes notes the disparity between different facets of American power: militarily the United States is obviously a force to be reckoned with, but without "the proper cultural, political, or even economic underpinning" this power is in actual fact "a pitiful form of weakness."[71] The United States' paranoid view of the world, its way, as Fuentes puts it, of "over-reacting neurotically to every setback and every challenge, seeing intrigue, ingratitude and Communist machinations wherever other people, having interests that do not coincide with those of the US, insist on pursuing them anyway" is a further symptom of the country's weakness.[72] Fuentes then adds another item to the list of American afflictions: the country suffers from a severe case of schizophrenia. Whereas in 1961 Fuentes had detected a basic continuity between the absence of real democracy on the domestic plane in the United States and the country's imperialistic foreign policy, by 1988 he is arguing that there is a fundamental contradiction between these two facets of American political life: "Why does the United States exhibit such a disparity between the way it acts internally (democratically) and the way it acts externally (through deception, intervention, violation of international law, and, if need be, violent military actions against weaker nations)?"[73] The United States is, in other words, a democracy inside and an empire outside. It is, Fuentes states in an article for *The Nation*, "Dr. Jekyll at home, Mr. Hyde in Latin America."[74]

In an article he wrote for the *Los Angeles Times* on the Iran-Contra affair, Fuentes again raises the specter of fascism, as he had done in 1961 in the wake of the Bay of Pigs invasion. Oliver North reminds Fuentes of the kind of "disgruntled soldier" who in an earlier time "opened the way for Hitler and Mussolini." "If this happened in the land of Kant and Beethoven," he muses, "why can't it happen again, in the land of Jefferson and Gershwin?" Fuentes's answer to his own question is somewhat ambivalent. At first, he appears to discard the possibility of a regression to fascism: in the United States, after all, everything eventually turns into entertainment. The fate of Oliver North and Fawn Hall is not to overturn the social order, but to be "played by Clint Eastwood and Morgan Fairchild." Yet he goes on to speculate that things may turn ugly after all: "the US may decide . . . to unify its imperial policies outside and inside. This would mean the end of democracy in the United States—or, more likely, an internal conflict of revolutionary dimensions to decide the issue."[75] This grim prediction appears to echo Fuentes's equally ominous statements about the United States in 1961, yet there is a significant difference: at the time of the Bay of Pigs crisis Fuentes did not regard his comment about the fascist traits of the United States as a speculation about the future, but as an observation about conditions in the present. Moreover, because the rise of fascism is part of a historical *telos* that leads to the destruction of capitalism, Fuentes conveys a certain satisfaction at seeing how events are following their predetermined course. By 1987, history has come to appear far less predictable, a circumstance that accounts for the entirely new tone of irony in Fuentes's observations about Oliver North and Fawn Hall, as well as for the less complacent interpretation of the general direction of U.S. politics.

Fuentes's revised perspective on the United States goes along with a different evaluation of the forces of resistance rising up in Latin America to oppose U.S. intervention in the region. To begin with, the two parts of the continent are no longer in total disaccord with each other: "We are both, North and Latin Americans, still projects of history, incomplete societies, working models."[76] There are other, less cheering resemblances. Fuentes's piece on Iran-Contra, "Hail to the Chief," opens with the assertion that "By following mistaken policies toward the Third World countries, the US itself ends up by acting as a Third World country."[77] This is not very flattering, either to the United States or to the Third World. Normally, however, Fuentes's statements on Latin America emphasize the positive over the negative. The principal positive force at work in the present is "a heterogeneous civil society invading the formerly homogeneous spaces of political, military, and religious power."[78] In 1987, Fuentes saw evidence of the emergence of such a civil society in both Argentina and Mexico.[79] The concept of civil society replaces the notion of the general will Fuentes had used in 1961. Although both concepts refer to situations in which people take control of their own destinies, Fuentes's later formulation places less emphasis on a unity of purpose among the people, and acknowledges instead that a variety of social and political goals may fruitfully coexist. Rather than lamenting the uncertainty and openendedness of such a situation, and its potential for generating conflict, Fuentes presents this heterogeneity as the most important desideratum in his sketch for a better society.

This leads into the final point of comparison between the two stages in Fuentes's thought: the question of the historical process, and, in particular, of the motor of historical change. By the 1980s, Fuentes has stopped appealing to the iron law of historical progress. The law continues to play an important role in his later thought, but it is a very different kind of law. When Fuentes claims that "our best shield against the excessive power of the US has always been the law,"[80] he is referring to the human-made laws of international agreements, not to the abstract law of history. Fuentes hopes that the tradition of the Spanish legal scholars Suárez and Vitoria, which affirms the principles of "non-intervention, self-determination, the peaceful resolution of conflicts, the coexistence of political systems,"[81] will ensure good relations between the United States and Latin America.

How does one get the United States to respect these laws? Presumably, the powers of persuasion of somebody like Fuentes are expected to play an important role in bringing about the desired changes. Fuentes believes Latin America must ultimately rely on a change of disposition among North Americans; for this reason, he addresses his readers in the United States and in effect asks them to make a conscious effort to understand their Latin American "Others," thereby contributing to a more just international order: "We are the strangers that the United States must understand first of all."[82] The historical process is conceived, in other words, in far less deterministic terms than was the case in 1961. Nevertheless, Fuentes does give us a sense of the overall direction in which he sees history moving, but, significantly, this movement is not toward the state of unity envisaged in the Marxist subtext of his earlier writings. The movement of history is instead conceived in what we might describe as Bakhtinian terms. Fuentes states that "the modern world" has made the "yearning for unity . . . materially impossible." We live in a world, he writes, in which "everything—communications, the economy, our sense of time and space, science, the new humanism—indicates that variety and not monotony, diversity and not unity, alternativity and not identity, the polytheism rather than the monotheism of values, shall define the coming century."[83] From identity to alternativity: the movement of Fuentes's thought could not have received a clearer expression. But what about his fiction? Does it undergo a similar change?

By the time of *Cristóbal Nonato* and *La campaña* we observe an important change in Fuentes's outlook. In these works, political values are no longer firmly grounded in a character's private life: the personal and the political each seem to go their own way and efforts to reintegrate them seem destined to fail. Both novels present characters who resemble Lorenzo from *Artemio Cruz*. Like Lorenzo, Ángel Palomar in *Cristóbal Nonato* and Baltasar Bustos in *La campaña* are young, politically engaged idealists whose behavior is largely shaped by their amorous impulses. Unlike Lorenzo, however, neither Ángel nor Baltasar experiences a wholly fulfilling erotic union with another person. Yet neither are their lives to be sacrificed in order to dramatize a social and political failure. I focus here on *La campaña* because the vexed relationship between private and public is not just one theme among many in the novel; it offers, rather, the basic parameters that define the actions of the novel's protagonist. It is around the very opposition between private and public that Fuentes has structured the plot of *La campaña*.[84]

Baltasar Bustos's exploits in the Spanish American wars of independence have a double motivation. On the one hand, he is driven by a vision of a better society; on the other hand, he wishes merely to impress the woman he loves, Ofelia Salamanca, who happens to be the wife of the Marquis de Cabra, one of the highest officials in the Spanish colonial government. The basic conundrum of the novel is this: How are these two strands in Baltasar's life related to each other? Roberto González Echevarría speaks of how *La campaña* "blends erotic and political desires,"[85] yet the novel is, in fact, much more preoccupied with showing how these two modes of desire enter into conflict with each other. *La campaña* constitutes a genuine break with the "romanticized history" described by Sommer. It illustrates the extreme difficulty of reading from the personal to the political and vice versa.

Baltasar's odyssey across the American continent begins with a kidnapping: on the night of the ouster of the Spanish viceroy and the installation of a junta in Buenos Aires, Baltasar sneaks into Ofelia Salamanca's private quarters, snatches her newborn baby, "destined for idleness and elegance," from his crib, and leaves in his place a black boy, "condemned to violence, hunger, and discrimination" (28/21). Baltasar believes that a political change must go hand in hand with a personal transformation. "It is not enough," he tells his friends Dorrego and Varela, the latter the narrator of the novel, "to denounce the general injustice of social relations, or even to change the government, if personal relationships aren't also changed" (26/19). The kidnapping of Ofelia's baby is not only a demonstration of Baltasar's willingness to put his ideals into practice, rather than merely to proclaim them in the abstract; it is also an illustration of his conviction that political upheavals must, in order to be truly meaningful, impinge directly upon people's personal lives.

Baltasar soon begins to have doubts about the course of action he has chosen. An unanticipated transformation takes place within him, one that involves first of all a revaluation of the relationship between the personal and the political. Baltasar discovers that there are different ways in which one can integrate the private and the public. When he switches the babies, Baltasar unites the personal and the political under the aegis of the political. He carries out his plan in the name of a political cause. After the event, Baltasar discovers that one can also grant priority to the realm of personal feeling. He reflects to himself: "Baltasar Bustos, you have mortally wounded the woman you think you love. You have committed an injustice against the most intimate nature of that woman. Ofelia Salamanca is a mother, and you, a vile kidnapper" (29/22). What matters now is not the larger cause, but the life of an individual. That is why Baltasar identifies Ofelia not according to her public station, which makes her his enemy, but as a mother. Baltasar similarly depoliticizes his own role: instead of being a revolutionary, he is now simply a criminal. He discovers that the private realm has a reality that is not merely an emanation of a person's public role, a point already illustrated by his own love for a woman whose political beliefs he must find repugnant.

La campaña is not, however, an argument for granting priority to the personal over the political; it seeks, rather, to illustrate the difficulty of stabilizing the relationship between the two. In *Cristóbal Nonato*, Fuentes had already announced the metaphysic (or antimetaphysic) that provides the foundation for this new understanding. At the end of the novel, the narrator evokes the figure of Werner Heisenberg in order to pronounce a ringing endorsement of the Uncertainty Principle: "There is no universality except relativity, the world is unfinished because the men and women who observe it still have not finished, and truth, unexhausted, fugitive, in perpetual motion, is only the truth that takes all arbitrary positions into account and all the relative movements of each individual on this earth" (561/529).

If everything is uncertain, then the relationship between private and public must be uncertain, too. In *La campaña*, Fuentes elaborates a similar conception of the truth, this time through a series of references to the different strands within French Enlightenment philosophy. Each of the three friends is associated with a different figure: Bustos with Rousseau, Dorrego with Voltaire, and Varela with Diderot. It is clear, however, that in the debate between these three figures Fuentes's sympathies lie with Diderot. After all, Varela is the narrator, so Diderot's voice occupies center stage in the novel. It is a voice that belongs to the same tradition of modernity as Cervantes and Shakespeare. The basic wisdom it communicates is not so different from the wisdom expressed through the allusion to Heisenberg in *Cristóbal Nonato*: it is "the conviction that everything changes constantly" (25/18).[86]

This view of the truth as something in perpetual transformation has interesting consequences for the disentanglement of *La campaña*'s plot. The novel concludes with a series of twists that serve less to reveal the truth than to suggest that it is impossible ever to reach any definitive conclusions, less to lead to a reconciliation than to remind the reader that every reconciliation is an uneasy substitute for some ineffaceable loss.

At the end of the novel, Baltasar learns several things. He learns that Ofelia in fact fought on the side of the rebels in their struggle against Spain. Yet he finds it impossible to believe in this version. He must live, then, not with the happy thought that there was, after all, no contradiction between his political and his amorous impulses, but with an unsettling sense of doubt. He learns, furthermore, that Ofelia's child was not, as he feared, lost in the tumult of the night of May 24–25, 1810. But here, too, his knowledge of the events of the past remains incomplete, for what he does not learn is that the boy, now his adoptive child, was, in fact, fathered by his friend Varela, who in 1809 and 1810 had conducted a secret love affair with Ofelia. The gaps in Baltasar's understanding are meant less to reveal a personal failure than to make a general point about the element of blindness in all human perception. And it is this blindness that frustrates the attainment of the ideal of unity to which Baltasar, as a follower of Rousseau, aspires: the unity of soul and nature, of self and history, of private and public.

Fuentes draws explicit attention to the trope of blindness in the closing pages of *La campaña*, and links it to another significant image: that of play. In the novel's final scene, we see Ofelia's son, now bearing the name Manuel Bustos, playing blind man's bluff and acting out war games. The mock execution which the boy stages is an image of the fate of all history: its transformation into theater. The images of play and blindness both presuppose the presence of a distance: between perceiver and perceived, between reality and representation. It seems appropriate, too, that at this very moment the woman with whom Baltasar will be united makes her entrance, and that this woman is Gabriela Cóo, the actress. As the woman who takes Ofelia's place in Baltasar's affections, she provisionally closes a chain of substitutions that runs through the novel: the substitution of the black baby for the white baby that sets the plot in motion, the substitution of Varela for the Marquis de Cabra in Ofelia's bed, the substitution of personal for political emotions and vice versa, the substitution of Fuentes's version of the struggle for independence in Spanish America for the one Gabriel García Márquez offers in *El general en su laberinto*.[87] The play of transformations reveals that *La campaña* is governed by a rule of displacement that effectively blocks the possibility of a Rousseauvian return to a state of wholeness. It also impedes the fusion of private and public that Fuentes had held up as an inspiring ideal in *Artemio Cruz*.

Making It New

A New Novel

In a 1972 interview with Herman P. Doezema, Fuentes stated that he "could never again write" novels like *La región más transparente, Las buenas conciencias,* and *La muerte de Artemio Cruz.*[1] When Doezema suggested that "*Cambio de piel* represents a very real break in your writing" (494), Fuentes heartily agreed. Yet from the present perspective it no longer seems plausible to regard Fuentes's first three novels as belonging to an early period in his career which he definitively put behind him with the publication in 1967 of *Cambio de piel.*[2] Fuentes's current habit of grouping all his narrative works (including works still to be written) under a single title, *La edad del tiempo,* indicates that he now views his entire oeuvre as an integrated whole.[3] By the 1980s, in fact, it had already become evident that the search for absolute novelty was making way for a tendency toward revision and recapitulation. In works such as *Gringo viejo* and *Cristóbal Nonato,* Fuentes began to go over ground he had already covered in *La muerte de Artemio Cruz* and *La región más transparente.* But for a period of time starting in the mid-1960s, Fuentes labored under the conviction that the genre of the novel was undergoing a profound crisis. Under such circumstances, only radical measures would do. *Cambio de piel* was intended as such a measure, in whose light Fuentes's first three novels came to appear as a type of work now clearly superseded.[4]

Cambio de piel differs from the novels that preceded it in Fuentes's career in two broad ways. It is, first, more ambitious in its thematic scope, and, second, more radical in its rejection of traditional novelistic form. The concern with Mexican history and culture that characterized Fuentes's early novels does not disappear in *Cambio de piel*. However, the Mexican theme is here folded into an investigation of Western civilization as a whole, an investigation that takes Ancient Greece and Nazi Germany as its two nodal points. As far as the formal issue is concerned, in the early novels (with the exception of the more conventional *Las buenas conciencias*) Fuentes's view of Mexico was mediated principally through the techniques of modernism. Although *Cambio de piel* does not amount to a rejection of these techniques, it does offer evidence of a desire to go beyond modernism. The modernist aesthetics of fragmentation and perspectivism with which Fuentes experimented in *La región* and *Artemio Cruz* are in the service of a fundamentally realist orientation. In *Cambio de piel*, however, the disruption of traditional narrative form is taken much further, amounting to a radical attempt to loosen the bond between text and reality. Fuentes's insistent questioning of the concept and practice of representation not only explains the novel's structural and linguistic opacity, but also constitutes a key element in his analysis of Western civilization. In this way, the two aspects of *Cambio de piel*'s innovativeness with regard to Fuentes's earlier work—its greater formal difficulty, and its critique of the Western tradition—are skillfully interwoven.

Throughout his career Fuentes has published critical and theoretical essays that offer clues to the intentions that governed the writing of his narrative works. The companion piece to *Cambio de piel* is clearly *La nueva novela hispanoamericana*. Although *La nueva novela* was first published in 1969, parts of it had already begun to appear as magazine articles as early as 1964. It appears, in other words, that Fuentes worked on *La nueva novela* more or less at the same time as he was writing *Cambio de piel*. If *Cambio de piel* was Fuentes's attempt to conquer new ground for the novel, then *La nueva novela hispanoamericana* was the critical codification of this endeavor. It was here that he spelled out why he believed the novel had entered a period of crisis, and what he believed could be done about it.

In his critical meditations from this period, both in *La nueva novela* and in the interviews he gave, Fuentes identified two related reasons for the need for a new kind of novel at this particular moment in time. In the first place, Fuentes spoke repeatedly of the threat posed to the novel by the rise of new modes of discourse. In the second place, Fuentes proposed that the traditional novel was no longer an adequate instrument for grappling with contemporary social and economic realities. In the interview with Doezema, Fuentes discussed the problems created for "the written word" by the "enormous expansion of the visual media," and referred to "cinema, reportage, sociology, psychology" (493) as forms of analysis and expression that had taken over the ground previously occupied by the novel. In his 1966 interview with Emir Rodríguez Monegal, Fuentes described a process whereby "a number of areas that seemed reserved for the novel have been taken over by the cinema, by journalism, by the psychopathological report, by sociological work in the manner of Oscar Lewis."[5] Fuentes restated this thesis concerning the annexation of the novel's territory by other forms of discourse in *La nueva novela*.[6] But what exactly was the terrain from which the novel was being forced to withdraw? And what options did Fuentes see for the novel to revitalize itself?

Fuentes's reflections on the state of the novel in these years were clearly informed by the widespread notion that the genre of the novel was dead. Recently, in looking back at the earliest years of his literary career, Fuentes indicated that he made his start as a writer under the shadow of this idea: "When I began to publish books, in 1954, I was constantly hearing some ominous words: 'the novel is dead.'"[7] In *La nueva novela* he developed a clear strategy for countering this verdict: he maintained that what had died was not the novel *tout court*, but just the bourgeois form of the novel. To make such a claim constituted in the first place a political statement, for it assumed that the decline of the bourgeois novel mirrored the decline of the bourgeoisie itself: "The end of the cycle of bourgeois fiction coincides with the death throes of the bourgeoisie itself"

(21–22). But what were the precise features of the bourgeois novel which Fuentes regarded as obsolete?

Fuentes answered this question in two different ways. At times, he identified the reasons for the exhaustion of the bourgeois novel in the term *bourgeois realism*. What he was suggesting, in other words, was that the new novel was discarding what he regarded as the bourgeois project of providing the reader with a faithful and convincing portrait of reality. In his interview with Fuentes, Doezema spoke of a new direction in the novel, describing it as "a direction away from a narrative presentation of a particular vision of the world" (491). If Doezema meant by this that he saw a turn away from referentiality in the novel, then it appeared that Fuentes wanted to count his own work as part of this movement, for he says to Doezema that in *Cambio de piel* "all the traditional psychological elements are in the novel, but they are there to be destroyed," and he goes even further, claiming that the novel itself "is there to be destroyed" (497). This view of the novel as a self-destructing artifact was clearly placed in opposition to the traditional conception of the novel as a mirror of the world.

Elsewhere, however, Fuentes made more modest claims for the new novel's difference from the bourgeois novel. Rather than saying that the representation of reality itself was no longer an interesting or viable enterprise, he suggested in *La nueva novela* that only certain types of subject matter, such as "psychological introspection" or "the depiction of class relations" (17), had been exhausted. As to why they were exhausted, Fuentes's answer was characteristically ambiguous. On the one hand, Fuentes claimed—and here we return to the point with which I began—that other forms of discourse were now in a better position to tackle the novel's traditional areas of interest, such as individual psychology or class relations. On the other hand, Fuentes suggested that the traditional categories of the realist novel had not so much been appropriated by the mass media and the social sciences, as they had in themselves become anachronistic. The world had ceased to revolve around individuals and social classes. It was here that Fuentes located the second reason for the crisis of the novel.

Fuentes argues in *La nueva novela* that the bourgeois novel encodes an outdated view of the world. If the novel is to survive, it must confront "the advent of a far more powerful literary reality" (17). According to Fuentes, the "true hallmark" of our era is not "the dichotomy between capitalism and socialism, but rather a series of facts—cold, marvelous, contradictory, ineluctable, newly liberating, newly alienating facts that are truly transforming life in the industrialized countries: automation, electronics, the use of atomic energy for peaceful ends" (18). But the list of features that characterize the new era seems distinctly anticlimactic in light of Fuentes's buildup at the beginning of the sentence. It is hard to think of the peaceful use of atomic energy as a stunning new development that makes the Cold War seem irrelevant. It is also difficult to see it as providing the foundation for a new orientation in the art of the novel. Yet the somewhat overheated language does conceal a serious argument.

In stating that technology had become more important than ideology, Fuentes was taking up a position that was surprisingly reminiscent of the end-of-ideology thesis put forward by Daniel Bell in the late 1950s.[8] The reminiscence is surprising not only because by the late 1960s, when *La nueva novela* appeared, the resurgence of ideological conflict in the West and elsewhere had made Bell's position appear superseded (although his ideas have experienced a kind of second life in recent years in the end-of-history debate), but also because it seemed out of character for a self-proclaimed leftist such as Fuentes to bow in this way before the power of technology. There were other aspects of Fuentes's analysis of the evolving social and economic order in Latin America that seemed out of character for a former writer for *Política*. For alongside the rise in importance of technology, Fuentes identified—and at times even seemed to celebrate—two other traits as central to the new era: the spread of consumerism, and the increasingly global nature of social and economic developments. In his interview with Rodríguez Monegal, Fuentes explained that *Cambio de piel* was on one level an attempt to legitimate "all the vulgarity, excess and impurity of our world," and then proceeded to associate these qualities with consumer society: "We are just as much part as any gringo or Frenchman of the world of competition and status symbols, the world of neon lights and Sears-Roebuck and washing-machines and James Bond movies and Campbell soup cans." Echoing a famous phrase Octavio Paz coined in *El laberinto de la soledad*, Fuentes clinched his argument by declaring that "the people of Mexico City or Buenos Aires or Lima are now contemporaries of all mankind in the realm of consumer products and fashions" (14),[9] a statement that shows how the argument about the rise of consumer society is at the same time an argument about the emergence of a global economic system.[10]

Given this analysis of the situation of the novel—on the one hand hemmed in by the rise of other discourses; on the other hand confronted with the emergence of an entirely new economic order—what is to be done? How will the novelist create a new novel?[11] One quality on which Fuentes placed considerable emphasis as a desideratum of the new novel was "ambiguity." But in *La nueva novela* there is considerable ambiguity in Fuentes's discussion of ambiguity.

Fuentes advocates ambiguity (along with complexity) as the proper literary response to the new socioeconomic situation. But to see how Fuentes arrives at this position, we need to look more closely at his account of the changes in the socioeconomic structure of Latin America, and in particular at what he says about the writer's location within this structure. In *La nueva novela*, Fuentes presents the reader with a fairly simple historical narrative: Latin America moves, in both history and literature, from a stage of "epic simplicity" to a stage of "dialectical complexity" (13). The first stage took place in the century after independence: it was the era of military dictatorships and native oligarchs (11). In the sphere of literature, these historical conditions resulted in the dominance of certain themes, such as the opposition between civilization and barbarism, and of certain forms, such as the naturalist novel. But the nineteenth-century Latin American writer's stance with regard to the issue of civilization and barbarism was considerably more ambiguous than Fuentes allows. Fuentes claims that the nineteenth-century writer "invariably chooses the side of civilization and opposes barbarism" and describes him as "the spokesman for people who cannot make their voices heard, a spokesman who sees his function precisely as that of denouncing injustice, defending the exploited and documenting the reality of his country" (11–12). But the second claim does not follow from the first. The very writer who offered the classic statement on the theme of civilization and barbarism in post-Independence Latin America—Domingo Sarmiento—was an advocate of "civilization," but not exactly a friend of the exploited and oppressed masses of his continent. One senses that Fuentes offers a simplified reading of the Latin American literary tradition so as to make it easier for him to stress the *complexity* of the work of his own generation.

Fuentes fits the naturalist novel into the same paradigm of epic simplicity. Its task was to bring about social change: "Novels were written in order to improve the lot of the peasants of Ecuador or the miners of Bolivia" (12). Fuentes sees the novel of the Mexican Revolution as the herald of a more complex sense of the world, and of the role of literature. Novelists such as Mariano Azuela and Martín Luis Guzmán introduced a powerful new aura of ambiguity into their works: "Heroic certitude is transformed into critical ambiguity, natural fate into contradictory action, romantic idealism into ironic dialectics" (15). But at the same time Fuentes proposes a reading of the Mexican Revolution that is wholly cleansed of irony or ambiguity: "For the first time in Latin American history we see a genuine social revolution, a revolution that aims not simply to replace one general with another, but to transform in a radical fashion the structures of a nation" (14–15). Even as he praises the novelists of the Mexican Revolution for having jettisoned the conventional opposition between heroes and villains, Fuentes proposes a conventionally heroic reading of the Revolution.

This ambiguity threads its way through much of *La nueva novela*, emerging very clearly in Fuentes's description of the contemporary situation of the writer. Once again, in the nineteenth century, everything was simple: "The choice between civilization and barbarism was clear and the radius of debate limited, so that the intellectual could take a position and affect the discussion with relative ease" (27). The nineteenth-century writer had a clear task before him: to

hasten the arrival of modernity in Latin America. But with the actual arrival of modernity in the twentieth century, everything becomes
immensely more complicated. The writer's social position changes.
He is no longer an elite figure with a clear vision of his society;
instead, the writer vanishes into the very social mass he was once
able to oversee and direct. Fuentes speaks of the modern writer as
"submerged in the petite bourgeoisie, facing the proliferating urban
masses" (28). As the writer disappears into the crowd, his or her
vision is increasingly impaired. The writer becomes an alienated
and disenchanted, solitary and anguished figure, filled with ambiguities and contradictions. He or she no longer has any answers to
offer, only questions. Yet alongside this portrait of doubt and disori-
entation, a different picture emerges of the writer as a person filled
with ideological certitudes. At the very end of the section of *La
nueva novela* in which he develops his argument regarding the new
type of writer, Fuentes suddenly informs us that "the Latin
American intellectual sees revolution as the only option" and that
"the example of the Cuban Revolution has led the majority of our
intellectuals to take up positions on the left" (29). Here the Latin
American intellectual emerges as somebody with unambiguous
political convictions. Instead of a divided, hesitant being who has
lost all confidence in his ability to have an impact on his society,
Fuentes depicts a figure with a strong *esprit de corps* and a firm sense
of how to help shape the future.

Along with "ambiguity," "language" emerges as a key word in
Fuentes's elaboration of a poetics for the new novel. But an analysis
of Fuentes's use of the concept of language in *La nueva novela* reveals
another cluster of contradictions. What Fuentes means when in his
interview with Rodríguez Monegal he says that in the new novel
"there is a search for language" (17) is open to different interpretations. The conjunction of the repeated invocation of the concept of
language with the persistent critique of the practice of realism suggests that Fuentes is advocating a type of writing that turns in on
itself, exploring the nature of language, and spurning the conventional connections of literature to the external world. This view of
the novel as self-reflexive and intertextual, rather than mimetic,

emerges in Fuentes's discussion in *La nueva novela* of Alejo Carpentier, whose work he claims draws attention to the fact that a novel is "in the first place writing," offering not a representation of reality, but a representation of a prior representation (56). This antireferential orientation is reinforced by Fuentes's use in *La nueva novela* of a vocabulary drawn from French structuralism. Fuentes repeatedly refers to the triad of "myth," "language," and "structure," and implies that the three terms are to some degree synonymous with each other (20). Such a view (derived from structuralism) has a number of implications: if literature is in the first place language, and if language is linked to myth, then literature is in effect lifted out of the realm of history. When Fuentes claims that the novel, in returning to a mythical style of thought, is at the same time approaching to the condition of poetry or anthropology (20), he is in effect proposing a view of the novel as essentially antihistorical. The point is made even more clearly a few pages later when Fuentes speaks (in the manner of Claude Lévi-Strauss) of "the universality of the mythical imagination" as inseparable from "the universality of the structures of language" (22). But he insists that this is a discovery of the new novelist: "*Madame Bovary* could only have been written by a nineteenth-century petit bourgeois Frenchman; *Pornografía* could have been narrated by a native of the Amazon jungle" (22).[12]

Yet alongside the argument that the new novel was the literary expression of certain universal and immutable patterns of human experience and consciousness, Fuentes developed a different argument that situated the language of the new novel in a more historical light. Fuentes repeated throughout *La nueva novela* that the new novel should be subversive; the notion was captured most vividly in the phrase "the enemy word." But subversion cannot take place in a void; it must operate against the background of a specific, historically circumscribed set of norms. This is indeed what Fuentes proposes in *La nueva novela*. He describes the language of the new novel as "the language of alarm, renovation, disorder and humor. The language, in sum, of ambiguity: of the plurality of signifieds, of the constellation of allusions: of openness" (32). To some extent, Fuentes regards these qualities as desirable in themselves, yet he makes it clear that they are especially desirable in light of certain specific traits of the Latin American cultural tradition. Fuentes describes Latin America as a continent of sacred texts, burdened with a long history of "lies, silences, academic rhetorics and complicities" (30). The new novel in Latin America has a specific antagonist: the false, anachronistic language of a closed, oppressive society. Under such conditions, to elaborate a new language is to pave the way for a new social order. And this is something only the novel can do.

There are two different stories in *La nueva novela*: one story is about the infinite ambiguity and complexity of the modern world and the novelist's response to that world; the other story is about the novelist's necessary enlistment in the great ideological battles of the day. The two stories correspond to the two positions Fuentes has simultaneously tried to occupy in the literary and intellectual field of his time: one is the position of the experimental novelist; the other is the position of the engaged intellectual.

Camp on the Edge

The emergence of new media and new discourses obliged the new novelist to answer the question of "what can be said through the medium of the novel that cannot be said through any other medium," as Fuentes phrased it in his interview with Doezema (493). Yet the way back into a distinctly novelistic practice might in fact necessitate an apprenticeship in other media. To Doezema, Fuentes also declared that the novel "has to take its *appuis*, its *apoyos*, in many other media so as to find a way into itself again" (493). Perhaps this explains the logic behind the inclusion of a series of photographs in *Cambio de piel*.

Inserted roughly into the middle of the book, there are two sets of three images each. The first series consists of a portrait of Friedrich Nietzsche,[13] a photograph of women and children being rounded up by German soldiers in the Warsaw Ghetto in 1943,[14] and a still from the German expressionist film *The Cabinet of Dr. Caligari*. The second series consists of a picture of Joan Crawford in *Whatever Happened to Baby Jane?*, a scene with John Barrymore and Joan Crawford from *Grand Hotel*, and a publicity photograph of John Garfield. Although these images appear to make up a fairly heterogeneous collection, they are all linked in some way to the text. The references to the movies reflect the importance of film to the education of several of the novel's characters. The photograph of Nietzsche and the frame from *Dr. Caligari* allude to the web of intertextual references Fuentes uses to characterize the novel's narrator, Freddy Lambert.[15] Placed alongside the picture taken in the Warsaw Ghetto, however, these two images can also be seen as referring to the novel's concern with Germany, and in particular with Nazism. A common exercise among historians and non-historians has been to track down intellectual or aesthetic artifacts in the German tradition that could be read as either paving the way for the Nazis or as sending a warning about their imminent rise to power. Both Nietzsche and German expressionism have been made a part of this narrative, which is what Fuentes may be doing here as well.

On one level, then, the pictures simply draw the reader's attention to prominent strands in the novel's thematic weave. But there is an alternative to reading the images in this referential manner. One might bracket for a moment the actual content of the images, and ask why Fuentes should have chosen to insert photographic images in what is after all a verbal artifact. It seems likely that the point of mixing media in this way has to do with the inherent qualities of the different media themselves. In other words, in the context of a verbal text, the photographs are a way of focusing the reader's attention on the nature of the photograph, or, more in general, the image, itself. One of the most notable qualities of the image is its immediacy, its ability to suggest that it exists in an eternal present. In his interview with Emir Rodríguez Monegal, Fuentes spoke of his desire to create in his work a "pure perpetual present," a project that seems more suited to a film than to a novel (11). Perhaps the inclusion of the photographs in *Cambio de piel* is one way in which Fuentes expressed his preoccupation with presentness and immediacy, and revealed his desire to share in the powerful new effects of the visual media.

Jean Franco has offered a more sociological version of this reading. In her view the images imply less an ontological choice in favor of a particular temporal dimension (the present) than an ideological choice in favor of a specific mode of socioeconomic organization. Franco focuses on Fuentes's claim in the interview with Rodríguez Monegal that Mexico has become part of the global reach of consumer society and suggests that it is this sense of the contemporary which the images in *Cambio de piel* are designed to capture. They reflect not the pure and absolute present of which Fuentes speaks in his interview with Rodríguez Monegal, but merely the false, illusory present evoked by the world of fashion and consumer products. Franco observes, however, that "the photographs included (many of them of old movie stars) convey a nostalgic rather than a modern impression."[16] In fact, in addition to being dated, the photographs also lack the slick, glossy quality we associate with fashion and advertising. They look more like negatives than fully developed photographs. The figures they represent have been reduced to their basic black and white outlines. As a result, they possess a rough, somewhat abstract quality which creates an effect of distance and defamiliarization rather than immediacy.

To understand the effect of the pictures in *Cambio de piel*, it may help to consider the notion of "camp," which artists and critics were beginning to discuss in these years. Around the time that he was putting the finishing touches to *Cambio de piel*, Fuentes published an article on camp in the cultural supplement of *Siempre!* Entitled "Tener sólo historia sagrada es vivir fuera de la historia," Fuentes's piece was part of a special section on camp that also included essays by Carlos Monsiváis and Luis Guillermo Piazza.[17] The interest in camp at this point in time owed a great deal to Susan Sontag's "Notes on Camp," included in her collection *Against Interpretation* (1966), and Fuentes duly begins his essay with an acknowledgment of his debt to Sontag: "If Hegel had cut off Holofernes's head, his name would have been Susan Sontag." After a somewhat campy description of Sontag doing the rounds in New York ("dressed like the Queen of Saba at the latest Andy Warhol show; like a pop Justine, black leather boots, mental whip at the *New Yorker* film ses-

sions"), Fuentes concludes that Sontag "is the most brilliant interpreter—even though she rejects the word—of the modern sensibility she herself embodies." Indeed, if we look at Sontag's definition of
camp, we will see that it provides some useful clues to understanding Fuentes's own attempt to express a modern sensibility.

Fuentes's interest in camp signaled the up-to-dateness of his
aesthetics, yet the camp sensibility itself stands in a somewhat paradoxical relationship to the new. For camp involves something very
different from a wholehearted and spontaneous embrace of the contemporary. An important element in Sontag's approach to camp is
her assertion that the "connoisseur of camp" delights in "the coars-
est, commonest pleasures, in the arts of the masses."[18] Camp represents an attempt to break down the barriers separating high from
low culture; it offers a lighthearted and playful alternative to the
severe, moralistic idea of culture associated in the Anglo-American
tradition with Matthew Arnold. Fuentes, too, draws attention to
this aspect of the camp sensibility: "camp . . . seeks to rescue the
vulgarity of the contemporary world by accepting it, by giving it an
aesthetic status (hence its kinship with pop art), camp discovers
that there is a good taste of bad taste and that this discovery is liberating." But this does not mean that camp advocates an indiscrimi-
nate appreciation of every facet of low culture. When Sontag
defines camp as "the answer to the problem: how to be a dandy in
the age of mass culture" (288), we may for a moment ignore the
confusion this statement expresses (inasmuch as the dandy was
himself a product of the age of mass culture), and note simply that
insofar as a dandy is somebody who likes to stand apart from the
crowd, camp necessarily implies a preference for detachment, rather
than for a direct involvement in mass culture. The obvious question,
then, is this: how does the person with a camp sensibility manage at
one and the same time to celebrate low culture *and* to maintain the
requisite distance?

Sontag offers two answers to this question. The dandy manages to reconcile these opposite demands in the first place because
of his ability to possess the objects of his pleasure "in a rare way"
(289). The assumption is that a sensibility is defined not only by

what cultural products it consumes, but also by *how* it consumes them. One doesn't become a person of camp sensibility simply by virtue of the fact that one enjoys low culture. If that were the case, the masses would have been camp all along. The point is to enjoy popular culture, but in a way that enhances rather than erases one's sense of distinction. One consumes the same products as the masses, but not in the same way. The trick is to introduce an element of irony into one's enjoyment by turning the very act of consuming mass culture into a kind of spectacle.

The second important technique for reconciling the somewhat contradictory demands that inhere in the notion of camp is for the person of camp sensibility to select for consumption objects from the mass culture of the past rather than the present. In Sontag's words, "the process of aging or deterioration provides the necessary detachment" (285). The cultivation of a taste for the anachronistic becomes the supreme mark of sophistication. The implication is clear: the camp sensibility turns away from the mass culture of the present. The self-conscious retrieval of the mass cultural products of an earlier period amounts to a rejection of the traditional canons of high culture, but also of contemporary mass culture, which after all operates on the principle of immediate consumption.[19]

The notion of camp helps clarify Fuentes's use of the photographic image in *Cambio de piel*. To begin with, the pictures convey a sense of novelty and excitement. They inform the reader that this is not yet another stodgy remnant of the age of literacy; rather, this is a work that seeks to participate in the powerful new effects of the increasingly prominent visual media.[20] Yet both the images chosen for inclusion in Fuentes's novel, and the way in which they have been reproduced suggests, at the same time, a desire to establish a distance with regard to the contemporary cult of the image. Both the selection of dated images, and the unpolished quality of the images indicate a refusal to be dazzled by the visual media. What Fuentes offers is a campy incursion into the images of the past. He evokes the image's drama and immediacy, yet he also places it in imaginary quotation marks.

There is something, however, that does not sit well in this analysis. For the photograph from World War II is profoundly unfitted to the kind of camp treatment that, we may agree, is given to the other pictures in the series. There is an evident tension between, on the one hand, the silent yet absolute terror conveyed by the picture of Jews being rounded up by German soldiers, and, on the other hand, the theatrical anguish emanating from the portrait of Joan Crawford. The somber reference to the millions destroyed in the Holocaust clashes in a decidedly grotesque fashion with the ironic allusions to a line of deceased cultural products. Perhaps Fuentes is drawing attention to the way in which in the age of the image, everything is reduced to imagery, and history and entertainment become indistinguishable. Perhaps the insertion of the theme of ultimate death in a camp framework is a way of underlining a feature of the camp sensibility pinpointed by Andrew Ross when he argues that camp, in its resurrection of outdated styles, acts as an obverse of the consumer culture of immediacy and disposability, and thus performs the function of "a kind of *memento mori*" (152). Yet even these explanations cannot take away the sense of incongruity in Fuentes's mixing of images.

To understand the nature and sources of this incongruity, it may help to turn once more to Fuentes's essay on camp in *Siempre!* The essay consists of two sections. In the first section Fuentes offers a brief summary of the principal features of the camp sensibility; in the second section he argues that Mexico itself is permeated with camp. What is interesting about Fuentes's account is that although it is clearly indebted to Susan Sontag, it departs in significant ways from her position. Fuentes begins by affirming that "Camp is a vision of the world from the point of view of style." He then adds that it favors a particular style: an extreme style of exaggeration and theatricality, a style that "transforms things into what they are not." Fuentes underscores camp's extravagance, its passion, while also observing, along with Sontag, that it spurns seriousness and exalts frivolity. It is at this point in his text that we see Fuentes veering away from a line of thought that is of considerable importance to

Sontag's depiction of camp. Fuentes echoes Sontag's opposition between camp and tragedy, but he does not develop as fully as Sontag the implications of this opposition. Of course, Fuentes is trying to compress into a much shorter space than Sontag a complex account of what Sontag herself calls a "fugitive sensibility" (277). Sontag has the leisure to approach her topic from a variety of angles; it would be impossible for Fuentes to do justice in a few pages to all of the ways in which Sontag's mind ranges over her subject. Even so, what Fuentes omits is significant.

Sontag states that "if tragedy is an experience of hyperinvolvement, camp is an experience of underinvolvement, of detachment" (288). This notion of disengagement is wholly absent from Fuentes's account. Like Sontag, Fuentes believes that "camp and tragedy are antithetical" to each other, but he sees camp not as a cool and playful aesthetic, but as an extreme and dangerous one. Camp, he claims, "arises from a sensibility that is passionate, irresistible, out of control," adding that "the camp sensibility refuses to see character in terms of development, seeing it instead as a state of perpetual incandescence, of a theatricalization of experience." By underlining camp's energy, intensity and extravagance, Fuentes downplays the element of whimsy and artifice. He converts an aesthetics of simulation into an aesthetics of authenticity. This shift in focus becomes especially evident at the start of the second section of his essay, where Fuentes links the camp sensibility to certain essential traits of Mexican culture:

> We tend to forget that Mexico is a country of radical intuitions, of gestations that antecede the formulas elaborated by culture. André Breton called Mexico the promised land of surrealism. Paradoxical? Extreme needs engender extreme desires. The distance between desire and its object invests them both in Mexico with an incandescent purity. The arc traced from the shore of longing to the shore of fulfillment leaps over any kind of realistic contingency: in Mexico all encounters are supra-real. Artaud and Michaux discovered new realms of perception here. All of Mexico is

permeated by an existentialism avant la lettre. The *now* has always been the country's response to an insecure, provisional life, without a probable future.

Note how in this passage Fuentes shows his true colors: a discussion of the camp element in Mexican life slides into an account of the existentialist quality in Mexican culture.[21] In associating the camp sensibility with the primitive, existential energy at the heart of Mexican life, Fuentes overlooks the profound differences that separate the thematics of camp from those of existentialism. At the same time he bypasses a fundamental distinction Sontag draws between three different creative sensibilities: "The first sensibility, that of high culture, is basically moralistic. The second sensibility, that of extreme states of feeling, represented in much contemporary 'avant-garde' art, gains power by a tension between moral and aesthetic passion. The third, camp, is wholly aesthetic" (287).

Fuentes's concern with radical intuitions, suprareal encounters, and extreme desires links his vision of Mexico to what Sontag calls the sensibility of "extreme states of feeling," rather than to camp. And it is of course this preoccupation with extremity, much more than the wish to be camp, that explains the presence of the Nazi theme in *Cambio de piel*.

On the Impossibility of Representation

There are clear parallels between Fuentes's use of camp elements in *Cambio de piel* and his deployment of the techniques of novelistic self-reflexiveness. Let us note to begin with that both camp and self-reflexive literariness are ways of making the world "wholly aesthetic," to borrow Sontag's phrase. In the case of the self-reflexive text this is a matter in the first place of downgrading, or even eliminating (to the extent that this is possible), the referential dimension of the text. That Fuentes had something like this in mind is clear from his statement in his interview with Emir Rodríguez Monegal that *Cambio de piel* is a novel that aims for a level of "absolute fictionality" (10). We must interpret this to mean that the novel does not presume to offer an imitation of the real world; instead, it is to be regarded as a novel about a novel, making no claim whatsoever to a referential dimension.

The self-reflexive novel is an elusive object much theorized about by structuralists, poststructuralists, and postmodernists. Patricia Waugh prefers the term "metafiction," which she defines as "a term given to fictional writing which self-consciously and systematically draws attention to its status as an artefact in order to pose questions about the relationship between fiction and reality."[22] One of the principal ways in which a text may pose questions about the relationship between fiction and reality is through the destruction of narrative. By making it impossible to reconstruct a story out of a text, the writer strikes a blow against the referential principle in general. Of course, a nonnarrative text need not necessarily be nonreferential, but a text that rejects reference almost by definition must reject narrative, too. One of the most common methods for undermining narrative is the juxtaposition of discrete textual segments, which, as a result of the effect of temporal dislocation, come to be projected onto a single plane of simultaneity. In the opening section of *Cambio de piel*, Fuentes attempts something of this kind. For about twelve pages, Fuentes alternates between the description of the arrival in Cholula of the four main characters of the novel on April 11, 1965, on the one hand, and the description of the siege of Cholula by Cortés and his men in 1519 on the other hand. This is exactly the kind of cutting and pasting technique employed by Mario Vargas Llosa in *La casa verde*, a novel that Fuentes describes in *La nueva novela* as "the supreme example of a novel that would not exist outside language" (37). Presumably what he means is that the elimination of conventional narrative sequence is a way of focusing attention on the text not as a window onto the world but as *writing*. In the opening section of *Cambio de piel*, Fuentes strives to establish a sense of simultaneity between different textual planes that might be read in a similar way. The disordering of conventional temporal distinctions is particularly evident from the fact that the passages set in the present are narrated in the past tense, whereas the historical segments of the text are cast in the present tense.

This undermining of the referential dimension of the text is carried even further in the next scene, in which we see two of the novel's main characters, Javier and Elizabeth, in their hotel room in Cholula. In the course of the first few pages of this section, selected fragments from the descriptions of Cortés's encounter with the Cholulans, and of the arrival of the novel's four protagonists in Cholula earlier the same day, are repeated, but now as parts of a conversation between Elizabeth and Javier. Thus, even while they discuss small things such as whether to unpack or to take a bath, Javier and Elizabeth pronounce phrases that the reader has already encountered in the previous section of the novel. For example, at one point, Javier turns on the tap in the bathroom and says, "after five hours of battle and three thousand dead in the streets" (30/20). We then see Elizabeth leaning against the door of the bathroom and answering in a low voice: "They are diviners. The gods divine treachery and take their vengeance. No power can resist them" (31/21). These passages were part of the account by an anonymous narrator of the massacre of the Cholulans by the Spaniards in the previous section of the novel. Fuentes now forces us to reconceive them as texts recited by particular characters within the novel. We must see them less as descriptions than as performances.

This shift of focus from the content of the narration to the act of narration is a characteristic device in *Cambio de piel*. Much of the novel consists of the conversations between Javier, Elizabeth, Franz and Isabel during their drive out of Mexico City, as well as during the night they are forced to spend in a hotel in Cholula after their car breaks down. These conversations often lead into extended reconstructions of the past lives of the various characters. But by constantly showing the reader how the remembrance of the past flows out of a dialogue that takes place in the present, Fuentes turns the act of telling a story into something as important, if not more so, than the story itself. In *Cambio de piel* the scene of narration is never allowed to fade into invisibility. To give a clearer sense of how this works, I will look briefly at one significant episode: the scene in which Javier meets Elizabeth at a party, then takes her to a cantina near the Plaza Garibaldi, where he receives a beating after he provokes the members of a mariachi band by throwing peanuts at them. The scene is reminiscent of the scene of Manuel Zamacona's murder in *La región más transparente*: both depict the violent encounter between an intellectual and the dark underside of Mexican life.

The episode is narrated on two separate occasions (122–32/103–14; 274–80/240–46). On both occasions Fuentes develops—as he does throughout the novel—a complex interplay between different narrative voices. In this particular episode, there are three different narrators: Javier, Elizabeth, and the novel's principal narrator, whose name (we learn at the very end) is Freddy Lambert. Freddy Lambert has a peculiar role as a narrator in *Cambio de piel*, for he is constantly fading in and out of the narrative. Sometimes he is a character in his own narrative; at other times he is not. Freddy Lambert's ambiguous status is reflected in this particular episode, for although most of his interventions appear to be in the context of the ongoing dialogue in which he engages with Elizabeth, there is also a suggestion that he is the taxi driver who takes Javier and Elizabeth from the party to the cantina, and then picks them up again after Javier has been bloodied up by the angry mariachis. Freddy Lambert's role as narrator is further complicated by the fact that while he speaks of Javier in the third person, he addresses Elizabeth (who he calls "dragon") in the second person. This mode of direct address is one more way in which the novel foregrounds the process of narration: by speaking directly to her, Freddy Lambert makes Elizabeth into a concrete presence in the scene of narration. This effect has its parallel in the way in which the narrative throughout this particular episode (in both its versions) maintains a double focus: on the one hand, we see Javier and Elizabeth in their hotel room in Cholula remembering the past, while on the other hand we see them on the fateful night itself. The narrative shifts back and forth in a sometimes dizzying fashion between the different temporal levels.

While the principal events in this episode—the rendezvous at the party, the taxi ride, the visit to the cantina, and Javier's beating—remain the same, the way in which these events are presented differs significantly from one version to the next. In fact, the differences are so numerous that I will limit myself to mentioning two key variations. In the first place, each version offers a different explanation for Javier's behavior in the cantina. In the first version (which is essentially Javier's), Javier's summing up of the episode in the phrases, "We had returned to Mexico, Ligeia. We were back" (132/114), added to Javier's depiction of the men in the cantina as typical *hijos de la chingada* (129/111), suggests that Javier is searching in some desperate way to bridge the distance separating him from his fellow Mexicans. Only by insulting them, and then suffering their revenge, can Javier establish the contact he seeks with the people. In the second version (which is essentially Elizabeth's), Javier's concluding statement refers not to the notion of home, but to the problem of his literary career. "They don't understand me. I've told you so before. It is impossible to do anything in Mexico. There is no criticism, no information," he says to his wife, and then refers to what apparently is a negative review of something he has just published: "Look, Ligeia, look what they say here about the story" (280/246). In light of these remarks, the beating administered by the mariachis acquires a completely different meaning: it can be seen as a kind of concretization of the punishment Javier feels he has received at the hands of the Mexican literary establishment.

A second important difference between the two versions of this episode is that Javier is far less explicit than Elizabeth as to what happens at the party where they meet. In her account, Elizabeth provides information about the nature of this meeting which is missing from Javier's account. Elizabeth explains that Javier draws her into a perverse game he seems to want to play with her in order to maintain a sense of freshness about their marriage. He tells her to be at the party at ten o'clock, but himself arrives much later, even though he is aware of the fact that Elizabeth does not know anybody at the party. When he finally arrives, Javier takes Elizabeth out onto the dance floor, but pretends that she is a woman he has only just met for the first time. In his imagination he turns her into a stranger: "A woman to be conquered. A new woman. A woman to be discovered" (276/242). Afraid of repetitions, longing for the exceptional, Javier erases the past, puts on a mask, and transforms Elizabeth into the creature of his desires. Elizabeth pretends to go along with her husband's performance, but in fact returns his caresses not because he is somebody excitingly new but because he is the man she has lived with for so many years: "I caressed you . . . because you were the same Javier as always" (277/242).

That Javier is seeking to defamiliarize the quotidian is corroborated by his own account of the events of the evening in question. Whereas Javier is a concrete presence in Elizabeth's version, Elizabeth remains an entirely shadowy figure in Javier's account. It is never clear whether Elizabeth is in fact the woman of whom Javier speaks. Javier never once in his version of the episode uses his wife's name, speaking instead of "she" or "the woman." To this extent, we might say that the two versions converge: Javier's distanced, impersonal perspective (reinforced by the way in which his account is laced with literary and mythological references) confirms Elizabeth's description of the game he plays with her. And yet, we cannot simply conclude that Elizabeth's version stands against Javier's as reality against invention. For the "real" Elizabeth of whom she speaks as an alternative to the "secret" woman of Javier's fantasies is herself presented as an unreliable construct. When Elizabeth says to Javier "you caressed me because I was a different woman, not Elizabeth Jonas, born in New York forty-two years ago" (277/243), we must recall that the novel elsewhere casts serious doubt on the "facts" concerning Elizabeth's background.

The insistent focus on the process of telling a story, as well as the presentation of different, incompatible versions of a single narrative sequence, have the same effect of undermining the referential dimension of the story. This process of derealization is taken so far in *Cambio de piel* that by the end of the novel we are unsure of the ontological status of sizeable chunks of the text. Did Javier and Elizabeth live on the Greek island of Falaraki in 1938? Did Elizabeth grow up in New York? The reader cannot provide a confident answer to these and many other questions. And if we cannot be sure what actually happens in the novel, then all we are left with is the text as text. From this we might conclude that

Cambio de piel is a purely self-referring artifact, or an extended performance sustained in language rather than through its connections with the world.

Yet the reading of *Cambio de piel* as wholly self-reflexive seems unsatisfactory. This is not just because Fuentes indicated in interviews from this period that the novel that exists only in and for itself was not the type of work he was interested in writing.[23] Nor can the sense of the inadequacy of the self-reflexive reading of *Cambio de piel* be assuaged by arguing that the novel's focus on its own narrative structure can be read as a commentary on our everyday real-life experience, inasmuch as it makes us aware of the role of narrative constructions in life in general.[24] Such a perspective would remain unsatisfactory, in that it applies the same distanced reading of novelistic conventions to the conventions of the real world, whereas in *Cambio de piel* one feels that Fuentes is less interested in instilling in his readers a skeptical, demystified view of the world than in confronting the reader with a raw, unprocessed vision of reality.

The point can be illustrated by returning to the episode of the mariachis. For however self-conscious, contradictory, and artificial the presentation of the entire episode may be, the anecdote contains a substratum of unexpungeable reality—the reality of violence. After all, the narrative does not cast any doubt on the central event of the episode—Javier's beating at the hands of the mariachis. One might even suggest that the fact that the episode is recounted on two separate occasions is a way of heightening its significance—a significance that resides in revealing the role of violence in human relations. It is evident that *Cambio de piel* is a novel obsessed with violence. I will not enumerate here all the examples of violence in the novel, except to say that they range from the relatively mundane—the psychological violence perpetrated by a husband on his wife, or a mother on her child—to the truly apocalyptic—the ultimate violence of the Holocaust. In an astute review of the English translation of *Cambio de piel*, David Gallagher drew attention to the tension between this level of violence in the text and the tendency of Fuentes's use of self-reflexive devices to make the world of the novel dissolve into insubstantiality: he "is not always content to accept the distance between all the events he describes and a more 'real' world. I felt that there was at any rate one phenomenon in the novel which was posturing as 'real': that is, that vital tiger underneath the skin not only of Mexico but also of Franz's 'German' and perhaps all of mankind."[25]

Yet there is a way in which technique and vision perhaps do merge in *Cambio de piel*. For to write about violence is to write about that which is beyond language. If Fuentes constantly undermines his own text, he does so in order to draw attention to the impossible nature of his subject: he leaves an incomprehensible violence in its full incomprehensibility.[26]

Why Javier Can't Write

Fuentes also explores the problem of writing in his portrait of Javier. Insofar as *Cambio de piel* is a novel that constantly threatens to self-destruct in the hands of the reader, we might say that it deliberately flirts with the notion of aesthetic failure. In this light, the fact that Javier is a failed writer acquires a special relevance.

Javier is a typical modernist artist, divided between his interest in the ordinary everyday dimension of life, and his allegiance to a theory of the autonomy of the aesthetic sphere. In the struggle between these two tendencies, the latter triumphs, a triumph that sets the stage for Javier's ultimate failure as a writer. The pattern is already apparent in Javier's first book of poems, *El sueño*. Javier's constructs his first poems out of the elements of his daily life: "this new and virginal poetry, fresh and solitary, made of the false shadows of his home, of Sundays on the lake and the solitary streets of the organ-grinders and servant girls and of Raúl's smell of soap and tobacco and of Ofelia's face of a little girl grown old." But in this same book Javier affirms that "only what is finished is perfect and enduring" (234/205); in the end, we understand that he writes not so much about everyday life, as against it. It is only in the closed sphere of art that Javier feels that he can save himself from the sense of waste that for him characterizes the realm of the quotidian. But in what can only be read as an illustration of the consequences of Javier's aestheticizing of life, the narrative shifts in the next few pages to the episode in which Javier and Elizabeth arrive home late one night and find a dead body cast on the sidewalk near the entrance to their building. Elizabeth wants to call the police, but Javier remains unmoved by the sight of the dead man. In Javier's opinion, the murderer did the dead man a favor in killing him: "He killed him so as to give him the totality of his life" (237/208). Only in death does life achieve closure, the closure of myth, and therefore also of art. To Elizabeth's horror, Javier transforms what the newspapers the next day describe as a random killing into an aesthetic event.

The oscillation between an art that aspires to the status of myth and an art of the quotidian also emerges from the contrast between two stages in Javier's personal and artistic trajectory. In 1938, Javier and Elizabeth spend part of the year on the Greek island of Falaraki, where Javier works on several projects, including a poem on "Greece as a point of departure and return" (264/231). But Javier's longing to return to the mythical origins of Western civilization comes to naught: the poem is never completed.[27] When he returns to Mexico, he appears to have discovered a new aesthetic orientation. Elizabeth describes his new project as follows: "You would roam the city in search of contrasts, masks, profiles; you would write the poetry of the quotidian" (150/131). Javier himself speaks of his desire to find, like Hart Crane in *The Bridge*, "a resonance of the city in poetry" (227/198). But there is only one scene in the novel in which we actually see Javier exploring the city. As far as we can tell, this scene takes place many years after Javier's initial return to Mexico. Yet it helps us understand why the poem of the quotidian was also never completed.

The passage in question is approximately twelve pages long and has no paragraph divisions. It describes the flow of Javier's thoughts one hot, dry day in March as he leaves his office (he is working for the United Nations at this point in his life) to wander about the streets of the city. In his cool, luxurious office, with its tinted windows and expensive furniture, Javier is surrounded by a web of institutional symbols. There is a photograph of Dag

Hammarskjold on the wall and a pile of documents on his desk. Javier carries an identification card that confirms "with its engraved lettering, its properly sealed photograph, its very official, very important-looking ornate script" that the bearer is a United Nations official (46/34). Yet Javier appears to feel estranged rather than sustained by these formal confirmations of his existence. A copy of the Carta de las Naciones in his office, "covered with finger-prints as if he could leave his personal mark on the world's constitution" (46/34), offers ironic witness to the futility of his existence. Javier ventures into the street to revivify himself, but everywhere he looks he encounters images of death, threats to his identity. He imagines he is walking along a beach, but he is afraid to look back and find "that he is not leaving any footsteps in the sand of the pavement" (47/35). He recalls a recurrent dream of a death by drowning, a dream he wants to—but cannot—forget. He imagines an innermost recess of his self: "a cloister where no sound pene-trates, not even the sound of his own voice as it speaks of that death in the dream of the sea" (48–49/36)—but he knows such a region does not exist. He imagines his own death, seeing in his mind's eye his corpse: "The map of his colorless face, with a beard that would continue to grow, like his nails, like the gases that would go on bub-bling in his discomposed stomach without realizing that his glassy eyes had stopped seeing, and his open, brutish, salivating mouth had stopped breathing" (55/42). In the shops, he sees the man-nequins: "truncated men" (49/37) and women with "mutilated glass legs" (50/37). Later, in the doctor's office, the other patients in the waiting room, reading old copies of *Life* and *Mañana*, remind him of wax dolls (56/43). He walks around with the taste of old coins in his mouth, and the light in the street is so bright that it blinds him. He sees a group of people in mourning coming out of a church. He enters the post office where he leans against a counter covered with telegrams that were never sent: "The marble counter was covered with telegram forms, some yellow, smooth, mute, others crumpled, discarded, rolled up by a mistaken or forgetful hand, seized by remorse, doubt or a final indifference" (55/42). Javier begins to read the telegrams. He might have discovered what he was looking for—the poetry of the quotidian—in these fragments of unknown lives. But for Javier they are just dead letters: they remind him of the other patients in the doctor's waiting room, engaged in what he calls "the act of fake reading" (56/43).

Because everything in the world around him appears degraded to Javier, he withdraws into the inner cloister of his identity. Unable to engage with the world, Javier cannot bring his literary projects to fruition. As a way of justifying his failure, Javier enunciates an aesthetics of silence. In one of his notebooks, Javier argues that to abstain from creating a work of art is the only proper response to the era in which he lives. The only way to be Byron in this time, is to remain silent. In Javier's view, he lives in a "monstrous era" (224/115) that does not even deserve the honor of being engaged with through art. But what is it exactly that makes the age so monstrous? According to Javier, it is that modern societies— both East and West—demand that their artists be "priests and acolytes of the cult of the external." Artists in this era have two options: either to sing "the glories of work" (East) or to sing "the glories of products" (West). Communist societies want to be consecrated in art, whereas capitalist societies already feel consecrated "because they distribute refrigerators" (225/196). Under such conditions, where the autonomous value of art is denied, only a kind of heroic abstention from aesthetic work is acceptable: "The entire work must remain within oneself, without externalization, without the weakness of giving to those who do not deserve it something that can only retain its value as long as it is not shared with anyone" (224/196).

The key to Javier's argument is the notion of aesthetic autonomy. What he repudiates is the way modern society wants to make the artist useful. Both communist and capitalist societies want to enlist the artist into the performance of some nonaesthetic goal. Javier contrasts this utilitarian approach to the conception of art upheld by what he calls barbaric (as opposed to modern) societies. In his notebook, he writes that "The beauty of the barbaric"—of which the ruins of Xochicalco offer an example—"is self-consuming, and thrives on its separation rather than its identification with

life" (220/192). Modern art operates according to an entirely different principle: "for us beauty is a model, an example and an incite-
ment to transfer it from its fixed expression to our vital experience.
. . . Hence its exhaustion in fashion" (220/192). Art is art by virtue
of its separation from life: Javier's doctrine is, of course, a common-
place of modern aesthetics, and is, in particular, highly reminiscent
of Wilhelm Worringer's work on the differences between primitive
and modern art. But adherence to a theory of the separation of art
from life proves profoundly unproductive. In the account of the fate
of one of Javier's literary projects, a novel titled *La caja de Pandora*,
Fuentes regales the reader with a reductio ad absurdum of the theory of aesthetic autonomy.

Terry Eagleton argues that the modernist work emphasizes its
autonomy so as to "fend off" the threat of being reduced to the status of a commodity. In order to prevent such reduction from taking
place, the modernist work "brackets off the referent or real historical world, thickens its textures and deranges its forms to forestall
instant consumability, and draws its own language protectively
around it to become a mysteriously autotelic object, free of all conta-
minating truck with the real."[28] Javier is clearly driven by the characteristic concerns of the modernists. Yet his solution to the problem
of art in a world of commodities goes a step beyond the one
described by Eagleton. Instead of creating mysteriously autotelic
objects, Javier ends by creating nothing at all. To understand why
Javier relapses into silence, we must examine the process whereby
La caja de Pandora fails to get written. The first thing the reader
learns about Javier's novel is that it is about "the secret of love"
(264/231). At the same time we learn that Javier conceives *La caja de
Pandora* as a self-reflexive novel, that is, a novel about the nature of
the novel itself. This is clear from the novel's opening sentence: "A
novel manifests what the world has not yet discovered and may
never discover for itself" (297/262). But if Javier's manifesto-like
opening statement suggests that a novel engages in a dialectics of
concealment and revelation, the fate of Javier's project indicates
that the process ends up being jammed by its own contradictions.
Because meaning comes from concealment, revelation proves to be

impossible. For Javier the novel is a novel by virtue of the fact that it contains a secret. This is in effect a reformulation of the doctrine of aesthetic autonomy, for to claim that the work of art is closed upon itself is to imply that it exists in a realm of incommunicability and irrepeatability. But if what the novel contains cannot be communicated or repeated then it cannot be known. The novel remains a secret as long as it withholds itself from the channels of circulation—in time and in space—through which all human creations must move. But the act of withholding can only be complete if the novel fails to be written. This is in effect what happens with Javier's novel. Toward the end of *Cambio de piel*, Javier asks Elizabeth to remind him of the plot of *La caja de Pandora*. She explains that the novel was to tell the story of a man and woman who loved each other, and who through their love arrived at "a new knowledge." They are the only couple ever to be able to "keep or capture" this knowledge, which is "a miracle of the flesh." They decide to share their secret with the world, but as soon as they communicate it to the world, the secret vanishes: "They reveal their secret to the outside world. The secret vanishes, ceases to be a secret, is misunderstood. The lovers are left naked, forever saddened. They opened Pandora's box." The moral of the story is that in secrecy lies the essence of love: "Love that can be known from the outside is no longer love." The secret of love is that love is a secret. But what is true of love is also true of art: insofar as the essence of art is in its secrecy (its autonomy), art too cannot be externalized. Javier explains that even though he was convinced of the beauty of his idea, the idea in fact made it impossible for him to write the novel: "The theme itself forbade me to write the book. It would have meant revealing the secret to the outside world. And this would have gone against the very logic of the work" (378–79/335–36). Once again the condition of love and the condition of art run parallel to each other. Javier concludes that it is futile to write a novel that communicates to the world that it is in fact impossible to communicate the world's most essential secrets. But in a broader sense he becomes convinced that it is futile to create *any* work of art once one has defined the essence of a work of art as residing in its secrecy.[29]

What To Do With the Monsters

What is the relationship between Javier's trajectory as a writer and Fuentes's own aesthetic choices in *Cambio de piel*? Clearly, there is a parallel between Fuentes's assault on traditional realism and Javier's resistance to the reduction of art to the status of a commodity. Yet there is also an obvious difference between the two: while Javier relapses into silence, Fuentes produces a long, vibrant and chaotic work that on some level embraces the very vulgarity of the modern world Javier so stubbornly spurns. Perhaps the explanation for the difference between Javier and Fuentes is that Javier fails as a writer because he demands from himself the perfection of aesthetic autonomy, while Fuentes successfully completes *Cambio de piel* because he manages to free himself from the demands of aesthetic perfection. Thus *Cambio de piel* can be viewed as an illustration of Jean Cocteau's dictum, "The only work which succeeds is that which fails." But Javier's aesthetic theories carry even broader implications in the novel. In effect, Fuentes links his analysis of the dilemmas of the artist to a sweeping conception of the nature of Western civilization. The best way to bring this to light is by looking deeper into the notion of secrecy.

Fuentes establishes in *Cambio de piel* a crucial link between secrecy and prohibition. This is clear from Javier's account of *La caja de Pandora*: what is not known is also a forbidden knowledge. Remember that he says about his project that "The theme itself *forbade me* to write the book" (my emphasis). Secrecy involves by definition an act of interdiction. That writing and interdiction go hand and hand is underlined in Javier's recollection of what may be regarded as the originative scene of his writerly vocation: "As a child, I used to write in the toilet the insults I dared not say out loud. Later I came to understand that writing books amounts to the same thing . . . insults transformed into names" (298/262). But this is a positive conception of writing as a mode of heresy and desacralization, which Javier, with his withdrawal into silence, does not manage to sustain. It is, furthermore, a stance that is fundamentally at odds with what according to Fuentes is the dominant tradition of the West, a tradition in which secrets are not violated, but repressed.

This view of Western civilization is developed in a series of discursive passages that crop up at regular intervals in *Cambio de piel*. In one passage the narrator traces the wrong turn taken by Western civilization back to the moment in which Orestes defeated the Furies: "Who told Orestes to pacify the Furies and send them underground where their sacred blood could no longer drain rivers dry and burn harvests?" (179–80/156). Before Orestes—"the before that circulates in our nocturnal memory"—the Furies were "part of the accepted order of a proliferating and inclusive nature" (180/156). In sending the Furies underground, Orestes merely prepared the way for their return in a more pernicious form: "In twisting their necks, he was only giving the Furies the advantage of negation, allowing them to reappear with their blood poisoned but wearing the mask of order, without the real spontaneity of their place in the world" (180/156). As Steven Boldy puts it, "When the Other is repressed, it is not always simply neutralized, but takes a sinister and evil form it did not have originally."[30]

The act of suppression perpetrated at the origins of Western civilization has produce a fundamentally dualistic culture. The narrator of *Cambio de piel* speaks repeatedly of the need to overcome "the old Manichaeism which since Plato has led us by the nose, forcing us to divide, to choose, to see things in black-and-white" (241/211), and of how it is imperative that we free ourselves "from all the false and fatal dualisms upon which has been built the civilization of the judges and priests and philosophers and artists and executioners and merchants" (269/236). Dualism is the result of repression and leads to catastrophe. Fuentes's interest in the Holocaust in *Cambio de piel* is linked to the fact that it illustrates this sequence. Nazism reveals how the originative act of suppression of the forces of monstrosity merely ends with the reappearance of those forces wearing the mask of order. Fuentes draws attention to the profound strain of irrationality informing Nazi ideology, but he is equally interested in showing how Nazism cloaks itself in the modern principles of rationality and efficiency. It is surely significant that the novel's main Nazi character—Franz Jellinek—is an architect, one who believes, moreover, that the architect's function in the modern era is to be "one more cog in the wheel of a collective enterprise" (282/248). Such a view of the architect makes Franz highly suited to the task to which he is soon assigned: the building of a crematorium for a Nazi concentration camp. It is also significant that the reader is first introduced to the Nazi theme in *Cambio de piel* through a very precise description of a concentration camp (80–83/65–66). The contrast between the crisp, clear sense of function conveyed by the narrator's depiction of the grounds and the horrifying deeds committed there stands as the perfect example of how in the modern world monstrosity hides behind the appearance of order.

One of the most interesting aspects of *Cambio de piel* is the way it links literature to the originative act of repression which set Western civilization on its twisted course. We saw earlier that according to the scheme proposed by the narrator of *Cambio de piel* the defeat of the monsters merely set the stage for their return in a diseased form. Literature is one of the vehicles for this return of the repressed: "The heroes of antiquity invented literature because they forced the powers of nature to hide and to reappear in disguise, and that's why we have epic and lyric and tragedy" (180/156). Literature, in this view, amounts to a masking, deflecting and denaturing operation performed on an original and inclusive order. Perhaps this is why the narrator proceeds to introduce Sherlock Holmes into the discussion at this point: "fuck all the Sherlocks . . . who, clutching their magnifying glasses, go hunting for the guilty" (180/156). Sherlock Holmes, with his rationalism, his desire for order, and his concern with doing good, becomes the embodiment of the literary enterprise itself. The writer emerges, in this account, as an ally of the priest and the politician: "all those who offer a different image of the world, an artificial and false image, an interpretation, an incantatory psalm" (350/310). This view of literature as the generator of "cold and artificial forms" (223/195) is, of course, perfectly captured in Javier's literary career, and, for that matter, in his personal life, too. When Javier wants Elizabeth to be "a mere representation of nature and not nature itself" we understand that he wishes to transform her into a work of art, an object he describes as "distant and motionless, restful and unreachable, circumspect and complete" (292/257), an object wholly removed, in other words, from the immediate, flowing and inclusive rhythms of the natural world. Art, then, becomes a technique for controlling and mastering an unruly reality.

Cambio de piel emerges as the embodiment of Fuentes's refusal to write this kind of literature. The novel's opacity serves to resist the very idea of representation, an idea Fuentes links to the freezing of reality in which Western civilization has been engaged since antiquity. But Fuentes has not made things easy for himself in *Cambio de piel*. For the question is how well this reading of Western civilization fits the Nazi theme which Fuentes so boldly introduces in the novel. On one level, as I suggested earlier, the Nazis, with their cruelty attached to a maniacal devotion to order, are the true endpoint of Fuentes's narrative of the trajectory of Western civilization. Nazism is the ultimate form monstrosity takes when the monsters are expelled from their place in a natural, free-flowing order, only to resurface in a perverted guise. Yet in *Cambio de piel* Fuentes entertains at the same time an entirely different reading of Nazism, one that sees it not as the logical culmination of a process inherent to Western civilization, but rather as a phenomenon that poses a profound challenge to the dominant tradition of the West. This view of Nazism not as the end-product of a repressive Western rationalism, but as a subversive and emancipating force is articulated most notably by Brother Tomás, the black man who takes up Franz's defense in the happening-cum-trial near the end of the novel. "The Negro," as he is referred to throughout this scene, presents the Nazis as bold rebels in search of a more authentic relation to existence. He depicts them as advocates of "the joyous acceptance of all of man's faces" (439/396), including the face that has been suppressed by "the centuries of Judeo-Christian barbarism which has mutilated mankind" (440/397). And accepting the whole human being means accepting evil: "we were liberators, not oppressors, we were the only men who when we felt the tide of evil within us, acted in the name of Evil, instead of mutilating that power" (442/400). To restore humanity to health: that is how the Negro sums up the Nazi program, even if doing so means recalling humanity to its diseased condition: "Somebody had to be Insane and Sick in a world which thought of itself as incurably Sane and Rational" (441/398).

There is something deliberately outrageous about this defense of Nazism, yet it is not at all illogical from the point of view of the reading of Western civilization proposed in *Cambio de piel*. For if the West's wrong turn can be traced back to the moment when Western man repressed the monster in him, and if the Nazis are the monsters of our own time, then to repress the Nazis would in a sense be to repeat the error at the source of Western history. It is for this reason that Fuentes entertains a kind of embrace of Nazism in *Cambio de piel*.

Yet in the end Fuentes veers away from the more extreme implications of his ideas. To begin with, it is suggested that the only right response to the defense of Nazism put forward by the Negro is irony. The narrator himself interrupts the Negro at one point in order to remind him of Jonathan Swift's *A Modest Proposal* for solving the problem of hunger in Ireland, thus implying that there is as little need to take the Negro literally as there is Swift. Moreover, the narrative introduces an explicitly moral perspective through the figure of Jakob Werner, a concentration-camp survivor who acts as prosecutor in the mock trial staged by the Monks at the end of the novel, and who sentences Franz to die for his crimes. The narrator appears to resist the ethical basis for Jakob's sentence, proposing instead that Franz must die simply as part of the necessary turn of the life-cycle: "It does not matter what he has done. He is the old. He must die. The cycle has ended and the new must arise on the ruins of the old" (492/451). Yet in both readings Franz's death implies the restoration of a notion of lawfulness, whether of an ethical or a biological kind. Thus, while on one level *Cambio de piel* denounces all forms of prohibition, and pleads for a recognition rather than a repression of monstrosity, on a different level it reestablishes a normative vision. The novel is seduced by the Dostoyevskian "everything is permitted," yet at the same time it takes on a fundamentally didactic point of view.

We saw earlier that there is a split running through *La nueva novela*, one that separates Fuentes the advocate of an art of irony and ambiguity, of linguistic play and self-reflexiveness, from Fuentes the champion of a confidently political art. In a number of ways, this division in Fuentes's essayistic self-image (for we can surely take Fuentes in *La nueva novela* to be talking about the kind of novelist he believes himself to be) corresponds to a division in *Cambio de piel* with regard to the fundamental problem of representation. The camp celebration of artifice is countered by the existentialist brooding over the problem of authenticity. The destruction of narrative serves to question the very possibility of reference, but it is also a way of evoking a realm of violence that exists beyond language. The interest in art as a mode of secrecy and silence unassimilable to the everyday circulation of goods and images in a consumer society is balanced against the enthusiastic embrace of the hectic, ephemeral rhythms of modern existence. The desire to challenge ordinary distinctions between good and evil runs up against the need to retain for the novel an ethical and pedagogical dimension.

On one level, the tensions in Fuentes's literary and critical positions can be regarded as the result of certain personal traits. Fuentes has always been remarkable for the voraciousness of his intellectual appetites. He has displayed throughout his career an exceptional capacity for the appropriation of literary, cultural and ideological trends, yet, perhaps inevitably, his absorptive capacity has resulted in a certain loss of cohesiveness in his work. On a different level, however, one might argue that the heterogeneity of literary and ideological orientations embodied in Fuentes's work reflects a fundamental heterogeneity at the heart of the notion of modernity itself. For the one thing that appears to unite the varied aspects of Fuentes's work is a uniform will to be modern. Yet to be modern means different things in different contexts. Fuentes's statements on topics such as consumerism, globalism, and the mass media indicate that developments in these areas fascinated him. He clearly saw the opportunities for tapping the energies unleashed by a range of social, economic, and technological innovations. At the same time, Fuentes's support for the Cuban Revolution can be read as a choice in favor of a particular strategy for bringing Latin

America into the modern world. *Cambio de piel*'s heady sense of up-to-dateness, as well as its strain of didacticism, can be viewed as reflecting the broader pedagogical and progressive orientation of modernity. Yet *Cambio de piel* also fits into a tradition of aesthetic modernity that has always been antithetical to modernity understood as a broader social and cultural phenomenon. Features of *Cambio de piel* such as its linguistic and structural opacity and its engagement with extreme subject matter can be seen as elements in the challenge modern art has consistently posed to modern society. To repudiate modernity in this way even as one is seduced by it is perhaps not so unusual a structure of feeling in a twentieth-century writer. Yet it may be that such self-division is experienced more acutely by the Latin American writer, who has generally felt more of an obligation than the writer in Europe or the United States to promote the social, economic, and political modernization of his continent, even while feeling a deeper sense of estrangement from the values of modernity than his coevals in the metropolitan centers of the world, for the simple reason that modernity has often been experienced in Latin American as an alien import. If Fuentes's work from the 1960s remains interesting and compelling even now, it is in large part because it so vividly embodies these conflicts.

After the New Novel

For how long can the new novel remain new? As time passed, the notion of the new lost some of its luster, and a different alignment emerged in Fuentes's thinking about the novel. A good place to examine the redistribution of Fuentes's theoretical emphases is "¿Ha muerto la novela?" the opening essay of *Geografía de la novela*. Here we find Fuentes's most recent and most fully developed statement on the role of the novel at the end of the century.

Some of the positions Fuentes takes in this essay echo arguments from *La nueva novela*. He constructs a narrative of the development of the novel in Mexico and Latin America, from the 1950s onward, that focuses on the new generation's rejection of the dominant literary codes of the mid century, codes Fuentes summarizes in three words: "realism," "nationalism," and "engagement" (14). When Fuentes claims that the writers of his generation rejected "the demand for a single reality, a single version of national identity, or a single political truth," and instead forged "a novel that would offer alternative, critical, imaginative viewpoints" (23), his position recalls the advocacy in *La nueva novela* of an open, critical, ambiguous, and multivoiced novel. Yet while the attachment to pluralism remains, Fuentes's views on how to advance and secure the interests of a genuinely pluralistic culture undergo some significant changes.

"¿Ha muerto la novela?" opens with a return to the theme of the competition between the novel and other modes of discourse: "what the novel communicated—we were told—was now communicated in a far more speedy and efficient manner and to a much larger audience, by film, television, and journalism" (9). But Fuentes evaluates the rise of the new media and of the social sciences very differently in 1993 than he did in 1969. Although Fuentes insists in "¿Ha muerto la novela?" that he feels neither disdain nor aversion for the modern mass media (12), there nevertheless enters into his treatment of the subject in this essay a dystopian note that was missing from *La nueva novela*. As he surveys in 1993 the impact of the mass media on modern societies, Fuentes strikes a tone of lamentation: "while it was true that we had never been better informed . . . it was also true that we had never felt so incomplete, so pressured, so alone, and, paradoxically, so deprived of information" (10). In the barren, lonely world created by the mass media, the task of the novel is to restore to its reader a more complete, richer culture.

That this notion of restoration implies some kind of return to the past is clear from an anecdote Fuentes relates in "¿Ha muerto la novela?" He recalls how in the first decade of this century his father and grandfather used to wait every month for the arrival in Veracruz of a ship from France. This ship brought "the latest news, recent issues of European illustrated magazines, as well as the latest novels by Thomas Hardy, Paul Bourget and Anatole France" (10). Although Fuentes recognizes the traces of a colonial mentality in his grandfather's longing for a link with the distant metropolis, he nevertheless sees something of great value in his grandfather's relationship to culture: "I am not expressing an opinion on my grandfather's literary tastes. I simply note the effort, the pause in time he imposed upon himself, the desire to know what was to be found behind his impatient monthly expectation" (10). What is interesting here is the characterization of an experience of culture in terms of a specific relationship to time. Opposite the hectic, ephemeral, and unstructured rhythms of the present era, Fuentes places the calm, regular, unstinting pace of the past. Fuentes expands on his notion of the "pause" on the next page, where he explains that the imagination can only carry out its necessary work in the space created by the "pause": "What is the imagination if not the transformation of experience into knowledge? And doesn't this transformation require time, a pause and a desire: the time of the pause and the desire of my grandfather and my father, holding hands on the pier at Veracruz, in the year 1909?" (11).

In *La nueva novela*, Fuentes presented Latin American history as a nightmare from which the new novelist was going to awake the continent. He saw the work of Cortázar, García Márquez, Carpentier, and others, as sharing in "a magical atmosphere" (67) that presented a deliberate alternative to "the historical nightmare" and "cultural schizophrenia" (68) of Latin America. The new novel was an escape from "the monolithic impositions of history and geography" (68). By 1993 the problem has become not the excess weight of the past, but rather the loss of a sense of history. And so the novel has a new task: to oppose the process of "de-historicization and de-socialization of the world in which we live" (13).

Does the echo of Joyce in his definition in *La nueva novela* of the novelist's task mean that in 1969 Fuentes spoke as a modernist? And can the return to history called for in *Geografía de la novela* be seen as a turn to a postmodernist conception of the function of the novel? These questions do not admit of a simple, straightforward answer, given the vexed and contested status of the notion of history in the modernism and postmodernism debate. A number of influential critics have indeed defined postmodernism as a healthy, historicizing reaction against the ahistoricism of the modernist period. Matei Calinescu, for example, reads the idea of modernity as

involving a "radical criticism of the past" and a "definite commitment to change and the values of the future," and sees this stance as
most clearly embodied, in the aesthetic realm, in the avant-garde's
adherence to a "logic of radical innovation" at the expense of the
"old, the institutionalized past, the library and the Museum."
Postmodernism, by contrast, is characterized by a willingness to
"*revisit*"and engage in "a lively reconstructive dialogue" with the
past.[31] Linda Hutcheon identifies, among the postmodernists, "a
new desire to think historically," and believes that this "return to
history is no doubt a response to the hermetic ahistoric formalism
and aestheticism that characterized much of the art and theory of
the so-called modernist period." Evoking the same Joycean image
as Fuentes, Hutcheon states that "modernism's 'nightmare of history' is precisely what postmodernism has chosen to face straight
on."[32] Yet there are also critics who take an exactly opposite view of
postmodernism, seeing it not as a sign that we are once again thinking historically, but rather as a symptom of the annihilation of the
very sense of history. Fredric Jameson, for example, regards postmodernism as the cultural mode of "a society bereft of all historicity."[33] This loss of historical orientation is tied to the emergence of "a
whole new culture of the image or the simulacrum,"[34] and, in an
even broader perspective, to the appearance of a new economic
world system—late or multinational capitalism—which, in its awe-
some and bewildering complexity, blocks and frustrates the kinds
of cognitive operations we associate with the possession of a historical sense.

Of the two models—postmodernism as a return to history or
postmodernism as a turn away from history—the latter is of more
use in grasping the development of Fuentes's work. For one thing,
Calinescu's and Hutcheon's views of postmodernism imply a reading of modernism that does not properly apply to Fuentes's positions of the 1960s, nor, in fact, to important strands within the modernist tradition. When Fuentes speaks in *La nueva novela* of escaping
from the nightmare of history, he is referring not to an escape from
history as such, but from a particular conception of history that had
imposed itself in Latin America. Fuentes sees the new novelists as

foes of a deterministic, static view of history, and as proponents of a mobile, critical, and ambiguous relationship to the past. In my analysis of *La nueva novela* and *Cambio de piel* I showed how in these texts, alongside the fascination with myth and with a self-reflexive literariness, there is also a strong desire to forge an active engagement with history. Such a combination of traits does not, in fact, place Fuentes outside the modernist paradigm. When Hutcheon speaks of modernism's "ahistoric formalism and aestheticism," she is betraying a rather limited conception of modernism. It is a view that does not properly apply to Joyce (in spite of the much-abused line about the "nightmare of history"), nor, for example, to Faulkner, whose perspective on the past constitutes a key model for Fuentes's own forays into history in the early phase of his career. It is worth noting, moreover, that Calinescu, in depicting postmodernism as a return to history, is led to contrast it not with modernism, but with the avant-garde, where the iconoclastic stance with regard to the past is much more evident. Yet even the avant-garde was not as single-mindedly devoted to the new as Calinescu implies, for its attacks on the institutionalized past often opened the way for the search for more authentic sources of creative inspiration, sources that were often found in alternative histories.

The definition of postmodernism as a return to history is questionable not only because it presupposes a very partial and unsatisfactory conception of modernism as a turn away from history, but also because the supposed return to history of postmodernism is conceived by a critic like Hutcheon in such a manner as to finally drain the notion of history of much of its significance. Hutcheon writes under the influence of French poststructuralists such as Derrida and Foucault, and of American metahistorians such as Hayden White. This infuses her entire approach to history with a radical skepticism that must ultimately lead to a denial of our ability to know the past. Jameson gets it exactly right when in an implicit criticism of Hutcheon's notion of "historiographic metafiction" (the form postmodernism takes in the domain of the novel) he writes, "This historical novel can no longer set out to represent the historical past; it can only 'represent' our ideas and stereotypes about that past."[35] For

Jameson the kinds of cultural artifacts in which history recedes behind a screen of semiological systems do not constitute evidence of a return to history. Quite the contrary, they reveal a grave weakening of the sense of history.

If Jameson's conception of postmodernism seems more applicable to Fuentes's work than Hutcheon's, it is in large part because Fuentes folds his call in *Geografía de la novela* for a literature that returns us to history into an analysis of the current socioeconomic dispensation that echoes the one offered by Jameson. Fuentes, too, argues that we live in a culture of the image or simulacrum, a situation he attributes to the increasing dominance of the media. He alludes to Baudrillard's idea that the explosion of information has led to an implosion of meaning (10). But there is absolutely nothing liberating about this situation. Fuentes describes the power of information as "the true tyranny of our era" (12). The media impose "an irreversible communication that leaves no room for any response" (12). It is this process which the writer, who in Fuentes's words lives in a "a slow, sedimented time" (12–13), is called upon to resist, a resistance that takes the form of a return to history and community. But history and community are not conceived here in a narrow, restrictive fashion. Fuentes explicitly rejects the fundamentalist view of the past as embodied in a "rigid, sacred, untouchable tradition" (27). He offers instead a conception of history as open, dynamic, and unfinished. It is the novel — "an arena of languages where nobody ever has the last word" (27) — that constitutes the ideal vehicle for articulating such a conception of history. Following Mikhail Bakhtin, Fuentes defines the novel as "a meeting-place of languages and distant historical eras, which otherwise would not have the chance to connect with each other" (27–28). He adds that this conception guided him when he wrote *Terra Nostra*. Fuentes's observations help us see even more clearly what separates him from postmodernism. For the technique of projecting different historical eras onto a single textual plane, which according to a postmodernist reading would have to be regarded as an illustration of the fictional nature of our reconstructions of the past, is viewed by Fuentes as a way of keeping the past alive: "Tradition and the past are only real when they are touched—and sometimes overpowered—by the poetic imagination of the present" (27).

In *Geografía de la novela* Fuentes criticizes the aesthetic and ideological dogmas embodied in the words "realism," "nationalism," and "engagement." Yet one should not take Fuentes to be rejecting these concepts outright. Rather, throughout his career Fuentes has argued for a more complex sense of realism, a less restrictive notion of nationalism, and a more varied conception of the modes and possibilities of engagement. Once we see this, we will have understood that Fuentes's work has never been characterized by a pure celebration of the new.

CHAPTER V

Utopia and the State

The Writer and the Journalist

In building up an oeuvre as a journalist alongside his work as a novelist, short-story writer, and essayist, Fuentes fits a familiar Latin American pattern. Although economic necessity has often drawn Latin American writers away from their more strictly literary work, journalism has also afforded them a way of showing their engagement with the political issues of the day in their societies. Burdened by a sense of the huge task of social, economic, and political transformation still waiting to be carried out throughout the continent, Latin American writers turn to journalism as the most effective way of contributing to this transformation.[1]

Fuentes has regularly distinguished his journalism from his fiction by arguing that he channels his political concerns into the former and his aesthetic interests into the latter. Fuentes stated this position very clearly in a 1962 interview with Lee Baxandall:

> I think the creative writer should be creative when he is a writer, when he is a novelist or poet, and should be political when he is a political writer. The point is not to mix the two things. One approach is that of the creative writer, who cannot be sectarian, or abstract, or dogmatic; and another is the approach of the political writer who is defending a cause.

One must not confuse the two things; one must be able to give both of these professions their due.[2]

Fuentes reiterated the view that his fiction and his nonfiction, his aesthetics and his politics run along separate tracks in a 1980 interview with Jason Weiss, in which he explained that his journalism allows him to publicize his political opinions, while in his fiction his primary goal is to "serve . . . literature."[3]

In approaching Fuentes's work from the first half of the 1970s, it seems advisable to keep in mind his injunction not to confuse the "political" with the "creative" writer. At no other time in Fuentes's career has the bifurcation between his two roles seemed as pronounced as during these years. The early 1970s are the years of Fuentes's most direct involvement in Mexican politics. Returning to Mexico in 1969 after a number of years spent living in Europe, Fuentes soon came out in strong support of Luis Echeverría, president of Mexico from 1970 to 1976, a support for which he was eventually rewarded with his appointment as Mexico's ambassador to France in 1975. As a result, Fuentes came to be closely identified in these years with the interests of the Mexican state. Yet this is also the period in which Fuentes wrote *Terra Nostra* (1975), perhaps the most self-consciously literary and certainly the most difficult and innovative novel of his career. There is a striking contrast, then, between the direct, polemical quality of Fuentes's political commentaries of this period and the arcane, experimental nature of his fictional work. Yet it is a mistake to separate the different aspects of Fuentes's production as a writer. not so much because fiction and nonfiction ultimately come down to the same thing but for the more interesting reason that Fuentes deals with the same concepts in both types of writing, yet at the same time treats these concepts in noticeably divergent ways. Although in his political commentaries Fuentes argues for a strong Mexican state, and at the same time attacks a certain brand of leftism for its irresponsible attachment to utopian visions of radical social and political transformation, in *Terra Nostra* Fuentes celebrates utopianism and condemns all forms of authority, including, of course, the authority of the state. It is this paradox I will attempt to describe and explain in this chapter.

The Novelist and the President

In the letters he wrote from Europe in the 1960s, Fuentes frequently lamented the deplorable state of Mexican cultural life. In a 1967 letter from Paris to Fernando Benítez, he describes Mexico as a culturally underdeveloped nation.[4] On other occasions, he complains bitterly of the narrow-mindedness and provincialism of the Mexican intellectual world.[5] So convinced was Fuentes of the destructive effects of Mexico's cultural environment on the country's most creative minds that he conceived a plan to purchase a tower in a medieval village a hundred kilometers from Rome, which he would offer on a rotating basis to writers from Mexico, thus helping them escape at least temporarily from the noxious effects of Mexican literary life.[6] Yet even as Fuentes relished the freedom his distance from Mexico afforded him, he remained tied to his homeland. The massacre by the Mexican army of hundreds of peaceful demonstrators at Tlatelolco in Mexico City on October 2, 1968, two weeks before the opening of the Olympic Games, deeply affected Fuentes, and appears to have moved him to reestablish a closer involvement with what was happening in his native country. On November 1, 1968, Fuentes wrote a letter to José Donoso explaining that the constant attacks on him in the Mexican press as a "defiler of the nation, traitor to the motherland, and vile expatriate" had made him definitively reject the idea of returning to what he describes as "the resurrected kingdom of Huitzilipochtli."[7] A few months later, Fuentes nevertheless embarked on the return journey to Mexico. In 1995, Fuentes described his decision as follows: "The student massacre ordered by President Gustavo Díaz Ordaz on October 2nd in Tlatelolco so as to assure a peaceful Olympic Games deeply affects him and he decides to return to Mexico."[8] The implication is clear: the severe political crisis through which Mexico was passing led Fuentes to seek a new role for himself in his country's public life.[9]

Before long Fuentes found the role he was looking for: when Luis Echeverría assumed the Presidency and announced that he was going to bring about an *apertura* (opening) of the Mexican political system, Fuentes decided to give the new president his backing. But Fuentes's involvement with the Mexican government did not last long: in 1977, when Echeverría's successor, José López Portillo, named Echeverría's predecessor, Gustavo Díaz Ordaz, ambassador to Spain, Fuentes resigned his own diplomatic post in protest, for he did not wish to serve his country alongside the man responsible for the Tlatelolco massacre. It seems appropriate that a conflict over Díaz Ordaz led to Fuentes's resignation, inasmuch as Díaz Ordaz had cast a shadow over the entire period of Fuentes's involvement with Echeverría. At the time of the Tlatelolco massacre, Echeverría was interior minister. It was hard to believe, in other words, that he had had nothing to do with the events of October 1968. Worse yet, there was another massacre in Mexico City not long after Echeverría became president, a massacre which according to at least one observer could not have taken place without the president's authorization, and of which the president, moreover, never provided a full accounting.[10] It was never completely clear to what extent Echeverría had broken with the authoritarian and repressive heritage of the system of which he himself was a product. However, up until the moment of Díaz Ordaz's rehabilitation, Fuentes seemed prepared to work with the system.

Fuentes explained his reasons for supporting Echeverría in various articles, interviews, speeches, and personal letters from these years. Before examining these texts, however, it is important to see—as I have tried to show in my account of Fuentes's return to Mexico after the Tlatelolco massacre—that Fuentes was looking for a way to channel his sense of political responsibility. Throughout his career Fuentes has fit the traditional mold of the Latin American intellectual as somebody who has a commitment not only to his creative work, but also to the social and political transformation of his country. The late 1960s were a period of intense political crisis in Mexico; it made sense, given Fuentes's predisposition to political involvement, that the need to carve out a space for himself in the political life of his country would seem especially urgent in this period. Given, moreover, the enormous powers vested in the president and the consequent belief that only the president can bring about significant changes in Mexico, it is not surprising that Fuentes should have allied himself with Echeverría, for

Echeverría's power constituted the most effective political tool in the country. This is not to say, of course, that Echeverría's specific political positions had nothing to do with his success in gaining the support of intellectuals like Fuentes. I will look at Fuentes's analysis of these positions in a moment. I am merely arguing that there were also other factors that influenced Fuentes's decision to support Echeverría.

Fuentes outlined his political position in these years first in "La disyuntiva mexicana," the closing essay in *Tiempo mexicano* (1971),[11] and second in "Opciones críticas en el verano de nuestro descontento," an article published in the August 1972 issue of *Plural*, the journal of culture and politics founded in Mexico City by Octavio Paz the previous year.[12] The latter article is more vehement, and therefore, perhaps, more revealing. Fuentes's key argument in "Opciones críticas" is that Mexico needs a strong state at this particular moment in its history. Insofar as Echeverría's policies are designed to fortify the Mexican state, he deserves to be supported. Fuentes derives the need for a strong state from two basic considerations: the first has to do with the economy, the second with foreign relations. Fuentes discusses both issues in relation to the lessons of the Mexican Revolution.

In his discussion of the Mexican Revolution in "Opciones críticas," Fuentes puts forward—as he has done on many other occasions—a view of the Mexican Revolution as first and foremost an act of national self-discovery. It was the first time in the nation's history that the "many Mexicos" (the phrase is Lesley Byrd Simpson's) that compose it came to the surface in a total and simultaneous act of national self-revelation. As Fuentes puts it here: "All the traditions of a country characterized by the plural coexistence of opposed, suffocated, mutilated, latent ways of life, sometimes existing only in dreams, sometimes kept alive only through the laborious effort of imperfect memories, came together in the Revolution" (3). The Mexican Revolution is in this reading both an act of restoration—the past is for once fully integrated into the present—and a new foundation—the future must be shaped in accordance with the ideals embodied in the Revolution.

For Fuentes the movements led by Pancho Villa in the north and Emiliano Zapata in the state of Morelos constituted the most authentic and valuable strains within the Mexican Revolution. In "La historia como toma de poderes," an essay from *Tiempo mexicano*, Fuentes speaks of how the Zapatistas managed briefly to fulfill the dream of a society that combines personal freedom with communal bonds.[13] Furthermore, in a country whose history according to Fuentes has been characterized by the disjunction between text and reality, the Zapatistas struggled to heal this rift, and to make text and reality into "a single, inseparable entity" (131). "La historia como toma de poderes" is primarily concerned with the Zapatistas, but Fuentes also speaks of the contribution made by the Villistas to the Revolution's project of self-discovery: "Villa's epic cavalcades were the expression of a powerful and intuitive urge to break down the watertight compartments of Mexican life, to contaminate Mexico with its own songs, colors and passions" (133). Yet the Revolution was aborted, as Fuentes explains in "Opciones críticas":

> But this total resurrection of Mexico may have been prema-
> ture. . . . The tradition of centralized power, kept in place
> from Izcóatl to Porfirio, triumphed (Obregón defeats Villa,
> Carranza assassinates Zapata) and imposed, by excluding
> the local, nascent, recovered promises of the Revolution, the
> promise of which it made itself the keeper: that of a basical-
> ly liberal, capitalist, "modern" project of development,
> though corrected by our equivalents of the Anglo-Saxon
> checks and balances: safeguards for workers and peasants,
> the latitude granted to the state to intervene in the economy,
> the eventual power of the state to modify the regime of
> property. (3)

Although Fuentes's narrative is by no means unconventional, it does contain a manifest paradox. For two very different stages may be distinguished in Fuentes's account of the Revolution. In the first stage, the centralist tradition in Mexican politics confiscates and betrays the pluralist and localist energies of the Revolution, whereas in the second stage, the power of the state secures at least some of the benefits for which the Revolutionary armies fought. In speaking of the current situation in Mexico, Fuentes states, "On the negative side, we are the heirs of a centralist and paternalist tradition, oppressive and arrogant in the exercise of power. On the positive side, we are the heirs to a popular and communitarian tradition, always harassed, yet surprisingly resilient" (6). Yet the centralist tradition to which Fuentes attributes the crushing of the Mexican Revolution's most positive aspects fed into the state power that Fuentes presents as the last bulwark against the capitalist reaction of the postrevolutionary period. In the 1970s, the state continues, in Fuentes's analysis, to occupy an ambiguous position in Mexican life. On the one hand, the state acts to concentrate power in the hands of the few; on the other hand, the state is the only force that can provide for a more equitable distribution of economic resources in Mexico.

In "La disyuntiva mexicana," Fuentes argues that one of the Revolution's principal achievements was to place important sectors of the country's economy in the hands of the state (175). From the 1940s onward, this achievement was discarded, as Mexico's rulers imposed on the country a capitalist model of development, a model that, according to Fuentes, has led to an increased imbalance in the distribution of wealth, as well as a gradual surrender of economic decision-making powers to foreigners. The only way to alter this situation is by expanding once again the role of the state in the economy. Only the state can direct the economy away from the wasteful activities Fuentes associates with a system of private enterprise. And only the state is capable of protecting the national interest against the economic interference of the United States. Echeverría, too, believed firmly in a state-directed economy, and for this Fuentes applauded him.

In referring to the Mexican economy's relationship to international economic forces, Fuentes is in effect introducing the issue of foreign policy. It is precisely in the area of foreign policy that Fuentes discovers the second important reason for seeking a stronger Mexican state. For Fuentes believes that only a strong Mexican state can safeguard Mexico's independence. The history of the Mexican Revolution already teaches this lesson. For there is one sense in which the defeat of the Zapatistas—and therefore of the localist dimension of the Mexican Revolution—was inevitable and even necessary. In "La historia como toma de poderes," Fuentes argues that Zapata's movement could afford to be "internationally irresponsible" (140). Their perspective was a local one; for the Zapatistas the United States seemed very far away. What Fuentes calls the "national revolution"—embodied in the constitutionalist forces led by Carranza and Obregón—could not afford to take such a narrow view: "it was forced to resist the constant pressure of North American power and the explicit threat of a foreign intervention" (140). Insofar as a Zapatista victory might have led to the dismemberment of Mexico, it is in a sense fortunate that the faction that stood for a project of nation-building ultimately triumphed. This analysis of the trajectory of the Mexican Revolution is relevant to Fuentes's assessment of the situation in the 1970s, inasmuch as he believes that Mexico is still engaged in the work of national consolidation. Because the United States still constitutes a threat to Mexico's independence, the nation must continue to rely for its very survival on the same centralist tradition that is at the root of so many of the country's ills.

Fuentes's description of the international order of the early 1970s is shaped to a considerable degree by the fact that these were the years of détente between the superpowers. Fuentes interprets the thaw in the relations between the United States and the Soviet Union from the perspective of a nation on the periphery of the global order. The view from Mexico is not encouraging: Fuentes believes the accommodation between East and West is merely a way for each side to legitimize the other's imperial ambitions within its "sphere of influence." Fuentes reiterated this view in an interview with James R. Fortson in June 1973: "The fact is that the great powers have divided up their zones of influence between them. There will be no further confrontations between the two superpowers. What we will see from now on are confrontations between each superpower and the nations on their periphery."[14] This means that for Mexico the principal threat comes from the United States. In

"Opciones críticas" Fuentes predicts that the situation will deteriorate even further if Nixon is reelected later that year: "Nixon's reelection would also represent the greatest threat that Mexico, and all of Latin America, have experienced in their already long and dramatic history of aggressions, mutilations and exploitations" (6).

Given the existence of such a serious external threat to its independence, the nation's top priority must be to ensure its own survival: in "Opciones críticas" Fuentes writes that "our bare survival as a viable national community has become our top priority" (6). But where can the national community turn for the defense of its independence? Fuentes believes that only the Mexican state can take on this task. In fact, in all of Latin America the state constitutes the principal barrier against U.S. imperialism: "Are there any movements of the people in Latin America that are strong enough to combat this situation? I don't see them. The sole, minimal line of defense consists of certain nation-states" (6). Hence Fuentes's support for President Echeverría: "On the international level, Echeverría is acting in the interests of the Mexican national state, of its viability, of its existence and development in a world that is day by day making it more difficult for national decision-making centers to survive" (6). Only a strong Mexican state, led by a strong president, can preserve the nation's independence: such is the basic rationale behind Fuentes's support for Echeverría.

Fuentes occasionally assumed a strident tone in defending his position: in "Opciones críticas" he accuses intellectuals who refuse to support Echeverría of committing a "historical crime." In a letter to Fernando Benítez written shortly after the overthrow of Salvador Allende in Chile, Fuentes declares that "Our choice is not between Echeverría and socialism, but between Echeverría and fascism."[15] Given such options, it was hard not to favor Echeverría. Even so, Fuentes realized that his support for Echeverría appeared to contradict political positions he had been defending for many years. In the very articles in which he speaks out in favor of Echeverría, Fuentes criticizes the personalist and antidemocratic nature of the Mexican political system and praises an ideal of local self-government, which he regards as deeply rooted in the Mexican cultural tradition.

Fuentes uses two strategies to reconcile the apparent inconsistency in his positions. In the first place, he argues that even though Echeverría was formed within the system, he unexpectedly became, thanks to a kind of conversion he experienced in the course of his electoral campaign, a proponent of democratization. In "La disyuntiva mexicana" Fuentes evokes the figure of Lázaro Cárdenas, president of Mexico from 1934 to 1940, in order to suggest that it is possible to carry out reforms from within the system (162). In the second place, Fuentes argues that a strengthening of the state does not necessarily result in a weakening of democracy. In these years, Fuentes regularly describes civil society as the arm of democracy. In "La disyuntiva mexicana" he alludes to Antonio Gramsci's definition of civil society as "the world that always escapes from the direct intervention of the state" (190). In his interview with Fortson, he explains that by civil society he means "a society that is dependent neither on the powers of private enterprise nor on the powers of the state, but rather exists for itself and claims rights for itself" (119). Yet even though on a conceptual level "state" and "civil society" are opposites, Fuentes insists that a stronger civil society need not mean a weaker state. In fact, Fuentes argues that the strengthening of civil society will result in a simultaneous strengthening of the state: in "Opciones críticas" he writes of the need to "strengthen the nation-state with the elemental sap of local, popular institutions of self-management" (8). This vision of the mutual reinforcement of the centralist and localist traditions in Mexican society amounts to an effort on Fuentes's part to cut across the contradiction that had opened up in his discussion of the Mexican Revolution, which is at the same time the contradiction in his own position.

The trickiest issue Fuentes faced in lining up to support Echeverría was what to say about the still unresolved matter of the massacre of June 10, 1971. In "Opciones críticas" Fuentes offered a reading of the massacre and its aftermath, according to which Echeverría was the victim of a conspiracy hatched by right-wing elements in the state apparatus who wanted to undermine his policy of democratization: "On the 10th of June of 1971 all the reactionary forces of Mexico conspired to set a trap for Echeverría, to stigmatize the new regime, and to discredit the difficult and carefully planned democratic option with which the new president tried to overcome the deep crisis of 1968" (8). In his interview with Fortson, Fuentes restated this theory. By this time, however, Fuentes did sound somewhat more critical of the president, though he significantly refrained from holding him responsible for the tragedy itself, and limited himself to deploring the loss of credibility that Echeverría had suffered as a result of his failure to provide the public with a full accounting of what had happened (139–40). Throughout, one senses Fuentes's eagerness to continue supporting Echeverría. For this, he was roundly castigated by some of his fellow intellectuals.

The poet and essayist Gabriel Zaid published an open letter to Carlos Fuentes in *Plural* in which he argued that Fuentes's position signified nothing less than a surrender of intellectual independence. He claimed that it made no sense to support Echeverría for his policy of *apertura*, and even less sense to say that a failure to support Echeverría constituted a historical crime, as long as Echeverría continued to fail the key test of this policy—whether he would provide a full accounting of the events of June 10, 1971. Zaid urged Fuentes to convince Echeverría of the fact that the massacre "is not just a little hair in the soup of the *Apertura*, but rather the public proof of whether he believes we can democratize ourselves or whether he thinks, like don Porfirio, that we are not yet ready for democracy."[16]

This was not the end of the debate, however. A month later *Plural* published a special supplement entitled "México 1972: Los escritores y la política." Both Fuentes and Zaid were among the writers invited to deliver brief statements on the topic. Fuentes took the opportunity to respond to Zaid's criticisms; he did so in the first place by sketching out a general position on the nature of politics itself. Fuentes claims to favor a critical, rational, and pragmatic approach to politics. Such a stance implies a rejection of two other attitudes commonly assumed in relationship to politics: the messianic and the puritanical. By the former Fuentes means "the transfer of the faith in a transcendent church to a historical church that is governed by religious commands and punishments." The latter he defines as a "whining abstention" from the world of politics, a "scandalized defense of one's virginity." Both attitudes evade the need for "concrete political solutions" and lead according to Fuentes to a sterilization of public discourse.[17] As for Zaid's suggestion that he present Echeverría with an ultimatum—namely, that the president either provide a full accounting of what happened on June 10, 1971, or that Fuentes withdraw his support—Fuentes rejects it as Manichaean.[18]

Fuentes returned to this theme in his interview with Fortson. He speaks repeatedly in the interview of the need for "a serious political organization" (109), by which he means "slow, modest and difficult, but also concrete and reliable political work" of which the rewards are the winning of "small daily battles" (127). Fuentes contrasts this realistic approach to politics with the tendency to think "in apocalyptic terms or in terms of radical confrontation, that things may change overnight" (127). Elsewhere in the same interview, Fuentes speaks disparagingly of people whose political engagement takes the form of "a sporadic Saturnalia" (109). He dismisses as entirely ineffective the "carnivalesque eruptions" that characterize a certain brand of leftist politics (109).[19] In a letter to Fernando Benítez, Fuentes praises his friend for seeing that it was futile at this point in history to hope for an "instantaneous socialist paradise."[20] Such utopianism is not just utterly unrealistic; it is actually politically dangerous. For in opposing and undermining Echeverría, the utopianist faction in practice prepares the way for the only real alternative to the current régime, "a military fascism subject to the US."[21] To opt for Echeverría, as Fuentes did in the 1970s, is to opt for the state, and to opt for the state is to acknowledge that a socialist revolution is merely a utopian dream, and that therefore the nation's first priority must be to avert a fascist takeover.

Revolutionary Millenarians: Protofascists or Early Moderns?

In an article published in *Plural* in June 1976, the historian Gastón García Cantú responded in acid tones to two speeches

Fuentes had presented in Mexico in the previous months. Fuentes had just published *Terra Noʃtra*, and García Cantú was struck by the resemblance between the novel and the speeches: "The two reports, like *Terra Noʃtra*, are dominated by a millenarian spirit."[22] García Cantú was right about *Terra Noʃtra*, but wrong about the speeches.

Both of Fuentes's speeches were implicitly addressed to José López Portillo, who had been selected by Echeverría to become Mexico's next president.[23] García Cantú probably felt the speeches expressed a millenarian spirit because of Fuentes's repeated allusions to a potential catastrophe looming over Mexico's future. In his first speech, Fuentes spoke with great urgency of the need to support López Portillo: "If he fails, we all fail, and if Mexico fails, our people will face bitter years of hunger, violence, repression and foreign intervention."[24] In the second speech, Fuentes described the current political situation in Latin America in utterly dark tones: "A nocturnal tide is rising up from the hemisphere's Southern Cone. It is wearing the black uniform of fascism. Its final objective is Mexico, a weak, isolated, disjointed Mexico, cornered between the prisons of the north and the prisons of the south."[25] But whereas the millenarian spirit exults in the image of an imminent apocalypse— because the complete destruction of the present order must necessarily precede the beginning of the millennium—Fuentes views the threat of a cataclysm as just that, a cataclysm. Insofar as the apocalyptic note in the two speeches to which García Cantú alludes serves as a warning, it is clear that these texts remain within the parameters of the antiutopian outlook that characterizes Fuentes's explicitly political statements from these years.

In turning from Fuentes's journalism to his major work of fiction from the 1970s, *Terra Noʃtra*, we will see that a striking shift in attitude and emphasis emerges.[26] *Terra Noʃtra* is a novel of extraordinary range: at its core it develops a sustained meditation on the history and culture of Spain in the period from 1492 to 1598, yet Fuentes also takes the reader backward to the Roman Empire at the time of Tiberius and forward to Paris at the end of the present millennium. One element that binds the different historical eras represented in *Terra Noʃtra* together is the theme of heresy. At every stage in Fuentes's history of the world, the forces of heresy appear to be pitted against the forces of orthodoxy. Fuentes has indicated that in developing his picture of the heretical spirit in *Terra Nostra* he owes a debt to one source in particular: Norman Cohn's *The Pursuit of the Millennium: Revolutionary Millenarians and Mystical Anarchists of the Middle Ages*.[27] It is clear from this source that Fuentes identifies the spirit of heresy with visions of the millennium.

The link between *Terra Nostra* and *The Pursuit of Millennium* is common knowledge. Yet nobody seems to have reflected on the possible pertinence of the ideological orientation of Cohn's book to an understanding of Fuentes's novel. Fuentes's critics have viewed *The Pursuit of the Millennium* purely as a source of information about a particular dimension of medieval European history, and have ignored the broader vision that informs Cohn's book. Yet *The Pursuit of the Millennium* is of interest not only as an astonishing feat of historical reconstruction, but also as a bold attempt to uncover the origins of certain key phenomena of twentieth-century European history. In brief, Cohn's argument is that the millenarian movements that are the subject of his book prefigure the totalitarian ideologies of our own century. Although he maintains a calmly descriptive tone throughout most of his book, Cohn in fact approaches his subject from a deeply unsympathetic point of view. He believes the millenarian movements were fueled by irresponsible fantasies that resulted in widespread violence and destruction. He notes that among the emotions unleashed by the upsurge of millenarianism was a virulent anti-Semitism that not infrequently led to the perpetration of horrifying massacres. In describing the techniques of terror used by the Anabaptists when they attempted in the 1530s to create a new social order in the German city of Münster, Cohn clearly expects the reader to see in this episode a prefiguration of the revolutionary regimes of our own era. In the closing pages of his book, Cohn draws explicit attention to "the relevance to our own times" of the "story told in this book." He mentions the anti-Semitism of the Nazis, and the "phantasies of a final, exterminatory struggle" of the Communists.[28] For Cohn, the revolutionary millenarian movements represent the ugliest currents in European history.

Like Cohn, Fuentes situates the millenarian movements in the context of a broad interpretation of the course of European history. But Fuentes tells a very different story from Cohn. This is immediately evident when we place *The Pursuit of the Millennium* alongside certain passages from *Cervantes o la crítica de la lectura* (1976), a long essay Fuentes himself describes as "a branch of the novel that has occupied me for the past six years, *Terra Nostra.*"[29] One of the principal themes of this book is the emergence of modernity in Europe, an event Fuentes associates with the transition from the Middle Ages to the Renaissance, that is, according to Fuentes, the transition from a closed to an open society. But the Middle Ages are not so closed, in this reading, that there is no room for countervailing tendencies. In fact, Fuentes believes the revolutionary millenarian movements fulfilled a key role in the slow undermining of the monolithic edifice of medieval ideology. Fuentes describes medieval society as controlled by the rigid orthodoxy of the Roman Catholic Church. But he adds that "Behind the unified façade of the Church of Rome, there existed a diversity in ferment." And he finds the clearest expression of this ferment in the "messianic movements . . . which . . . led the poor, the dissatisfied, the neurotic, the rebels and the dreamers of medieval Europe to the concrete actualization of heresy." Fuentes concludes this passage with the suggestion that the various movements described in Cohn's book amounted to "the sign that Europe was turning its back on the Church and its univocal reading of the world, and was embarking upon the ocean of history with its multiple tides and tensions" (24). In other words: the millenarian movements prefigured and perhaps even helped pave the way for the Renaissance. In Cohn the millenarian movements are the forerunners of Hitler and Stalin, whereas in Fuentes they are the precursors of Copernicus and Cervantes (and himself). A more striking difference in interpretation is difficult to imagine.

The interpretation Fuentes offers of the revolutionary millenarian movements in *Cervantes* is largely in agreement with his presentation of these movements in *Terra Nostra*. The view that the heretical sects were allied to a new set of social forces, as well as to a new way of thinking, that were eventually to transform Europe, is articulated with particular clarity in "The Rebellion," one of the longest and most important chapters, which deals with the 1521 uprising of the *comuneros* (townships) against the Spanish monarchy. In *Cervantes*, Fuentes explains that historians have put forward widely divergent interpretations of the historical significance of the rebellion and its defeat. Conservative historians claim that the rebellion "was nothing more than a kind of anachronistic outbreak of feudalism, an insurrection of the nobility against the modern concept of absolutism embodied by Charles V" (53). These historians maintain that the Hapsburg Empire in Spain and the Americas "represented a step forward that brought us up-to-date with the development of the unified modern state via anti-feudal absolutism, as was the case in England and France" (53). Fuentes rejects this view, claiming instead that Charles V "did not defeat a ghostly feudal nobility, but rather transferred to Spain the universalist ideal of the Holy Roman Empire . . . and crushed the pluralistic and democratic tendencies of a medieval Spain in transition to modernity" (53). The *comuneros* included a broad array of social groups that had joined forces in order to demand the democratization of the Spanish political system. Their defeat constituted not an advance but a setback on Spain's road to modernity.[30] Whether Fuentes agrees with the proposition put forward by the conservative historians that in France and England the absolute monarchy prepared the way for the modern state is not clear. In the case of Spain, Fuentes emphatically denies that such a development took place. The unifying impulse of Charles V had profoundly regressive rather than progressive consequences for Spain.

Fuentes's version of the rebellion of the *comuneros* in *Terra Nostra* departs in one significant regard from his account in *Cervantes*. Whereas in *Cervantes* Fuentes presents the rebellion as a secular movement—a movement calling for institutional reform and speaking in the name of "the general will of the people"—in *Terra Nostra* Fuentes accords a substantial role in the rebellion to the revolutionary millenarian movements. When Fuentes once again narrated this episode from Spanish history in nonfictional form in *The Buried Mirror*, he again made no mention of a possible role in the rebellion of the townships for the heretical sects.[31] But Fuentes does have a respectable source for the view he develops in *Terra Nostra*: it is José Antonio Maravall's *Las comunidades de Castilla*, the work that overturned the conservative thesis concerning the 1521 uprising. It is from Maravall that Fuentes derives the argument he puts forward in *Cervantes* that the rebellion of the *comuneros* was carried out in the name of pluralism and democracy, that it was, as the subtitle to Maravall's book states, "a first modern revolution."[32] Maravall concedes that both the nobility and the bourgeoisie played important roles in the rebellion. Yet he sees the rebellion first and foremost as a mass movement in which the people as a whole participated. And he argues that in joining the rebellion, the masses imprinted on the movement a certain irrationalist, mystical character. Maravall points out that in the early sixteenth century a variety of prophetic and messianic beliefs circulated in Europe. Furthermore, he notes that elements of fanaticism are frequently encountered in revolutionary movements. For these reasons, it is not surprising that the rebellion of the *comuneros* should have included millenarian strains.[33]

What needs to be emphasized, however, is that the attention Maravall pays to the element of religious fanaticism in the *comunero* uprising does not divert him from his central thesis concerning the key role of the rebellion in what he calls "the history of democratic freedom in Spain."[34] Maravall does not provide much detail concerning the exact nature of the prophetic and messianic beliefs that fed into the *comunero* uprising. Fuentes supplies what is missing in Maravall with information from Cohn. "The rebellion" alternates between quotations from a variety of historical documents connected to the uprising and Fuentes's own version of the events. The former passages appear in italicized form, and have most likely been taken from Antonio Ferrer del Río's *Historia del levantamiento de las Comunidades de Castilla*.[35] Most of the documents Fuentes quotes are letters in which the townships that have risen up against the King express their grievances and state their demands. The writers ask for an end to tyranny and the recognition of their rights of self-government. They do not express a millenarian outlook. The townships want an end to the Inquisition: they are concerned with religious toleration, not with the end of the world. Yet in the sections of this chapter written by Fuentes himself, the entire panoply of heretical sects reappears. Mixed in with a moderate vision of reform and democracy, the reader encounters the overheated language of millenarian expectation.

Fuentes thus presents the millenarian groups as allies of the forces of pluralism and democracy, and turns them into forerunners of the spirit of modernity, a spirit which in this episode of *Terra Nostra* is at least temporarily crushed by the regressive forces of medieval Catholicism. Whereas Norman Cohn's *The Pursuit of the Millennium* offers a clear warning of the dangers of a utopian-apocalyptic outlook—dangers that have to do in the first place with a sectarian spirit of intolerance—Fuentes transforms Cohn's religious fanatics into the precursors of modern relativism.[36]

Fuentes's interest in the emancipatory dimension of the millenarian spirit is particularly clear from the role of eroticism in his depiction of the heretical sects. Fuentes does not shy away from portraying the more horrific aspects of some of the rituals practiced by the revolutionary millenarian movements. The opening chapter of *Terra Nostra* includes a detailed description of the spectacle of a band of men engaging in an elaborate public ritual of self-flagellation (23–25/19–21). Fuentes bases this description on Norman Cohn's account of the flagellant movement. This movement offered a communal and organized form of the practice of penitential self-flagellation that had been adopted for the first time in certain monastic communities in Italy in the early eleventh century. In Cohn's words, "Medieval self-flagellation was a grim torture which people inflicted on themselves in the hope of inducing a judging and punishing God to put away his rod, to forgive them their sins" (127). At times, the flagellants saw their mission in much broader terms: they viewed their penance as "a collective imitatio Christi" that was meant to secure "not only their own salvation but that of all mankind" (128). But Fuentes has no difficulty making the transition from the grim to the festive: at the end of the opening chapter a description of the fearsome destructiveness of the revolutionary millenarian groups—"They're assaulting and destroying the monasteries, churches and palaces . . . they kill anyone who refuses to join their crusade" (33/28) — shifts suddenly to a mesmerizing account of the beautiful visions that inspire these people: "life in the new millennium must eradicate all notions of sacrifice, work and property, in order to instill one single principle, that of pleasure" (33/29). In a later chapter, we learn of the unconstrained sexual practices to which the deification of pleasure leads: "Beneath the cold moonlight, in remote forests . . . bodies are coupling in cleansing pleasure so that they may reach the heavenly kingdom free from sin" (59/54).

One of the sources for this description is Cohn's account of the heresy of the Free Spirit, particularly his depiction of the Adam-cult frequently found among the adepts of this heresy.[37] Once again, a look at how Fuentes handles his source is instructive. Cohn explains that the members of this cult asserted "that they were restored to the state of innocence which had existed before the Fall" (180). It is worth noting that Cohn accepts the view that the Adamites "did at times practise ritual nakedness, just as they did at times indulge in sexual promiscuity," but discounts the claim "that this cult involved communal sexual orgies" (180). In the description of the sexual practices of the followers of the Adam-cult in *Terra Nostra*, Fuentes appears to be writing the claim about communal sexual orgies back into the record. This fits in with the larger differences between Cohn and Fuentes on the issue of the role of eroticism in certain millenarian movements of the Middle Ages. For it is clear that Fuentes does not share Cohn's highly skeptical view of the erotic dimension of the cult of the Free Spirit. Cohn speaks of "an eroticism which, far from springing from a carefree sensuality, possessed above all a symbolic value as a sign of spiritual emancipation" (151). This is the worst charge one can make about eroticism, that is, to say that it is not erotic. In Fuentes, on the contrary, the sexually liberated practices of the Adamites and others are described in an approving manner. We may conclude this from the quality of the descriptions themselves, as well as from our knowledge of Fuentes's work in general.[38] But it is particularly clear from the position occupied by the heretical sects in the overall thematic structure of *Terra Nostra*. For the novel pits the forces of heresy against the forces of orthodoxy embodied in the figure of El Señor. And to the extent that the ghastly, death-enamored El Señor represents everything the novel repudiates, his fiercest enemies inevitably appear in a favorable light.

The key position of eroticism in *Terra Nostra* is revealed with particular force in the novel's conclusion. Fuentes's final chapter offers a dizzyingly complex superimposition of textual and historical dimensions. The narrative gathers together in Paris on the eve of the next millennium an array of characters who have appeared in earlier chapters of the novel itself, but also of characters from other works of literature. The heretical sects resurface and are linked to an evocation of the Holocaust, as the references to the "final solution" and to "night and fog" (779/775) indicate. A group of characters Fuentes borrows from other works of contemporary Latin American fiction—Pierre Menard, Horacio Oliveira, Cuba Venegas, Santiago Zavalita, and several others—take leave of the many utopian visions that have shaped Latin American history, bidding farewell to Utopia itself, to the City of the Sun, to Vasco de Quiroga, to Emiliano Zapata, and many more (767–768/763–764). One character—Polo Febo—is confined to a suite in a hotel, where he reads a set of manuscripts that appear to contain the very book we as readers hold in our hands. He dreams, like a character from *Cien años de soledad*, of a "second opportunity" in life (778/774), but concludes mournfully that history always repeats itself: "its axis the necropolis, its root madness, its result crime" (779/775). Yet this dizzying multiplication of textual and referential frames is finally brought to a halt in a scene that imagines the ultimate form of the resolution of contraries. Two characters—Polo and Celestina—engage in a delirious sex act which culminates first in the creation of a new hermaphroditic being, and second in the vision of a new genesis for humanity, a genesis, moreover, which explicitly echoes the biblical text, while deliberately removing from that text the notion of sin: "and unto dust shalt thou return, without sin, and with pleasure" (783/778).[39]

We have reached the point now where it is possible to summarize the picture developed here of the relationship between

Fuentes's fiction and his journalism. In his political commentaries from the early to mid-1970s, Fuentes sees the state as a positive force. In Mexico, the state acts as guarantor of national independence, while at the same time it secures certain rights for the weakest sectors of society. In tandem with this favorable evaluation of the role of the state in contemporary politics, Fuentes argues that the injection of millenarian expectations into political discourse could only have damaging effects on the country. One needs to be cautious in suggesting that *Terra Nostra* inverts this scheme, for although it is clear that the novel presents millenarianism in a largely positive light, it is less clear whether El Señor, as the enemy of the millenarian sects, can be regarded as the embodiment of the state, at least in the modern form Fuentes has in mind in his political journalism. Yet even while it would be absurd to suggest a parallel between El Señor and Luis Echeverría, it is not at all misleading to draw attention to the way in which *Terra Nostra* consistently aligns itself *against* the idea of unity, a concept that is integral to any adequate theory of the state. Fuentes's concern with the pernicious effects of all attempts to impose unity on a people or society is clear from the portrayals in *Terra Nostra* of a whole series of forces that represent in different ways the drive for a centralization of power, from the Emperor Tiberius Caesar in the chapter "Manuscript of a Stoic" to the "world council on depopulation" (772/767–68) that makes a brief appearance in the novel's final chapter. The novel speaks repeatedly in favor of the values of multiplicity, of diversity, of pluralism, and of dispersal. But while Fuentes portrays such values with great imaginative power in *Terra Nostra*, it appears he had considerable difficulty imagining an appropriate role for such forces in the immediate sociopolitical context of 1970s Mexico.

How do we account, then, for the peculiar configuration of Fuentes's work at this particular moment in his career? One might speculate to begin with that Fuentes was merely responding to the fact that different moments in history cannot be read according to a single, inflexible set of presuppositions. *Terra Nostra* focuses on sixteenth-century Spain—a key period in the history of Spain and of Spanish America. Yet the terms used to interpret this period are not necessarily applicable to the context of the 1970s. One might even argue that insofar as Echeverría became in the 1970s a symbol of Third World opposition to the reigning global order, support for Echeverría might be read as a heretical gesture.[40] Although this is a plausible argument, the historical sweep of *Terra Nostra*, as I pointed out earlier, actually takes us far beyond sixteenth-century Spain and Mexico. As a result, it seems acceptable to read the novel as propounding a series of universalizable political principles, primarily the principle of respect for multiplicity. It seems equally acceptable then to draw attention to the fact that in the political context of the 1970s support for Echeverría is not what one would automatically have expected from the author of *Terra Nostra*.[41]

There are two possible ways of looking at the contradiction in Fuentes's work. In the first place, one might view the contradiction itself as the symptom of a fundamental divergence between the aesthetic and the political realms. As a novelist, Fuentes was working within a paradigm that valued qualities such as innovation and defamiliarization. Brian McHale has pointed out that *Terra Nostra* is "one of the paradigmatic texts of postmodernist writing, literally an anthology of postmodernist themes and devices."[42] In developing an aesthetics of estrangement, Fuentes was drawing on the long tradition in twentieth-century avant-garde thought of equating a revolution in artistic form with a revolution in society. In *La nueva novela hispanoamericana*, Fuentes had put forward a view of writing as "the enemy word," which he defined as a "heretical" use of language that was always on the side of "those who dissent from power."[43] Yet when Luis Echeverría became president, a complex set of motives led Fuentes to modify his views on the necessary enmity between the writer's language and the language of power. The fact that relations between intellectuals and the state in Mexico have traditionally been uncommonly close, may perhaps helps us understand how it happened that Fuentes was drawn in this way into the orbit of state power.[44] But Echeverría's skill in presenting himself as a different kind of president was also an important factor in inducing Fuentes to take this step. In making himself into a spokesman for the Third World, and a critic of U.S. imperialism, Echeverría could plausibly claim that in the realm of international politics his was a voice of dissent from power. On the level of domestic politics, in the meantime, Echeverría was that curious hybrid, the reformer from above. In confronting such a phenomenon, it is always difficult to know whether to focus on the policies (of reform) being advocated, or the position (of power) from which they are advanced. Fuentes chose to place his confidence in Echeverría. But in doing so he distanced himself from the utopian tradition by which his literary work was in large measure inspired, and uncovered the gulf that separated the world of aesthetics from the world of politics.

Yet there is a different way of looking at the relationship between Fuentes's fiction and his nonfiction in this period, one that sees continuity rather than discontinuity between the two realms of Fuentes's work. When Brian McHale states that *Terra Nostra* is a "paradigmatic" postmodernist fiction, he is suggesting that it is a novel primarily concerned with its own status as a fiction. According to McHale, the transition from modernist to postmodernist fiction occurs when writers abandon the characteristically modernist concern with "attaining to reliable knowledge of *our* world" and instead decide to "fictionalize."[45] The aim of postmodernist writers is to draw attention to "the fundamental ontological discontinuity between the fictional and the real."[46] Yet one cannot apply such generalizations to *Terra Nostra* without seriously distorting the novel. For Fuentes does not fictionalize history in order to demonstrate the distance between text and reality. Hidden within the fiction of *Terra Nostra*, there is a reading of the past that we as readers are meant to take with utter seriousness. The fact that Fuentes alters the past in an apparently arbitrary fashion in *Terra Nostra* does not mean that for Fuentes the past offers no ground to stand on. *Terra Nostra* proposes a clear thesis about the nature and origins of Spanish American culture: in brief, the notion that it possesses at its source a democratic, pluralist, and utopian dimension that it must struggle to recapture. Insofar as *Terra Nostra* articulates a message of this kind, Fuentes was clearly not writing postmodernist fiction as defined by McHale. And insofar as *Terra Nostra* indeed contained this type of didactic orientation, Fuentes was evidently using his fiction in a

manner not that different from the way he used his political journalism: as a way of expressing his ideas about history, culture and
politics.[47]

Redemption Through Culture

Much has changed in Mexico in the roughly twenty years since
the publication of *Terra Nostra*. But the PRI continues in power.
And as long as the PRI sustains its symbiotic relationship with the
Mexican state apparatus, the question of the role of the state in
Mexican society and politics retains an urgency not all that unlike
the urgency it had in the first half of the 1970s. At the same time, a
new set of developments—above all the processes of transnational-
ization in culture, communications, and economics—appear to be
diminishing the importance of the state in Mexico and elsewhere.

The topic of the state surfaces regularly in *The Buried Mirror*,
Fuentes's sweeping 1992 history of Spain and the Hispanic world.
In thinking about the role of the state in the story he tells, Fuentes
varies his point of view in interesting and revealing ways. The
thread of his reflections on the state can first be picked up in the
chapter on the Roman conquest of Spain—a conquest that left a
lasting imprint on the Hispanic tradition. Among the more powerful
of Rome's legacies, Fuentes mentions "the idea, formed through language and law, of the state as cocreator of development and justice."
And, he adds, "All of those theaters, aqueducts, roads, and bridges
were but the exterior signs of Rome's decision to impose progress
and economic development through the benevolent authority of the
state" (41). The "genius of Rome," in Fuentes's estimate, is that it
created in Spain "a growing sense of community," yet also "fostered
change, openness, mixture, and circulation" (43). Unfortunately,
this balance between a central authority and local liberties was not
maintained in the other historical periods Fuentes surveys in *The
Buried Mirror*.

The state occupies an important place in Fuentes's map of the
main social and political forces in Spain during the centuries of the
reconquista and its aftermath. Fuentes describes the history of this

period as a struggle between three main groups: "strong feudal organizations based on the land, rising mercantile and artisanal activities based on the townships, and princes struggling to recapture the Roman sense of authority and statehood" (70). An alliance between the kings and the townships helped bring down the feudal lords (80). The monarchist cause was further advanced by the union of Isabella of Castile and Ferdinand of Aragon in 1469, an event that helped prepare the way for the defeat of Islam in 1492 and the unification of Spain under Catholicism. But with the crushing of feudalism, the stage was set for the monarchy to turn against its former allies, the townships. All along, the true aim of the kings had not been to promote the development of institutions of local self-government, but rather to change "the status of each person from that of a *vassal* of a lord to that of a *subject* to themselves" (80). When in the sixteenth century the unified Spanish monarchy faced "the challenge of rising independent townships and their democratic demands" (127), it responded by crushing these demands. It is at this point—as he narrates the episode of the 1521 rebellion of the *comuneros*—that Fuentes returns to a passage in Spanish history he had already covered in a similar fashion in *Terra Nostra* and *Cervantes o la crítica de la lectura*; when Fuentes states that Carlos V "consolidated the central state" (155) during his reign, it is clear that this process produced not the capacious and flexible state of Roman times, but rather the vertical and authoritarian state that would eventually share responsibility for Spain's long decline in the centuries to come.

The next stage in Fuentes's history of Spain and the New World in which the state plays an important role is the Mexican Revolution. The outlines of Fuentes's account are familiar from his earlier writings on the subject. He once again describes the split between the revolution of Villa and Zapata, which "favored a decentralized, self-ruling, communitarian democracy, inspired by shared traditions," and "the national, centralizing, modernizing revolution led by Carranza" (304). And he restates his view that the victory of the national revolution over the local revolution was both necessary and inevitable, primarily because only the national revolution was in a position to avert the very real threat of U.S. intervention. But Fuentes cannot wholeheartedly applaud the outcome: "The epic had become a tragedy" (306).

This is a striking conclusion to Fuentes's account of the Mexican Revolution. It is striking because at different times in his career Fuentes has argued that in our era both tragedy and epic have become impossible. Of the two, the impossibility of epic is the more fully elaborated topic in Fuentes's oeuvre. The passing of epic is closely tied to the rise of the novel—a story Fuentes tells in *Cervantes*. The death of tragedy is a topic that emerges later in Fuentes's thinking—and even then it is only hinted at. In the 1960s the call for a renewal of the tragic vision was a constant in Fuentes's essays and interviews. It is an especially prominent motif in *Casa con dos puertas*. But it also appears in *La nueva novela*, which, after all, came with an epigraph from Jean-Marie Domenach's *Le retour du tragique*. In his interview with Emir Rodríguez Monegal, Fuentes even argues that what distinguishes the new novel from the naturalist novel of Ciro Alegría, Jorge Icaza, and Rómulo Gallegos is the discovery of "an infinitely complex reality in which there is a certain tragic destiny because we realize that the just and the unjust are both guilty and from there arises the tragic tension."[48] This Nietzschean understanding of tragedy is one of the informing principles of *Cambio de piel*. Yet in a 1988 interview with Debra Castillo, there arrives a powerful and revealing moment in which Fuentes appears to bid farewell to the possibility of tragedy in our world: "I don't think . . . we can restore a 'sentimiento trágico de la vida' which I would like. It is one of the great achievements of the human spirit to be able to understand life and recreate it in the tragic manner, but perhaps we can't do that anymore. We're destined to farce and irony and it's the best solution we have at hand."[49]

Fuentes's observation to Castillo may account for the predominantly comic tone of novels such as *Cristóbal Nonato* and *La campaña*. It can also cast light on a work such as "Las dos orillas," a recent story in which Fuentes rewrites the history of the Spanish conquest of Mexico in such a way that it is the Aztecs who sail across the Atlantic and conquer Spain, a contrivance that seems to turn history into something of a joke.[50] But does the impossibility of tragedy also have an impact on the assessment Fuentes gives in his nonfiction of the political struggles of our own time? It would seem that the seriousness with which Fuentes views his role as a spokesman for his culture would preclude him—at least in his nonfiction—from reading the history of his continent, or its present situation, in a farcical or ironical light. This is clear from his reading of the Mexican Revolution in *The Buried Mirror*; it is also clear from the sketch he provides on the final pages of this same work of recent changes in society and politics in Latin America. For Fuentes emerges here not as a detached and ironical commentator, but rather as a committed spokesman for a new civil society, or for what, following Carlos Monsiváis, he calls "the politics of permanent social mobilization": "Professionals, intellectuals, technocrats, students, trade unions, agricultural co-ops, business associations, women's organizations, religious groups, neighborhood communities—the whole spectrum of society—are quickly becoming the protagonists of our history, outflanking the state, the army, the church, even the traditional political parties" (355). In effect, the reading of the Mexican Revolution in terms of tragedy prepares the way for the attempt to demonstrate the renewed vitality of the localist, pluralist tradition in Mexican politics.

Fuentes's position at the end of *The Buried Mirror* intersects in interesting ways with a new conception of politics that emerged in the 1980s. To the extent that this new conception flowed out of the critique of the grand narratives of modernity,[51] it could be labeled a postmodernist politics. In this light, the concluding paragraph of *The Buried Mirror* might be regarded as a sign that Fuentes had become a postmodernist in politics. Yet before we reach such a conclusion we need a somewhat more detailed account of the politics of postmodernism. A good place to look for such an account is Martín Hopenhayn's contribution to the recent *boundary 2* special issue on "The Postmodernism Debate in Latin America." According to Hopenhayn, postmodernist discourse declares the obsolescence of four principal ideas: the idea of progress, the idea of a vanguard, the idea of modernizing integration, and, finally, ideologies in general (the idea of ideology).[52] Given the disqualification of these categories, what do the postmodernists offer in return? In Hopenhayn's eyes, postmodernism celebrates "diversity, aesthetic and cultural individualism, multiplicity of languages, forms of expression and life-projects, and axiological relativism" (97). But what are the specific consequences of postmodernist discourse for our conception of the state? Hopenhayn notes that the rejection of the idea of the vanguard is tied to the rejection of "the category of the directionality and rationality of history" (96). The result is that "whether in politics, science, art, or culture, and whether the vanguard is the party, the state, the educational elite, or an aesthetic movement, no one can claim to constitute the group chosen or destined to establish totalizing orientations" (96). From the perspective of postmodernism, the state appears as a unifying, coercive, homogenizing entity whose claims to legitimacy can no longer be upheld. Postmodernists envision politics as taking shape through the interventions of a multitude of local, autonomous, ad hoc social and political groupings. The combined energies of these new social actors overwhelm the traditional normative and regulatory powers of the state.[53]

When Fuentes speaks on the last page of *The Buried Mirror* of the "outflanking" of the state by a host of social groups, we might be inclined to say that he speaks as a postmodernist. Yet such a label does not sit comfortably on Fuentes. To begin with, it is important to recall that even while Hopenhayn's list of top postmodernist themes echoes values for which Fuentes has often been a spokesman, Fuentes himself has always identified diversity, multiplicity and relativism as modern rather than postmodern values. Hopenhayn acknowledges that there is a party to the debate on postmodernism that sees postmodernism as "no more than modernity reflecting on itself and explaining its unresolved conflicts" (93).[54] Given the persistence of Fuentes's affiliation with modernity, as well as the paucity of his references to postmodernism, it makes more sense to think of him as somebody engaged in the self-critique of an incomplete modernity—even when he appears to incorporate postmodern themes into his reflections. Moreover, one should place

Fuentes's talk of the "outflanking" of the state in the context of other statements Fuentes has made on the continued importance of the state in Latin America. To give but one example, in a lecture he gave at the Coloquio de Invierno held in Mexico City in February 1992, Fuentes spoke of how critics should not "throw the nation-state overboard" and instead should demand of the state "that it go on a diet so that it may better perform certain indispensable functions in the areas of social justice and development."[55]

But there is a more important reason for declining to place the postmodernist label on Fuentes. For *The Buried Mirror*, even while it concludes with the irruption of the forces of multiplicity and heterogeneity onto the stage of Latin American history, clearly belongs to the genre of the totalizing narrative, which postmodernism so firmly repudiates. In *The Buried Mirror*, Fuentes narrates the story of Hispanic civilization from its origins to the present day. In doing so, his aim is to uncover the cultural continuity that holds together the history of this civilization. Fuentes places particular emphasis on the culture of the Hispanic world because he believes that culture can compensate for the devastation wrought in Latin America by politics and economics. In the introduction to *The Buried Mirror*, Fuentes draws attention to the painful split in the Latin American world: on the one hand, we have the crisis of Latin America's political and economic systems; on the other hand, there is the incomparable wealth of the continent's cultural heritage (9). Fuentes argues that Latin America must draw on its rich cultural tradition in order to discover a more satisfying political and economic identity.[56] This vision of redemption through culture is already present in *Terra Nostra*, for, as Lois Parkinson Zamora has argued, *Terra Nostra* proposes that it is in the literary tradition "that utopia may be located."[57] But such a view of literature and culture is profoundly foreign to the postmodernist paradigm. In this light, we might argue that if there is a common element between Fuentes's fiction and his nonfiction, it is to be found in the shared distance with regard to a set of postmodernist principles.

Reading *Terra Nostra* in conjunction with Fuentes's nonfiction allows us to see more clearly the dilemma that has shaped Fuentes's career as a writer. On the one hand, he has always placed great value on aesthetic innovation, in part no doubt because in the modern era this has been the surest path to consecration as a writer. In the 1970s, innovation meant breaking with the realist orientation of earlier fiction. On the other hand, Fuentes has wanted from the beginning of his career to play the role of the engaged intellectual. Given the long tradition in Latin America of involvement in politics on the part of writers, one could say that in this regard Fuentes did not need to invent a new position for himself in the field of intellectual production. The role had already been defined by innumerable precursors. In any event, it proved impossible for Fuentes to keep the two aspects of his role separate. This is utterly clear from *Terra Nostra*: a formally innovative novel that verges on the unreadable but at the same time contains a diagnosis of the ills of Hispanic culture, as well as recommendations for remedying these ills.

Critics of *Terra Nostra* have divided into two main camps, pitting those who view Fuentes's novel as a fundamentally open and subversive text against those who see *Terra Nostra* as the work of a literary despot intent on lording it over his readers. The first group includes Margaret Sayers Peden, who believes the novel "poses, but does not answer, questions."[58] Djelal Kadir offers a more complex version of this argument when he suggests that in *Terra Nostra* Fuentes "records the terrible dangers that lurk in abandoning the timely human dimension in favor of overweening structure and ideology's mystified illusion."[59] Carl Gutiérrez similarly claims that in *Terra Nostra* Fuentes "is actively engaged in rethinking alternatives to linear modes of history," a project Gutiérrez regards as emancipatory inasmuch as the ideology of history Fuentes overthrows "played a principal role in the despotic control of colonial and postcolonial populations."[60] Luz Rodríguez Carranza, finally, reads *Terra Nostra* as a novel that reveals an "infinity of possible worlds."[61] The first blast from the opposite camp came from José Joaquín Blanco, who not long after the novel's initial publication asserted that "rarely does one find in Mexican literature a writer so *radically* solitary and monological."[62] But it was Roberto González Echevarría who put forward the most often cited version of the argument that

Terra Nostra itself displayed the closed and tyrannical mind-set which the novel appeared to be criticizing. González Echevarría describes *Terra Nostra* as a "novel of cultural knowledge," a novel, that is, that makes an anachronistic claim to a privileged understanding of Spanish American culture.[63] For González Echevarría, the view that a work of literature possesses a "deep insight" into a culture's identity is sheer mystification, a mystification undone not only by his own deconstructive reading of Fuentes's novel, but also by the general turn in the Latin American novel towards "fictions in the vein of Sarduy and Puig," with their emphasis on "indeterminacy in all realms and the 'universalizing' force of popular culture."[64]

My own view is that *Terra Nostra* is not nearly as "open," "subversive," "multiple," or "infinite" as the first group of critics claims. Although *Terra Nostra* has clear affinities with the venerable modernist and postmodernist tradition of textual self-critique, it also has affinities with the activist, engaged qualities of Fuentes's other textual productions. At the same time, I do not regard the propositional dimension of *Terra Nostra* as quite as misleading or sinister as Blanco and González Echevarría think it is. Blanco is wrong to suggest that Fuentes regards Mexico as a nation forever condemned to barbarism because of its Hispanic and Indian roots. In fact, as I have shown, Fuentes wishes to rescue in *Terra Nostra* the pluralist heritage of Mexico's cultural and political tradition. González Echevarría, in turn, is wrong to dismiss the very legitimacy of the issue of cultural identity. A cultural identity may be extraordinarily difficult to define, it may be multileveled and in a constant process of change. But this does not mean that it does not exist. Fuentes's notion of redemption through culture may seem overblown, but if the alternative is to throw out the very notion of culture, with all that it implies — language, religion, history, custom, and more — then Fuentes's position may in fact be the more fruitful one, if only because he does not foreclose the possibility of debating an issue that will clearly not go away.

CHAPTER VI

The Nation as
Unimaginable Community

Two Mexicos

George Orwell once claimed that politics gave him the sense of purpose he needed to write good prose. Mexico has played the same role in Fuentes's writing as politics in George Orwell's, with the difference that for Fuentes it is not so much good writing as writing *tout court* that appears to have been enabled by the possession of a literary polestar. Consider the fact that an autobiographical essay Fuentes first published in *Granta* as "The Discovery of Mexico" became "How I Started to Write" when it was later included in *Myself With Others*, a collection of Fuentes's essays. One can hardly imagine more vivid proof of the conflation, in Fuentes's conception of his own career, of two processes: the encounter with Mexico, where he did not go to live permanently until age sixteen, and the emergence of a literary vocation.

But although the idea of the nation has sustained Fuentes's literary imagination throughout his career, he has not always returned the favor by sustaining the idea of the nation. Fuentes has regularly put forward a heroic vision of the Mexican nation as a unified, self-knowing whole, but he has been equally, if not to say more, inclined toward a view of Mexico as a violently conflicted, divided entity. A brief example from *La muerte de Artemio Cruz* — perhaps the most obviously "nationalist" text in Fuentes's corpus — will give a sense of

how Fuentes swings between the celebratory and the deconstructive in his rendering of the Mexican nation. Eric Hobsbawm has
noted how the "travelogue or geography lesson" is a common technique for inculcating a sense of the nation as "a coherent whole,
deserving love and patriotic devotion."[1] The school is obviously the
preferred medium for the transmission of such lessons, but they are
also to be found in literary texts. Near the end of *Artemio Cruz* there
is a long, evocative section about Artemio's relationship to his country that includes a kind of tour of the nation's territory. At first, the
sheer variety of the Mexican landscape is still reconciled within a
notion of unity-in-diversity (a common strategy in definitions of
national identity):

> It's a thousand countries with a single name. . . . You will
> bring with you the red deserts, the steppes of prickly pears
> and maguey, the world of the nopal, the belt of lava and
> frozen craters, the walls with golden church cupolas and
> stone battlements, the cities of stone and mortar, the cities of
> red *tezontle*, the towns of adobe, the villages of reed huts, the
> paths of black mud . . . the fine bones of Michoacán, the
> diminutive flesh of Tlaxcala, the light eyes of Sinaloa, the
> white teeth of Chiapas, the short-sleeved *huipil* blouses, the
> bow-shaped combs, the Mixtec tresses, wide *tzotzil* belts,
> Santa María shawls, Puebla marquetry, Jalisco glass,
> Oaxaca jade . . . you carry them with you and they weigh
> you down . . . they've gotten into your guts. (275/267)

It is above all the experience of the Mexican Revolution, seen as an
"amorous encounter," the expression of a "strange, common love"
(276/268), that ensures that the multiple realities of Mexico can be
reconciled within a higher unity. But a few pages later, the speaker
imagines a profound and unbridgeable faultline running right
through the heart of the nation. "There will be a frontier here," the
voice declares, "a frontier no one will defeat" (279/271). It is a frontier that separates a "dry, immutable, sad" Mexico, a Mexico
belonging to the "stone cloisters and imprisoned dust of the high

plateau," and linked to the Aztec past, from the Mexico of "the half-moon of Veracruz," a Mexico tied to another history, a different world, the sensuous, voluptuous world of the Antilles, and, beyond, of the Mediterranean (278/270).

Agua quemada, a collection of four linked narratives first published in 1981, marks a return in Fuentes's work to the concern with the immediate sociopolitical realities of Mexico that had characterized his early novels.[2] The stories offer one of the more intriguing and skillful explorations in Fuentes's fiction of the idea of Mexico. The two epigraphs Fuentes selected for this volume speak of Mexico from the perspective of loss and fragmentation, thus indicating from the start that *Agua quemada* aligns itself with the deconstructive pole in Fuentes's thinking about his country. The first epigraph is from Alfonso Reyes's "Palinodia del polvo," an essay in which Reyes laments the disappearance of a purer and more beautiful Mexico. The second epigraph consists of four lines from Octavio Paz's "Vuelta," which describe modern-day Mexico as a heap of fragments unconnected to any larger purpose. The stories of *Agua quemada* offer a narrative interpretation of these images of disintegration.

Figurations and Disfigurations of the Nation

The descriptive passages I quoted from *Artemio Cruz* are one way of representing the nation in a work of fiction. But the novelistic representation of the nation may be lodged less in such isolated passages than in certain structural features of the text. Benedict Anderson identifies a structure of simultaneity in the novel that has allowed it to become one of the fundamental forms of imagining the nation. He evokes a standard novelistic plot in which a series of disparate events are described as occurring simultaneously, perhaps in order to interlock at some later point, perhaps in order to diverge. Anderson then wonders why the two characters in his imaginary plot who never meet, who "can even be described as passing each other on the street, without ever becoming acquainted,"[3] are nevertheless connected to each other. He offers two answers. On the one hand, he sees a modern notion of a uniform and measurable clock-time as providing a frame within which to enclose a wide variety of events. On the other hand, he speaks of the embedding of these events in certain "sociological entities of . . . firm and stable reality."[4] Anderson undercuts his own argument about the privileged relationship between the novel and the nation by offering as examples of such societies entities (Wessex, Lübeck, Los Angeles) that are not nations. Even so, his suggestion that the nation offers a point of reference that ensures the unity of certain works of fiction provides a useful framework for an analysis of Carlos Fuentes's *Agua quemada*.

Even though Anderson's discussion is concerned with the novel, his remarks can help us read *Agua quemada* because the four stories that make up the collection are all carefully linked, and so can be seen as constituting a single universe in a way that is not so different from what we typically encounter in a novel. An examination of the nature of these links will give us an initial sense of Fuentes's conception of the community he is representing. It will also provide us with an insight into some flaws in Anderson's interpretation of his own model.

Each of the four stories in *Agua quemada* deals with a different set of characters, but each story intersects briefly with one or more of the other stories. Doña Manuela in "Estos fueron los palacios" was once a servant in the home of General Vicente Vergara, the main character in "El día de las madres." The General continues to pay Manuela's rent in a building owned by Federico Silva, the protagonist of "Las mañanitas." The Aparicios in "El hijo de Andrés Aparicio" also used to live in one of Silva's buildings. Moreover, Bernabé Aparicio's grandfather was an aide de camp to General Vergara during the Revolution, and two of his uncles now work at a gas station owned by the General's son Agustín.

Fuentes's picture of a single spatiotemporal continuum within which several life stories cross paths would appear to offer a fitting illustration of Benedict Anderson's idea about how a novel imagines a national community. Yet the existence of a common frame does not necessarily mean that what occurs within that frame constitutes a *genuine* community. Anderson appears insensitive to the uses of irony and so does not see that a particular literary technique can be used to question as much as to imagine a community.

The links between the different stories in *Agua quemada* serve to turn a collection of disparate narratives into a general survey of an entire community. But the glancing nature of these connections creates a paradox: the connections, precisely because they are so tenuous, become an image of disconnectedness. This fragmentation of the social body is an all the more bitter reality because it is so often the result of deliberate refusals on the part of individual characters to preserve and respect the bonds that tie them to their fellow citizens. General Vergara fires Manuela after the death of his wife because she triggers too many memories in him. He discontinues the invitations to the Aparicios for breakfast on the anniversary of the Revolution, perhaps for the same reason. Federico Silva knows absolutely nothing about the people who live in his buildings, which he has never even visited. Later we learn that he raises the rent "mercilessly" (102/193) on the Aparicio family when the rent freeze is lifted, forcing them to move to a different part of the city. It seems, then, that whenever two stories in the collection are linked to each other it is in order to depict an act of severance, to describe an erosion of the sense of community.

This sense of erosion is also conveyed through the way in which space is mapped in the stories. *Agua quemada* attempts to cover different points on the map of Mexico City, as well as to trace the interrelations between these points. We move from the exclusive Pedregal neighborhood where the Vergaras live to the old colonial center with its half-abandoned palaces, then to Federico Silva's house sandwiched between the Zona Rosa and the Colonia Roma, and finally out to a nameless squatters' community on the outskirts of the city. But the inclusive gesture only serves to uncover a general loss of cohesion in the urban fabric. Two motions stand out: on the one hand, the city, as it spreads, becomes shapeless, loses solidity, as we see in the description of the nameless district where Bernabé Aparicio grows up, "a temporary place, like the cardboard and corrugated tin shacks" (97/188); on the other hand, the city erects barricades against itself, as in the description of the attempt at "urban chastity" (37/51) in the fortresslike Pedregal neighborhood.

The description of the city as chaste evokes the image of the community as a body. Octavio Paz remarks in *Corriente alterna* that "the nation is a projection of the individual,"[5] a link that provides another basis for the imaginative representation of the nation. *La muerte de Artemio Cruz* offers an excellent example of this technique: the vicissitudes of the protagonist's life are emblems of different stages in the modern history of Mexico. The hero's psychological disintegration (captured in the tripartite structure of the novel) and his physical dismemberment (most vividly depicted in the concluding image of the surgeon's scalpel slicing open Artemio's stomach for the final, unsuccessful operation) point to the disintegration and mutilation of the nation as a whole. In *Agua quemada* the image of mutilation crops up again: Federico Silva's throat is slit in the course of a robbery in his house, an incident foreshadowed in Silva's own detailed and gloating description earlier in the story of the workings of a guillotine. Silva, we are told, resembles "the lost perfume of the ancient lake of Mexico" (74/156); he belongs, in other words, to a vanished Mexico. Like the victims of the guillotine in France, he is an anachronism. The fact that the woman who participates in the fatal robbery in Silva's house is named Pocajonta gives a further, paradoxical twist to Silva's role: he belongs to an older Mexico, but he is also an intruder, an outsider, a colonialist in his own country. And in this story, of course, the native princess will not reach out to save the doomed foreigner.

The depiction of Silva as both a native and a foreigner, both insider and outsider, reveals the instability of the notion of national identity. But the most effective vehicle Fuentes chooses in order to demonstrate this instability is not the individual, but the family. One of the strands that ties together the different stories in *Agua quemada* is the motif of the missing relative. In "El día de las madres" the mothers themselves are dead. In "Estos fueron los palacios" Manuela's daughter Lupe Lupita has run away from home. In "Las mañanitas" the protagonist Federico Silva is a convinced bachelor who is led to think at the end of his life about the son he never had.

In the final story of the collection "El hijo de Andrés Aparicio" it is precisely the father named in the title who never appears. The case of "El día de las madres" is particularly interesting, however, and therefore deserving of a more extended analysis. Here the theme of loss is given an especially bitter twist: the absence of the mothers turns out to be not a symptom of familial disintegration, but rather the sine qua non of domestic harmony. The men of the Vergara family can only continue to live together thanks to the violence they perpetrate on women. They bond over the dead bodies of their wives and mothers. To the extent that the history of the Vergara family is meant to recapitulate the history of twentieth-century Mexico, the story reveals that national unity is entirely a function of violence and repression. The mourning of a loss masks the fact that the loss energizes the survivors.

On a more or less explicit level, "El día de las madres" offers two answers to the question of what it is that brings all Mexicans together into a single, unified community. Near the beginning of the story we see General Vicente Vergara thinking nostalgically of "the years of the Revolution and the battles that had forged modern Mexico" (11/25). Here it is a shared, and, significantly enough, violent, past that has created the nation. Later in the story, the General's grandson Plutarco, who is also the narrator of "El día de las madres," in the course of querying his grandfather about his somewhat contradictory stance with regard to the Church says, "you also say that the Virgin unites all us Mexicans" (18). This time it is a shared symbol—and the fact that it is a feminine symbol is what needs to be underlined—that acts as the guarantor of the nation's unity. But what the story shows is how both these techniques for making the nation are fraught with terrible contradictions. The violent past makes but also cripples the present, while the idealization of womanhood is merely the gentler way of excluding actual women from the national community.

The relationship to the past and the relationship to the feminine are the focus of the story's opening lines: "Every morning Grandfather vigorously stirs his cup of instant coffee. He grasps the spoon as in other times my dear-departed grandmother Clotilde had grasped the pestle, or he himself, General Vicente Vergara, had grasped the pommel of the saddle now hanging on his bedroom wall" (11/24). In just two sentences, Fuentes gives us a complex structure of comparisons and contrasts that prepares the way for the story's subsequent trajectory. The present brings forth the past; a simple domestic task evokes the heroic, violent days of the Revolution. But the resemblance between now and then, between the grandfather and the military hero, immediately collapses under the weight of a merciless irony. The similarity between the two actions, the grasping of the spoon and the grasping of the pommel of the saddle, is promptly stripped away to reveal an unbridgeable gulf separating the past from the present. The passage offers no more than an illusion of continuity. The unobtrusive shift from one name to another, the Grandfather of the first sentence becoming the General of the second, cannot conceal the fact that these two figures have very little in common, for only in the slightly hallucinatory world of an old man overcome with nostalgia can preparing coffee and fighting a military battle entertain a genuine resemblance with each other. Having established the link between past and present, the narrative proceeds subtly to draw attention to the distance that has been traveled between them through the detail of the saddle, which, hanging on the General's bedroom wall, has acquired a merely ornamental value in a thoroughly domestic setting.

Toward the end of the opening paragraph, the General himself, even while he has been busy recapturing the past in a cup of coffee, acknowledges that times are no longer the same. He remembers a time when "men were men" (11/24), taking pleasure in getting drunk and going to war. The present, then, is characterized by the decline of machismo, a decline that affects the General himself, for the other link established in the opening lines of "El día de las madres," besides the one that connects Vicente Vergara's present self to his past self, is the one that connects him to his deceased wife, and, therefore, to the realm of the feminine. In the act of preparing himself a cup of coffee, Vicente Vergara takes the place of his wife, and so becomes a domesticated, feminized figure. But as was the case with the crossing over between past and present, the exchange between masculine and feminine qualities proves to be illusory. The story's opening image of the feminized grandfather gives way in the course of the narrative to the portrait of a man (a community of men, really) fundamentally cut off from womanhood.

The relationship between past and present is embodied in the relationship between General Vergara and his grandson Plutarco. Near the beginning of the story Plutarco speaks of the "anguish of a cornered mouse" (12/25) that seizes him every time he sees General Vergara "purposelessly wandering through the rooms and halls and corridors" (12/25–26). But Plutarco feels this way less out of pity for the aimlessness of his grandfather's existence than because the old man constantly reminds him of the futility of his own life. Immediately after the above passage, Plutarco runs out of the house, as if to escape from his grandfather's oppressive presence. He hops into his Thunderbird (an obvious symbol of Americanization, and hence of the distance between Plutarco and the General) and heads for the ring road around the city, where he will finally feel free and at ease: "I could circle the city once, twice, a hundred times, as many times as I wanted, driving thousands of kilometers with a sensation of never moving, of being simultaneously at the point of departure and the destination" (13/27). But the structure of Plutarco's action is ambiguous: on the one hand, he flees from his grandfather; on the other hand, he ends up imitating him. After all, the aimlessness of Plutarco's highway drive simply replicates the purposelessness he had sensed in his grandfather's wanderings through his house.

It is this ambivalence that offers the key to the relationship between Plutarco and General Vicente Vergara. To the extent that the General, having fought in the battles that had forged modern Mexico, is a national hero, and as such a kind of embodiment of the nation, the complexities of his relationship with his grandson are symptomatic of the impasse that has struck the nationalist project. This impasse is captured most vividly in the following conversation between grandfather and grandson:

"I love you very much, Grandfather."

"That's good, boy. The same goes for me."

"Listen, I don't want to have everything served to me on a silver platter like you say."

"Can't be helped. Everything's in my name. Your father just manages things. When I die, I'm leaving everything to you."

"I don't want it, Grandfather; Grandfather, I want to begin from the beginning, the way you did."

"Times are different. What do you think you could do now?"

I half smiled: "I wish I could have castrated someone, like you did." (23/37)

It is worth examining this passage in some detail so as to unravel the structure of the relationship between Plutarco and his grandfather. The first two lines of the dialogue set up a dynamic of repetition and imitation: the grandfather's feelings for his grandson are the same as the grandson's feelings for his grandfather. Their emotions mirror each other. But Plutarco's desire to be like the General runs into insurmountable difficulties. Plutarco wants to imitate his grandfather, but his grandfather prides himself precisely on never having imitated anybody. If Plutarco wants to begin anew, to create himself, like his grandfather, he must begin by freeing himself of his dependence on the old man. In other words, if Plutarco wants truly to imitate the General, he will have to reject him. The impossibility of reconciling these two imperatives causes Plutarco's paralysis. And it is the nature of time itself that is responsible for this situation, as the General acknowledges with serene simplicity when he says, "Times are different." In a sense, he means that times are never the same. One of the ways in which time becomes concrete is through the succession of the generations, and it is the fact of generation that places the children at a permanent disadvantage in the struggle for originality. Plutarco says that he would have liked to castrate somebody, as his grandfather did, but we are given to understand that in effect his grandfather, simply by virtue of his priority in time, has already castrated him.

The rivalry between the General and Plutarco points to the presence of an Oedipal paradigm in "El día de las madres." The pattern is confirmed when we learn that Plutarco's first experience of sexual arousal occurred at age thirteen when a friend showed him a picture of a girl in a bathing suit. The girl turns out to be Plutarco's mother, who died when Plutarco was five. Both the incest wish and the wish to take the place of the father-figure express what Freud calls the child's "wish to be the *father of himself*."[6] That this particular reading of the sources of the Oedipus complex is most pertinent to Fuentes's story is clear from the fact that what is at stake in the struggle between Plutarco and his grandfather is, as I have tried to show, the desire of the younger man to be self-created. We have seen, however, that Plutarco's desire to engender himself is paradoxically intertwined with his desire to imitate his grandfather. The doubleness of this structure can be elucidated with the help of René Girard's reading of the Oedipus complex in *Violence and the Sacred*.

Girard looks at Freud's writings on the Oedipus complex through the prism of his theory of triangular desire. Girard argues that desire is never the spontaneous movement of a subject toward an object. Instead, desire is always borrowed desire. The subject, according to Girard, does not "choose the objects of his own desire."[7] Desire is instilled in the subject by a model or mediator, a third person to whom the subject attributes a desire for a certain object. The subject will begin to desire this same object only because of the "illusory value" conferred upon the object by the rival's desire.[8] The subject's desire, in other words, is mimetic rather than autonomous. In *Violence and the Sacred*, Girard argues that the mimetic structure of desire can give us a better understanding of the Oedipus complex. Picking up on Freud's notion that the male child seeks identification with his father, Girard concludes that this must mean that the son will "desire what the father desires."[9] Principal among these objects of desire, of course, will be the child's mother.

In the scene in "El día de las madres" where Plutarco contemplates, in a state of sexual excitation, the photograph of his mother, there is no sense that Plutarco's desire is modeled on his father's desire. However, there is another passage where the structure of

rivalry to which Girard grants so much importance is vividly present. Plutarco deplores the impoverished quality of his sex life, and
compares it to his father's: "I never got any farther than a whore-
house on Saturday nights, alone, without friends. I wanted to
seduce a real lady, mature, like my father's mistress, not the proper
girls I met at the parties of other rich kids like myself" (26/40). It is
likely that Plutarco desires a mature woman only because of his
father's prior desire for such a woman.

The more important father-figure in "El día de las madres,"
however, is the General. Girard points out that the child's relationship to his father results in a "mimetic double bind."[10] On the one
hand, when the son conceives a desire for the mother he "is simply
responding in all candor to a command issued by the culture in
which he lives and by the model himself,"[11] that is, the command to
imitate his father. On the other hand, when the two desires, the
father's and the son's, converge on the same object, the stage is set
for a terrible conflict. This results in an injunction that contradicts
the first one; now the command is *not* to imitate. This notion of the
double bind is clearly applicable to the relationship between
Plutarco and his grandfather. Here, too, the two commands, to imitate and not to imitate, are spoken simultaneously. Conversely, the
two desires, to be like his grandfather, and not to be like his grandfather, surge up side by side in Plutarco.

The story reaches its climax in the nighttime scene in which the
General and Plutarco visit various nightspots in the city and end up
in a brothel. In the midst of the drunken revelry, the General cannot
stop talking about his military exploits. The entire scene becomes a
mock replay of the battles of the Revolution. The General calls the
mariachis he has hired for the night his troops, and when he gets into
a fight in a nightclub he orders the piano's guts ripped out "the way
they did to the horses at Celaya" (32/47). But the General must finally face the unheroic nature of the present when he fails in bed with
the prostitute Judith. When Plutarco takes over from his grandfather and has sex with Judith, we can see this as an act of revenge
both on Judith (who is blamed for the General's impotence) and on
the General (for having tried to figuratively castrate his grandson).

The General watches sadly "as if he were seeing life being born anew, but it was no longer his life" (35/49). Plutarco takes the place of his grandfather, and takes possession of his own life. In the next few pages of the story, Plutarco's suddenly more mature and reflective voice takes center stage. The General falls asleep as Plutarco drives him home; when they arrive, Plutarco must carry his grandfather into the house, "like a child" (38/52). The order of the generations has been reversed. But if Plutarco feels sad in spite of what he regards as a victory over his grandfather, it is because the double bind described by Girard continues to haunt him. The son's appropriation of the father's desire entails the destruction of the latter, but this immediately leads to the cessation of the son's desire which cannot exist without the father's mediation. Plutarco wants to take the place of his grandfather, but he cannot do so without destroying his grandfather and thus nullifying his own project of imitation.

The women in this model are turned into a medium for the expression of inter-male rivalry. This is true for Judith, but even truer for Evangelina, Plutarco's mother. Plutarco's father and grandfather conspire to murder Evangelina. What did she do to deserve this? In essence, her sin was that she was not her mother-in-law. Clotilde, the General's wife, was war booty. Evangelina, by contrast, chose her husband. She actively desired him, where Clotilde passively accepted her fate. But as Becky Boling points out, Evangelina's challenge to "the patriarchy's exclusive right to power or desire" makes her a "pariah" for General Vergara.[12] Her death reaffirms the patriarch's authority and restores the bond between the men of the Vergara family. René Girard speaks in *Violence and the Sacred* of a society's need to find a scapegoat onto whom to deflect intracommunal violence. The sacrificial process allows a community to establish the sense of unanimity it needs to sustain itself as a harmonious entity. This process is reflected in "El día de las madres." The victimization of the women allows the men to fortify their sense of connectedness. But Girard believes that the sacrificial process is at the origin of human culture, that it is a way of finding a socially acceptable outlet for humanity's violent instincts. In Fuentes's story, however, there is nothing acceptable about the violence of the Vergara men.

Instead of a community, Fuentes depicts a parody of a community. In this way, he questions the nationalist project in Mexico.

History as Inheritance and Disinheritance

Una familia lejana relates the histories of two New World families, both of them named Heredia.[13] The reconstruction of these histories is carried out via a series of embedded narratives: the main narrator, a man named Carlos Fuentes (not to be confused with the Carlos Fuentes who wrote *Una familia lejana*), tells the story of the story he heard, one afternoon in Paris, from an elderly French aristocrat named Branly, whose narrative consists in large part of the stories he heard from Hugo Heredia, a Mexican archaeologist, and Víctor Heredia, a mysterious Frenchman of Spanish American descent who lives in a villa near Paris. The novel's intricate structure draws attention to the act of narration, specifically to the way in which narratives are passed from one person to another, like inheritances.

The notion of inheritance both helps clarify the structure of *Una familia lejana*, with its complex process of narrative transmission, and plays a key role in the actual historical narratives the novel relates. Hugo Heredia is obsessed with the past as a lost inheritance. As an archaeologist, he believes his task is to repair the past. For Heredia, to restore Mexico's pre-Columbian past is not only to revive the period of Mexico's greatest grandeur; it is also to recreate a society in which the past was never sacrificed on the altar of the present. He sees the modern era as an era that is enamored of the new, and disdainful of the past. But in the pursuit of novelty, the present itself evaporates, leaving the modern individual to live in an "illusory time" (16/11), a time that will itself be reduced to oblivion by the future (164/170). Premodern societies, by contrast, "refuse to abandon the old ways in favor of the new; rather than being cast aside one after the other, some realities accumulate in a permanent accretion" (16/11). The profoundest lesson of Mexican antiquity, for Hugo Heredia, is that everything is interrelated. It is this vision he wishes to recapture.

The irony of Hugo Heredia's quest is that he himself is a product of the very culture that destroyed the possibility of the type of spiritual integration for which he longs. Hugo's ancestors arrived in the New World in the first half of the sixteenth century, and built up a fortune in the usual way, that is, by appropriating the land and labor of the indigenous population. In the history of his family, Hugo recognizes in compressed form the entire Spanish American history of abuse and exploitation. But the history in which the Heredias participated meant not only the end of the unified vision of the indigenous civilizations; it also spelled the death of European universalism. At one point in the narrative, Branly explains to Fuentes that the New World was the tomb of European universalism: "Never again, following that century of discoveries and conquests, was it possible to be universal. The new world proved to be too large, on a different scale" (121/124). The fate of Europe is sketched out in the trajectory of the Heredia family: "There we all became Heredias: enervated creoles" (121/124). The encounter between the Old World and the New shatters the hope for order and wholeness on both sides of the ocean.

To recover the lost inheritance of ancient Mexican civilization Hugo must in a sense deny his own family inheritance, in that the Heredias, as we have seen, helped bring about the destruction of the world Hugo now wishes to reconstruct. At the same time, however, Hugo's quest to revive the pre-Hispanic past serves as a form of compensation for his own family's disinheritance. For with Mexican independence, the fortunes of the Heredia family begin a downward spiral. Having struggled to maintain their social and economic position under the "capricious regimes" (161/168) of the nineteenth century, the Heredias receive the definitive "coup de grâce" (162/168) during the Mexican Revolution. By the time Hugo is born in 1931, only two options are available: "find a profession or live by my wits" (162/168). Bereft of the privileges of his ancestors, he must confront what he calls "democratic oppression" (162/168), that is, a world in which everybody has a right to everything. In response, he seeks a refuge in the ruins of the indigenous civilizations, though he does so in full awareness of the paradoxical nature of his quest: "I, a Creole in search of lost grandeur, could find it only among the monuments of my victims' past" (162/169).

The failure of Hugo's quest is embodied in his relationship with his son Víctor. The father fails to inculcate in the son the veneration he himself feels for the past, a failure captured in the scene in which Víctor finds a perfect object—so perfect that it cannot be described—among the ruins of Xochicalco, but then, filled with hatred for this symbol of the ancient civilization his father reveres, smashes the object with a stone until it breaks in half. Yet Víctor's act of desecration should not be read as a rejection of the past per se. It is simply that he has learned a different lesson from the past, not the lesson of the lost civilizations of the New World, but the lesson of the usurpers of those civilizations: "the conviction that we belonged to a superior caste endowed with innate privileges that entitled us to reclaim the authority usurped from us by a world of parvenus" (164/171). Víctor fails to inherit his father's passion because of the inherently contradictory nature of the past as both goal and obstacle of Hugo's quest. Hugo strives to bring back the perfect unity of ancient Mexican civilization, but in order to do so he must forget what he calls the "black utopia" of New World history (187/196). This black utopia is the consequence of the Conquest, a wound that never heals, an inheritance that leaves Mexicans in a permanent state of disinheritance.

The notions of inheritance and disinheritance also play an important role in the story of the other Heredia, Víctor (not to be confused with Hugo's son). Víctor Heredia's family history abounds in what Hugo calls "glaring inconsistencies" (184/192)—the dates in his narrative simply refuse to be strung together in any logical fashion. At the same time, Víctor appears to be not one, but several people. He lives in a villa near Paris, but in Hugo's narrative he shows up in Caracas and Monterrey. Yet Víctor's speech and behavior do reveal a certain consistency: he is described as a man marked (or disfigured) by a lack of courtesy and an attitude of resentment. His resentment is provoked by Branly's aristocratic background, and is linked to his own sense of dispossession. Whereas Branly is the inheritor of a centuries-long tradition of social distinction, Víctor

Heredia's family history is distinguished by acts of delusion, betrayal, and revenge. The key event in this history occurs during the Spanish American wars of independence, when a French merchant, having exhausted the fortune he once built up in Haiti, emigrates to La Guaira, together with the beautiful daughter he hopes to use as a bait with which to renew his wealth. When he marries her off to a young man named Francisco Luis de Heredia, the disappointment proves to be mutual, for Heredia's parents "had cut him off because of his rebel doings" (105/107), and so he "married Mademoiselle Lange believing she was an heiress, as Lange thought Heredia was an heir" (106/108). What ensues is a nasty story of greed and revenge. From this past Víctor Heredia inherits a rancor that appears to have sprung from the double act of disinheritance with which the family history originates.

The complex pattern of inheritances and disinheritances which *Una familia lejana* traces reveals the impossibility of ever stabilizing a family identity. This theme is taken up on a different level in the images the novel offers of the intertwining of the histories of the Old and the New Worlds. Thus, Víctor Heredia is partly of French, partly of Spanish American descent, while Hugo is married to a Frenchwoman, which means that his son Víctor, like his homonym, is also part French, part Spanish American. The identities of the characters to whom the histories of the Heredias are relayed constitute an extension of this theme: first Branly, a Frenchman, and second, Carlos Fuentes, who turns out to be a French immigrant of Spanish American origin. Branly explains: "In 1945, Fuentes, you decided to live in Buenos Aires and Montevideo; you did not return to your native Mexico; you became a citizen of the River Plate region, and then in 1955 you came to live in France. You became less of a River Plate man, and more French than anything else" (204/215). At the same time, Branly imagines the life his friend might have led had he returned to Mexico in 1945: "Imagine what would have happened if you had returned to Mexico after the war and put down roots in the land of your parents. Imagine you publish your first book of stories when you are twenty-five; your first

novel four years later. You write about Mexico, about Mexicans. . . .
You remain forever identified with that country and its people"
(204–5/215). The reader immediately recognizes in this alternative
scenario the story of the real Carlos Fuentes's life. Fuentes thus
imagines in *Una familia lejana* another history for himself—one in
which he retraces the footsteps of a distinguished progeny of
French writers of Spanish American background. Yet at the same
time, by making the Carlos Fuentes of the novel the ultimate destination of the novel's many narratives, Fuentes turns his alternative
self into the inheritor of the very past from which he imagines an
escape. In this to-and-fro movement—between the past as
inescapable inheritance and the past viewed from the perspective of
an outsider—is captured the unresolved nature of personal, familial,
and cultural identity in *Una familia lejana*.[14]

The Writer as Therapist

Perry Anderson has argued that the repudiation of the notion of
national character in Europe in the early part of this century was a
side-effect of the assault on the notion of individual character. Both
literary Modernism with its "widespread rejection of any stable ego"
and psychoanalysis with its weakening of "traditional assumptions of
individual character as moral unity" contributed to this development.[15] It is striking, in light of Anderson's observations, to note the
enduring link that exists in Mexico between psychoanalysis and the
discourse on national character. Samuel Ramos based his analysis of
the Mexican character in *Pérfil del hombre y la cultura en México* (1934)
on Alfred Adler's notion of the inferiority complex.[16] Octavio Paz rejected Ramos's interpretation in *El laberinto de la soledad*, arguing that
"the Mexican's solitude is vaster and profounder than his sense of inferiority."[17] But Paz continued to rely on a psychoanalytic model for
his reading of the national character, for in the key chapter of *El
laberinto*, "Los hijos de la Malinche," where he finds the sources for
the present-day Mexican's identity in the period of the Conquest,
Paz offers what is essentially a rewriting of Freud's parricide-incest

theme to fit Mexican history: "the distinctiveness of the Mexican resides . . . in his violent, sarcastic humiliation of the Mother and his no less violent affirmation of the Father."[18]

The reliance on psychoanalysis implies that there is a pathological element in the national character. Martin Stabb has drawn attention to the frequency with which the essayistic tradition in Latin America projects the image of the intellectual as a doctor whose task it is to cure the nation of its illnesses.[19] There is a specifically psychoanalytic version of this motif in which the intellectual appears in the guise of a mental therapist. Again, Paz offers a good illustration of this motif: in *Posdata* (1970) he calls explicitly for "a critique of Mexico and its history—a critique that resembles psychoanalytical therapeutics."[20] It is a call Paz answers in the very text in which he makes it, for the aim of *Posdata* is to trace Mexico's current pathologies—which erupted most dramatically in the 1968 Tlatelolco massacre—to the nation's Aztec past, in a hermeneutic maneuver that is parallel in structure to psychoanalysis. In excavating the nation's history Paz performs the exact same operation as the therapist who brings to light the patient's unconscious. In Paz's model of the Mexican character, the Aztec period comes to occupy the same position as the unconscious in the psychoanalytic model. And his concept of criticism is analogous to the idea of the talking cure in psychoanalysis. In bringing the past to light, Paz hopes to dispel its noxious effects on the present. The only difficulty, perhaps, in making the translation between psychoanalysis and Paz's concept of the critic's task is where to locate Paz himself, for Paz appears to be both the doctor prescribing a cure, and, as the intellectual who engages in acts of criticism, the patient who does the talking.

Roger Bartra describes Mexico as a "paradise for psychoanalytical expeditions."[21] He believes that these expeditions have normally produced negative views of the Mexican character. Bartra argues that such images serve a specific purpose: the act of defining (or defaming) the nation is designed to facilitate the ruling of the nation. The producers of the discourse on the Mexican national character describe the masses only in order to dominate them more effectively. In an argument that is clearly indebted to Michel Foucault, Bartra claims that the essayistic tradition in Mexico identifies a "*subject* of national history" in order to make it easier to keep the Mexican "*subjected* to a specific form of domination" (emphasis mine).[22] The uncovering of certain specifically Mexican character traits serves to justify the existence of an authoritarian political system that is presumed to *fit* the peculiarities of the Mexican character.[23]

To some extent, Fuentes follows in the footsteps of Ramos and Paz. "El día de las madres" is a good example of what Bartra calls a psychoanalytic expedition into Mexican society. But what conclusions should we draw from this? Does Fuentes denigrate the Mexican character so as to exalt himself? Does he fix the Mexican national identity in order to make it easier to subject the Mexican people to a project of political control? Several observations may be made in answer to these questions. In the first place, one can point to Perry Anderson's argument that a psychoanalytic perspective destabilizes rather than stabilizes the notion of national character. The example of "El día de las madres" lends support to this contention, for Fuentes uses a psychoanalytic framework in this story in order to reveal a structure of intergenerational rivalry that blocks the very possibility of transmitting the mentality and code of conduct associated with Mexican nationhood. This destabilizing effect is reinforced by the strong links Fuentes's work entertains with the other cultural phenomenon to which Anderson attributes the decline of the notion of national character—literary modernism. These links are particularly evident in *Una familia lejana*, a novel whose self-conscious narrative structure and preoccupation with the plasticity of time and memory envelop everything that occurs within it in a typically modernist aura of uncertainty, an uncertainty that has as one of its main corollaries the undermining of any notion of national character as something fixed.

My second point is that neither *Agua quemada* nor *Una familia lejana* should be viewed in isolation from the rest of Fuentes's oeuvre, in which we may find a celebratory as a well as a deconstructive vision of Mexico. As I have demonstrated in earlier chapters, this celebratory vision often hinges on a particular reading of the Mexican Revolution. To recapitulate, I will draw a brief example of this reading from *The Buried Mirror*, in which Fuentes describes the Mexican Revolution as an eroticized act of national self-recognition: "A country in which the geographical barriers of mountains, deserts, ravines, and sheer distances had separated one group of people from another now came together, as the tremendous caval-cades of Villa's men and women from the north rushed to meet Zapata's men and women from the south. In their revolutionary embrace, Mexicans finally learned how other Mexicans talked, sang, ate, and drank, dreamed and made love, cried and fought."[24] This kind of celebration of the nation's cultural distinctiveness breaks out of the confines of the model sketched by Bartra. Bartra sees only contempt in Mexicanist discourse. Fuentes mixes denigra-tion with boosterism.

To account for these contradictions we must see that Fuentes is the inheritor of two separate traditions. On the one hand, he has nourished himself on the skeptical, subversive tradition of modern literature. On the other hand, he has absorbed the traditional Latin American intellectual's sense of responsibility toward the communi-ty. The collision of these two paradigms is responsible for the curi-ously fractured quality of much of Fuentes's work. And it is this quality that helps us see that Mexicanist discourse need not be as monolithic as it appears in Bartra's account. The same writer can imagine a community, and unimagine it as well. Such ambivalence is understandable, for the nation itself is a Janus-like entity, especially in Latin America. On the one hand, the nation has long been regarded in Latin America as the first and most important line of defense against imperialism; on the other hand, nationalist ideology has regularly been placed in the service of oppressive political agen-das. Insofar as the nation has been a tool for emancipation, Fuentes has wished to contribute to its making. Insofar as the nation has sti-fled the life of a community, Fuentes has sought to contribute to its demystification.

The Real Nation and the Legal Nation

A Brief History of an Idea

The mismatch in Latin America between the "real" nation and the "legal" nation is a persistent theme in Fuentes's work, a theme that links him to numerous precursors in the Latin American essayistic tradition who have remarked upon and worried over the deeply disjunctive nature of Latin American reality. A look at some examples from this tradition reveals that the absence of a cohesive sense of nationhood is generally attributed to the rift between what is native and what is foreign to Latin America. Yet we will also see that the somewhat schematic opposition covers an extraordinarily complex and sometimes even contradictory set of ideas concerning the desired relationship between the two forces in question.

At the very dawn of Latin American independence, Simón Bolívar, in an address to the Venezuelan Congress in Angostura, where the Constitution of 1819 was drafted, warned of the dangers of blindly imitating the political institutions of Europe and the United States. From Montesquieu's *L'Esprit des Lois*, Bolívar drew the lesson that "laws must be related to the physical properties, the climate, the quality of the terrain, the situation, and the extension of the country, and to the way of life of the people."[1] Bolívar urged the legislators to refer in their deliberations in the first place "to the religion, the inclinations, the wealth, the number, the commercial activities, the customs, and the manners of the country's inhabitants,"[2] reminding them that "the excellence of a government does not derive from its theory, nor from its mechanism, but from its appropriateness to the nature and character of the nation for which it has been instituted."[3] In Venezuela, according to Bolívar, one must look soberly upon the facts of political immaturity and racial heterogeneity and evolve a mode of government appropriate to such conditions. One must resist the lure of foreign models, for what works in one place does not necessarily work elsewhere. Many legislators wanted to copy the federalist system of government from the United States, where it had enjoyed an evident success. But Bolívar insisted that Venezuela, a nation marked by the composite nature of its population, could not afford such a loose system, for it would aggravate rather than counter the disintegrative tendencies already at large in Venezuelan society. Bolívar's assessment of the Venezuelan situation led him to prescribe a centralist system of government with a strong executive for the country. Yet clearly Bolívar's quarrel was not with imitation itself, for in the same address he advocated the creation of a hereditary senate in Venezuela, and referred to the British House of Lords as an appropriate model for such an institution. In this case, the foreign model fit the Venezuelan circumstance.

Sarmiento appears less preoccupied than Bolívar by the dangers of transplanting ideas and institutions from Europe or North America to South America. In fact, Sarmiento attributed the Revolution of Independence in Argentina to the impact of European ideas, and he believed the progress of civilization in Argentina could be measured according to the degree of "Europeanization" undergone by the country.[4] Yet even as he seemed to commend the citizens of Buenos Aires for viewing their city as an extension of Europe,[5] Sarmiento drew attention to the gulf that separated Argentina from Europe. In a characteristic twist, Sarmiento invoked the critique of Enlightenment universalism launched by French thinkers such as Tocqueville, Thierry, Michelet, and Guizot, in order to remind his readers of the need for a political thinker to know something about "races . . . inclinations . . . national habits . . .

historical antecedents,"[6] for only thus could one avoid applying inappropriate epistemological principles to Argentina. On the one hand, then, Sarmiento advocated the spread of European civilization throughout Argentina, while on the other hand he made himself into the spokesman for a vast zone of Argentine reality that remained profoundly alien to everything European.

The historical experience of Latin America in the nineteenth century, in particular the failure of the liberal model in politics and economics to produce the same results in Latin America as in Europe and the United States, seemed to justify the fears expressed forcefully by Bolívar and intermittently by Sarmiento concerning the distortions that would result from the uncritical adherence of Latin Americans to foreign models of any kind. The task of disentangling autochthonous from nonautochthonous elements in Latin American culture and society became a prime preoccupation for Latin American intellectuals. José Martí offered a classic denunciation of the divorce between the abstractions imported from Europe and North America and the concrete reality of what he called "our" America: "With a decree by Hamilton one cannot halt the pushing of a plainsman's horse. With a phrase by Sieyès one cannot make the stagnant blood of the Indian race flow again."[7] José Carlos Mariátegui took up the problem of creating "a more Peruvian, more autochthonous order" from a Marxist perspective,[8] arguing that the fundamental problem of Peru—the problem of the exploitation of the country's indigenous population—could never be solved through legal or administrative measures, which Mariátegui regarded as essentially artificial, but instead required a transformation at the level of the country's economic structure.

It is Octavio Paz, however, who developed the version of this theme that has most obviously helped shaped Fuentes's views on the subject. Over the course of his long career, Paz has repeatedly pondered the problem of the inauthentic, inorganic nature of the Mexican historical process. It is a problem Mexico shares with the rest of Spanish America, originating, according to the account Paz gives in *El laberinto de la soledad*, in the disjunction between the ideology mobilized by the Spanish American revolutionaries in their struggle for independence and the actual political and economic interests they represented. In brief, in Spanish America the imported ideology of liberal democracy served only "to dress up the survivals of the colonial system in modern garb."[9] The lack of congruence between ideas and reality transformed Spanish American political culture and intellectual discourse into a realm of simulation, a condition that reached its apogee in Mexico during the regime of Porfirio Díaz, when the accentuation of the country's feudal character was masked by the official adherence of the government and its intellectual supporters to the ideals of progress, science, industrialization, and free trade, all the ideals, that is, of European liberalism.[10]

Although the description of the problem of the gap between the legal nation and the real nation is generally clear, it is often less easy to say how different authors believe this gap might be closed. Should the legal nation make a more sustained effort to mold the real nation according to its ideals, or should the legal nation allow itself to be shaped by the forces springing up from the real nation? In a 1976 essay, "El espejo indiscreto," Paz offers a reformulation of the problem that reveals the difficulty of resolving this dilemma. Paz describes Mexican independence as an act of self-negation: the break with Spain signaled Mexico's desire to become a modern nation, but because everything in the Mexican tradition was antithetical to modernity, such a step "demanded a sacrifice: that of ourselves."[11] Yet the impossibility of denying the weight of history meant that the project of modernity was destined to fail. Paz sums up the result of this misstep at the very inception of Mexican nationhood: "We are still not modern, but since then we wander in search of ourselves."[12] Mexico must become modern, but it must at the same time preserve its own identity. But how to reconcile these two demands?

A similar complication emerges from Fuentes's essayistic meditations on the real nation and the legal nation in Latin America.[13] Fuentes links this opposition to the opposition between localist and centralist energies in Latin American culture and politics, identifying the local with the real, and the central with the legal. But his portrait of the local—the bedrock of Latin American reality—is itself a deeply divided one. On the one hand, Fuentes presents the local as the source of a genuinely democratic Latin American culture. In *The Buried Mirror*, Fuentes rebukes Simón Bolívar for his promotion of a centralist, semidespotic system, and for his failure to consider "the alternative models of self-rule based on cultural loyalties that survived in many agrarian communities."[14] In *Valiente mundo nuevo*, the work in which he offers the most sustained discussion of the problem of the real nation and the legal nation, Fuentes attributes Latin America's political troubles to "the contradiction between a de jure central authority and the development of multiple de facto local authorities."[15] On the other hand, however, Fuentes also describes the real nation as profoundly retrograde and antidemocratic in nature. In *Valiente mundo nuevo* he proposes that from colonial times to the present the legal nation has always erected a façade that conceals "the unjust and squalid aspect of the real nation" (16). In colonial times the real nation was the world of "the haciendas, mines and small villages," a world dominated by the despotic power of "landowners, local bosses and foremen" (194). Described in these terms, the local dimension of Latin American reality can hardly be expected to function as the wellspring of an authentically pluralist culture.

In *Valiente mundo nuevo* Fuentes suggests that the disjunction between the real nation and the legal nation is not only the source of many of Latin America's political problems, but also of the continent's creativity: "between the real nation and the legal nation, the writers, artists and thinkers of Ibero America have struggled to outline an image of cultural continuity; a struggle that at times pitted them against their own fertile contradictions" (16). But to construct the image of Latin American cultural continuity may involve reflecting on the very schism—between the real nation and the legal nation—that presents the gravest obstacles to the achievement of continuity. This is precisely what we see happening in *La campaña*, a novel that deals explicitly with the topic of the real nation and the legal nation, a novel, moreover, in which the author's contradictory attitudes with regard to this problem can be seen to clash with the overarching goal of articulating a vision of cultural cohesion. In

Cristóbal Nonato, a slightly earlier novel that also includes a meditation on the theme of the real nation and the legal nation, the very
project of outlining a vision of cultural cohesion is discarded in
favor of an alternative vision of mobility and rupture.

The Dislocation of Culture

In a recent lecture at Rutgers University, Fuentes discussed the persistence of the problem of poverty in Mexico and elsewhere in Latin
America. He suggested that because neither the state nor the market can be counted upon to bridge the divide between the developed
and the underdeveloped segments of Latin American society, it is up
to civil society to tackle the problem, to bring about, as he put it, an
encounter between the two Mexicos, the two Brazils, and so on.[16]
The topic of civil society has been a staple of Fuentes's essays,
newspaper articles, and speeches for several decades now.[17] He has
also sought to use some of his novels as vehicles for the exploration
of civil society, though with somewhat more ambiguous and complicated results.

First published in 1987, *Cristóbal Nonato* is set in 1992, a year for
which Fuentes projects a series of catastrophes for Mexico of
almost unimaginable proportions. The national debt has reached the
staggering—and symbolic—amount of $1,492 billion (by the end of
the novel it has grown to the equally symbolic amount of $1,992 bil-
lion). The population of Mexico City now stands at 30 million, with
air pollution so severe that the city is generally known as
Makesicko City. At the same time, the nation has literally disintegrated: Northern Mexico has seceded in order to become part of a
new entity known as Mexamerica, U.S. marines have occupied
Veracruz, an oil consortium has taken over the southern states, and
Club Med controls the Yucatán. But Fuentes also evokes a catastrophe from the recent past—the earthquake of September 1985—and
sees in the response to this disaster the hopeful signs of the emergence of a civil society in Mexico.

Faced with the incompetence of the authorities, the people of
Mexico City improvise their own rescue operations, saving many

lives, and in the process demonstrating the irrelevance of all forms of officialdom: "They had organized by themselves, and they knew perfectly well what they had to do, without instructions from a government, a party or a leader" (49/40). Much later in the novel, Federico Robles Chacón, the son of Federico Robles and Hortensia Chacón from *La región más transparente*, and now a minister in the Mexican government, is charged with "theorizing" this episode in recent Mexican history: "What moved us that day? The sense of solidarity, a humanitarian feeling, the need to save our neighbors. . . . That morning, the man next to me was my fellow man. I was another fellow man. We went beyond institutions. . . . Civil society transcended the state" (469/442–43). Yet in the novel's present, Robles Chacón is engaged in a political enterprise that appears to involve not a strengthening but a defanging of civil society. In fact, Robles Chacón's role in *Cristóbal Nonato* reveals a much greater pessimism on Fuentes's part concerning Mexico's civil society than he has ever expressed in his nonfiction.

Robles Chacón has concluded that the key problem for Mexico is the symbolic legitimation of power. Against the belief of his fellow ministers in the power of statistics, Robles Chacón argues that only the imagination can resolve Mexico's crisis. What the government needs to prop up its authority is a powerful symbol. Robles Chacón finds what he is looking for in a young woman of unremarkable appearance from the secretarial pool in his ministry, transforming her into the bizarre creature of the country's dreams: "Mamadoc," Mother and Doctor of all Mexicans, emblem of national unity and continuity. One character, Homero Fagoaga, a grammarian and politician, admires Mamadoc because she represents a "singular synthesis" (69/60) of Mexico's different components. Although her name connects her to Papadoc, the infamous Haitian dictator, Mamadoc's effectiveness seems to derive in the first place from the fact that she is linked to both the great figures of traditional Mexican femininity (she is likened to Coatlicue, La Malinche, and the Virgin of Guadalupe) and to the most famous "gringa" movie stars (she is compared to Lana Turner, Marilyn Monroe, and Mae West). Mamadoc belongs in part to ancient myth, in part to mass culture. She builds a bridge between Mexico's roots in a native past, and its dreams of a universal future. Robles Chacón himself also possesses this synthetic quality, for he is compared both to Bishop Juan de Zumárraga, to whom the Indian Juan Diego in the year 1531 revealed the miraculous appearance of the Virgin of Guadalupe, *and* to Danton, the French Jacobin leader. The comparisons suggest that Robles Chacón's authority is rooted in myth and tradition, as well as in reason and revolution. He represents, in a sense, an encounter of the two Mexicos. Yet in Robles Chacón's case the encounter seems more absurd than inspiring.

Near the beginning of the novel, Robles Chacón reflects on Mexico's need for "new civic powers, a real civil society" (30/22). But instead of stimulating the growth of civil society, he creates Mamadoc, who takes the place of civil society while simultaneously blocking its development. Robles Chacón explains, "In ancient times, when the people's spirits were low, the emperors would give them bread and circuses" (40/31). In contemporary Mexico, when popular discontent is on the rise, the rulers resort to "a visit by the Pope or a fight with the gringos" (40/32). Mamadoc fulfils the same goal of distracting the population, but she does it better because she is "an institution all our own" (40/32). Mamadoc's regime is fueled by endless "contests and celebrations" (314/287), which provide the nation's citizens with a permanent source of distraction. Her slogan—"UNION AND OBLIVION" (314/287)—reflects her intent to smother the very thing Robles Chacón had proclaimed Mexico needed: an active, self-organizing, diverse civil society. Mamadoc promotes a sense of cohesion among all Mexicans, but it is the cohesion of a stupefied mass of people.

If civil society is the place where the real nation and the legal nation meet, then the Mamadoc plot in *Cristóbal Nonato* offers a farcical version of such an encounter. As the brainchild of a man consistently referred to as Dr. Federico Robles Chacón, Mamadoc is clearly one more invention of the nation's educated elite. Yet she has been conceived in such a way that the Mexican masses can sublimate in her all their unfulfilled desires. In fact, Mamadoc possesses "a vulva sewn up with golden thread and embellished with two dozen diamonds sharpened like tiny shark teeth" (41/33), just so that a convincing case can be made that "NO ONE SHALL POSSESS HER BUT THE PEOPLE" (45/37). In the description of the current of sexual desire that flows between Mamadoc and the masses, Fuentes offers a fiercely comical interpretation of the very notion of national unity. The idea of sex as an allegory of national unity is replayed in an equally satirical fashion in the conclusion of the Mamadoc plot. Mamadoc finally rebels against her role, refusing to perform any more symbolic ceremonies, and throwing herself at the feet of Robles Chacón, with whom she has fallen in love. As Mamadoc wraps herself around his legs, Robles Chacón insists she must not shirk her duties. "Laws are meant to be obeyed," he says, to which she replies, "But not carried out!" (511/482), an exchange that evokes the standard wisdom about how Spain governed its empire, and thus offers a comic modulation on the theme of the disjunction between the real nation and the legal nation. Here the meeting between the two can transpire only under the sign of mockery. In fact, the narrator refuses to tell us whether Robles Chacón succumbs to Mamadoc's pleadings, claiming that he wishes to leave the destinies of the characters of his novel in the hands of his readers. But the open ending of the Mamadoc sequence is not only a call for reader participation; it also reflects the unresolved nature of Fuentes's treatment of the topics of civil society and of the relationship between the real nation and the legal nation in *Cristóbal Nonato*. It is significant that after aborting the scene between Mamadoc and Robles Chacón the narrator shifts, in a chapter entitled (in honor of Norman Mailer) "What Are We Doing In Veracruz?", to a satirical account of an imaginary U.S. occupation of Veracruz, as if Fuentes himself, faced with the impossibility of projecting a convincing image of national cohesion, should have opted instead for a fight with the gringos.

Robles Chacón has rivals inside as well as outside the government. In the latter category we find a young man named Matamoros Moreno, also known as the Ayatollah. He first appears as an untalented writer who cannot get his work into print. Eventually, he channels his frustration and resentment into politics.

Building on a core constituency of long-haul truckers, he succeeds in mesmerizing the masses with an ideological mishmash composed of Mexican machismo, religious fundamentalism, and 60s-style liberationism. In some ways, the Ayatollah's movement appears to emerge from the depths of Mexican society, and to offer an attractive model of popular self-organization. The section of the narrative dealing with the Ayatollah's insurrection opens with a description of Mexico's highways as a kind of autonomous zone or liberated territory within the nation (439/413). The truckers are hardy individualists in search of some principle of solidarity. Yet when the masses mobilized by Matamoros converge upon Mexico City, they inspire terror more than anything else. One character sees the movement as a joyous carnival (462/435), but it is another character, named Fernando Benítez (based on the real Fernando Benítez, Fuentes's friend), who comes closer to expressing the novel's overall perspective when he warns, "Here the only thing we're going to see is force disguised as religion. We shall start out in the realm of the sacred and we shall end up with a government of priests" (452/426). Or, as the not entirely disinterested Robles Chacón says to Matamoros, "you reach into your hat for a paradise and you pull out a hell" (471/443).

In *Cristóbal Nonato*, Fuentes laments the disintegration of his country, but at the same time mocks and satirizes all attempts at reunifying Mexico around a transcendent symbol or utopian political project. Whereas in *Valiente mundo nuevo*, as we saw, Fuentes describes the Latin American artist's task as the creation of an image of cultural continuity, in *Cristóbal Nonato* he declines to offer a convincing representation of the civil society he regards as the best instrument for promoting such continuity, and instead chooses to celebrate the values of rupture, discontinuity, and incompleteness. This is particularly clear from a series of semiessayistic passages that offer meditations on such topics as the relativity of knowledge, the multiplicity of language, and the fragmented nature of modernity. In one passage, the narrator offers a brief history of modernity that encompasses don Quixote's discovery that the world does not resemble itself, Tristram Shandy's discovery of the divorce between language and reality, and Emma Bovary's discovery of herself as other than herself, and culminates with the image of Kafka turning into an insect (106).[18] This idea that modernity equals dislocation accounts for the novel's idiosyncratic, multileveled prose. It also seems to underlie one of Fuentes's most intriguing inventions in *Cristóbal Nonato*: a mysterious urban gathering-place known as the Bulevar, a space defined in the first place by the fact that it has no location: "The Bulevar changed location every week, sometimes every twenty-four hours. . . . It was . . . the place to see and be seen . . . but now with this scandalously wonderful singularity: where that meeting place was no one knew, as secret as language (the new languages) it mutated every day, every hour" (326/299). In this fluid space, the people of Mexico City can satisfy their desire for community while at the same evading the threat of external control. The Bulevar avoids the inertia of the real nation as well as the coerciveness of the legal nation. Yet it is significant that Fuentes's description of the Bulevar is essentially a set-piece; it plays no role in the development of the plot. As a result, the Bulevar remains, within the overall conception of the novel, a powerless institution (or anti-institution).

There are two possible explanations for the absence in *Cristóbal Nonato* of a strong vision of political hope for Mexico. This absence may simply constitute one more example of the disjunction between Fuentes's political vision and his literary imagination. In his political statements, Fuentes tends to offer concrete proposals for bringing about a better future for Mexico and Latin America. In addition, he presents a positive view of the role of the writer in the construction of such a future. Yet his literary imagination is often drawn towards satire, in particular the negative, destructive dimension of satire. The novel becomes a device for exploding Mexico's social and political illusions, rather than for exploring the possibilities of social and political transformation. However, it may be that Fuentes does have a vision of renewal for Mexico to put forward in *Cristóbal Nonato*, a vision for which the freedom of the Bulevar acts as an allegory. Yet insofar as this vision hinges on an experience of mobility and dislocation, it would clearly be inconsistent to stabilize any of the textual spaces that function as vehicles for this vision, including the Bulevar.

Carlos Fuentes, Author of the Quixote

Cristóbal Nonato imagines the future; *La campaña* reflects on the past. Fuentes returns in *La campaña* to the Spanish American wars of independence in order to reimagine the original crisis out of which the independent nations of the continent emerged. Indirectly, the novel also offers a meditation on where the Spanish American nations might have gone wrong in their efforts to forge an independent existence for themselves. In making a young Creole intellectual the protagonist of his novel, Fuentes centers the reader's attention on the role of *ideas* in the making of the Spanish American revolutions. Historians commonly assert that the impact of Enlightenment ideas on the educated elite in Spanish America was one of the principal causes of the movement for independence.[19] By opening his novel with a description of the intoxicating effects of the forbidden works of Voltaire, Rousseau, and Diderot on three young men, Varela, Dorrego, and Baltasar Bustos, Fuentes appears to be illustrating this thesis. Yet Varela (who is the narrator of the novel) insists that they are seduced not only by their "cosmopolitan readings," but also by "a new idea of faith in the nation, its geography, its history" (11/5). This passion for native realities had been stimulated by the Jesuit instructors who, returning in secret from the exile imposed upon them by the Spanish Bourbon régime in 1767,[20] had taught a new generation of Americans "that American flora and fauna exist, that there are American mountains and rivers, and, above all, that we have a history that isn't Spanish, but Argentine, Chilean, Mexican" (12/6). This double passion—for foreign ideas and native realities—and above all the difficulty of reconciling them with each other, establishes the terms for Fuentes's exploration of the Spanish American revolutions. The disjunction between ideas and realities prepares the way for a long list of related binary opposites which the novel brings into play: between theory and practice, rhetoric and action, institutions and customs, the universal and the local, intellectuals and the people, in sum, between the legal nation on the one hand and the real nation on the other. In relating the adventures of Baltasar Bustos during the Spanish American wars of independence, the novel stages a confrontation between Baltasar's conception of how the world ought to be and how it in fact is. For Fuentes, this clash provides a key to understanding the trajectory not only of the wars of independence themselves, but of the very project of modernity in Spanish America. For in a very real sense Spanish America can be said to have embarked on the struggle to create modern societies with the battle for independence, a process that involved the effort to remodel Spanish American societies according to a set of ideals largely imported from abroad as well as the attempt to determine the shape of a native identity.

Baltasar's encounter with the real nature of his continent is a humbling one. He must learn that the books he has read do not provide him with a reliable guide to the world he lives in. Baltasar derives his notion of how things ought to be from the Enlightenment philosophers: "Everyone knew that Baltasar Bustos had read all the books of the Enlightenment" (26/19–20). But in leaving his library in order to become a warrior, he puts his readings to a severe test. The narrator compares Baltasar to don Quixote for his "foolhardy . . . decision to test the validity of his readings in reality" (26/20). The comparison suggests that Baltasar behaves more like a character in a novel than like a person in the real world. Like don Quixote, Baltasar will have great difficulty recognizing the distance that separates books from life.

Paradoxically, it is from his reading that Baltasar derives his conviction of the need for a return to nature.[21] Baltasar is a follower of Rousseau: when he returns for a visit to his family's *estancia* on the pampa, he brings with him four of his favorite books, all of them by Rousseau. No doubt, it is his reading of Rousseau that shapes Baltasar's conception of his trip as an attempt to "to return to nature and in nature find 'the hours of solitude and meditation' that would enable him to be himself, without obstacles, truly be what nature wanted him to be" (39/31–32). Thus, it is from books, artifacts linked to an urban, cosmopolitan culture, that Baltasar learns that he must search for his true self in nature. But the pampa has a disappointment in store for Baltasar. At first, he is hopeful that with the city behind him the conditions are right for a wedding of spirit and nature (40/32). Yet it is not long before the promise of an ecstatic embrace of self with landscape begins to dissipate. The pampa loses its semblance of grandeur and serenity: "Its creeks, its peach trees, its leagues and leagues of hard lime soil inhabited only by mad ostriches struck him as so many bleak and contrasting accidents" (40/33). Everything is small, irregular, incoherent. Wherever he looks, Baltasar sees "problems, contradictions, untenable options" (41/33).

In the end, however, it is not the pampa itself but its inhabitants who pose the greatest problems for Baltasar. When he arrives at his family home—where his father and sister live surrounded by gauchos—Baltasar begins to sound more like a reader of Sarmiento than Rousseau. The gauchos fill Baltasar with revulsion. He recalls that it was from the savagery they represented that he fled to Buenos Aires at the age of seventeen in order to become a civilized person. The gauchos bring out the very worst in Baltasar: ignoring his father's advice that charity begins at home, Baltasar takes pleasure in humiliating them. He uses his reading to justify his failure to act according to his principle that all human beings are equal: he sees in each gaucho "a Genghis Khan, with his own personal history of violence, superstition, and stupidity, the kind Voltaire had condemned for all time" (44/36). What most offends Baltasar is the nomadic way of life of the gauchos, who he sees as "ambulatory negations of the sedentary life he identified with civilization" (44/36). All in all, the gauchos spoil the idyllic vision of the natural world that Baltasar has acquired from his reading of Rousseau. They provide the first of the novel's lessons on the disjunction between the nation as it exists in the mind of an intellectual and the nation as it is in reality.

On his visit to his parental home, Baltasar observes the first signs of the profound social changes that will soon obliterate the "slow, autarkic world" (70/62) to which his father belongs. The educated, urban elite wishes to remake the country according to its own ideals. Its preferred tool is the law. Baltasar's trip to the pampa coincides with the proclamation of a new law with which the government in Buenos Aires hopes to solve the "problem" of the gaucho: "The government of Buenos Aires had passed a law against nomads. The gauchos were to abandon their barbarous, wandering, unproductive customs and settle down on ranches or farms or in industry" (69/61). Gauchos who do not obey the new law will be condemned to forced labor, or drafted into the army. Baltasar is convinced that the new law will have beneficial effects on the country: "Most of these gauchos will end up in the army for being rebels. Then they'll demand that careers in the military be open to all" (72/64). By democratizing the army, the gauchos will indirectly democratize Argentine society. But the gauchos themselves demonstrate a much better grasp than Baltasar of the consequences of the new law. They do not actually speak for themselves in this chapter. But Baltasar's father reads their thoughts: "Who do these city folk think they are? Do they really think they can rule us from there? Maybe we ought to go there and govern those sons of bitches ourselves. Let's see who wants to take charge of the gauchos. Let's see who wants to be our chief. Whoever it is, we'll follow him to the death, against the capital city, against the law" (70/62).

The legal nation—the nation of laws and books, of rhetoric and reason—does not know how to come to terms with the real nation. In this particular episode, the legal nation is clearly undermined by its own contradictions. Baltasar hopes for a reconciliation between self and world, but he seems to think he can only have it if he can get the gauchos out of the way first. The liberal government in Buenos Aires believes in freedom and equality, but only on its own terms. The narrative does not at this stage present us with noble ideas or just laws foundering on a recalcitrant reality. Rather, we see ideals being jettisoned as soon as they have to be put into practice, and laws having effects that blatantly oppose the spirit that supposedly informs them.

In the next few chapters, however, the conflict between the real nation and the legal nation begins to take on a more complicated cast. As he follows the revolution into upper Peru, Baltasar begins

to change. He grows closer to the people, and becomes more skeptical of his own rhetoric. Yet the narrative neither denigrates
Baltasar's ideals nor romanticizes the native world. At first, Baltasar
is still his arrogant, short-sighted self. One of his first actions upon
arriving in upper Peru is to read out loud in the main square of a
local town a decree declaring the liberty of the Indians. Baltasar's
intentions are no doubt noble, yet the episode stands as one of the
most vivid, painfully ironic illustrations of the distance separating
Baltasar's world from the indigenous world.[22] To begin with, the
scene has been staged by a local priest and revolutionary who forces
Baltasar to read his proclamation while seated on a horse, explaining that in this land "the horse is authority. . . . The horse defeated
them" (82/72). Thus, Baltasar invests himself with the authority of
the conquistador in order to declare the end of the era of Indian
servitude. But worse than the contradiction between Baltasar's
speech and the position from which he pronounces it is the fact that
the Indians he addresses know no Spanish and so do not understand a word of what he says. In a letter to his friends Dorrego and
Varela back in Buenos Aires, Baltasar describes how as he sat on
his horse he felt the temptation of exercising his power with impuni-
ty over those weaker than himself. Yet even as he launches his radical decrees over the heads of the local population, Baltasar has a
secret intuition that the Indians have "their own roads to liberty, not
necessarily . . . those we have piously devised" (92/82).

But where lies the Indians' *own* path? After Baltasar comes
down from his horse, a series of episodes follow in which he is
brought face to face with the native world. In each episode, Baltasar
has a guide who leads him on his journey of discovery. His first
guide is the priest who had arranged for Baltasar to read his decree
to the Indians, the colorfully named Ildefonso de las Muñecas. The
priest proposes an exchange: he accepts the law Baltasar has pronounced, and offers him a woman in return (86/76–77). The next
scene shows Baltasar having sex with a nameless native woman.
The woman acts as a mediator: by engaging in sexual intercourse
with her, Baltasar obtains access to the world that surrounds him.
He experiences sex as a return to the earth, an encounter with the

senses, a recreation of the world. The native woman represents the realm of the concrete, and insofar as this is the case, she is inserted into an opposition with the realm of the abstract, represented in this context by the law. Thanks to father Ildefonso, Baltasar loses his virginity, and gains a knowledge of the Indian world. But this knowledge is in the first place a recognition of the distance that separates the palpable quality of native existence from the abstract codes Baltasar brings to bear on this world. This sense of disjunction between the two worlds is emphasized by the episode's conclusion. Baltasar wakes up to find that his lover has disappeared. Apparently the woman is dead, perhaps as a punishment for having slept with a Creole officer. In the meantime, father Ildefonso, now referred to as "the *caudillo* Ildefonso," instead of busying himself with the implementation of Baltasar's edicts, leads a raid on the local treasury. The aim is clearly to grab power, not to enforce the law. An old man explains the situation to Baltasar: "These auxiliary armies exist for themselves, not to serve the Buenos Aires revolution. Fortunately, or unfortunately, it is they who have filled the void between the Crown and the republic. They are here. You merely come, promise things that are never done, and then go" (90/80–81). The local caudillos spring directly from an autochthonous reality. This reality consists of deeply sedimented experiences that cannot be swept aside by the decrees of a remote, alien authority that does not even keep the promises it makes. As the old man puts it, "There will be time for laws. Eternity can't be changed in a day" (90/81).

The old man, whose name is Simón Rodríguez, guides Baltasar through the next stage of his encounter with the Indian world. Simón begins by instructing Baltasar that having first addressed the Indians from the heights, he must now descend down to their "poor land," which, as he will discover, has been "oppressed by the laws of poverty and slavery," but also "liberated by magic and dreams" (92/83). The point about magic and dreams is illustrated when Simón leads Baltasar into a cave, and from there to the edge of an abyss, from where they look out over a city made of light. Simón tells Baltasar that for him he has kept in reserve "the vision of El

Dorado . . . the city of gold of the Indian world" (97/87). But the lesson to be extracted from this vision of a hidden world is a complicated one. To begin with, it is not clear whether the city of light is real or just a projection of Baltasar's mind. For Simón, the meaning of El Dorado is that "everything you imagine is true. Today we happened on one fantasy among many possible fantasies" (99/89). But if this is so, can Baltasar be said to have learned anything about the world of the Indians? Also interesting—and disconcerting—is the fact that the vision produces feelings of vertigo and nausea in Baltasar. The light of El Dorado scribbles messages across every door and roof of the city. At first, the messages are illegible, but then, in points of light, a name appears before Baltasar's eyes, the name of the woman he loves, Ofelia Salamanca, repeated over and over again. Next, Ofelia herself appears, provocatively naked, mocking Baltasar's desire for her. Once again, Fuentes uses a woman's body, hovering ambiguously between presence and absence, between the real and the unreal, as an image of what is *other* for Baltasar. But Baltasar interprets the frustration of his desire as a sign that the romantic dream of a reconciliation of subject and object is indeed just a dream: "He was convinced that he'd reached the remotest past, the origin of all things, and that this magic origin of secrecy and illusion was not that of a perfect assimilation of man with nature but, again, an intolerable divorce, a separation that wounded him in the most certain of his convictions" (97/87). By the end of the chapter, Baltasar is seen in a house in Cochabamba recovering from his wounds and preparing for his next adventure.

The next person charged by the narrative with educating Baltasar is Miguel Lanza, the pale-faced, blue-eyed commander of an army of one hundred guerillas and five hundred Indians. Lanza's army operates in the space between the revolutionary army from Buenos Aires and the royalist forces from Lima. But although the *montoneros* are numerically inferior to the two other armies, they have the advantage of belonging to the region for which they fight. Lanza represents local interests. He knows the Inquisivi region, where he hopes to found a miniature republic, like the back of his hand. Everywhere he goes, he is accompanied by an Indian named Baltasar Cárdenas, a man suspicious of words, and wholly immersed in the realm of deeds: "There were so many things waiting to be done that saying them was unnecessary" (104/95). Baltasar Bustos, who has decided to admire everything he is not, throws himself into the life of a *montonero*: "He became identical to all the others; he ate what they ate, slept when they slept" (106/97). He listens to Lanza explain that the word liberty does not mean the same thing in Buenos Aires and upper Peru: "But if down there liberty became one with the law that proclaimed it, here . . . liberty was inseparable from an equality that had never before been known in these lands" (111/101). Liberty is inseparable from equality. But Lanza also stands for an ideal of fraternity (he treats Baltasar like a brother) which ends up undermining liberty (Baltasar will not be allowed to leave Lanza's territory). In Inquisivi, Lanza's will is the unwritten law, and everybody must think like him. In the end, Baltasar disguises himself as an Indian in order to escape from the prison Lanza has created for him.

La campaña is on one level a satire of the attempt to apply Enlightenment ideals to the specific conditions of Spanish America in the early nineteenth century. It illustrates the thesis that many of Spanish America's ills are attributable to the profound disjunction between, on the one hand, the ideas and rhetoric, the laws and books of a small educated elite, and on the other hand the practices and actions, the beliefs and customs of the vast majority of the continent's people. Fuentes's initial choice to write *La campaña* as a kind of Bildungsroman indicates that his aim is to rebuke Spanish America's cosmopolitan intellectuals for not knowing more about their own culture. By depicting in *La campaña* the process whereby a young idealist is initiated into the reality of his own continent, and by presenting this process as a beneficial and necessary one, Fuentes implies that the development of the nations of Spanish America will depend at least in part on the willingness of the continent's intellectuals to leave behind the abstract schemas of the legal nation in order to embrace the concrete life forms of the real nation. The novel proposes that its young hero, having received an education from books, must now receive a more important education from reality.

Yet underneath this polemical message, the novel puts forward a somewhat different perspective on the problem of the relationship between the legal nation and the real nation. Certain episodes in *La campaña* suggest that although the legal nation is clearly not up to task of creating new societies in Spanish America, this does not mean that the law is necessarily bad, nor that reality is necessarily good. Fuentes has often argued that the legal nation's failure to come to terms with the real conditions of Spanish American life created a void in Spanish American society that the caudillos rushed to fill.[23] Yet there is also an argument to be made that the caudillos did not emerge out of nowhere in order to fill the gap between the real nation and the legal nation, but rather that the caudillos are themselves the expression of the real nation. But as manifestations of local realities, the caudillos are highly ambiguous figures. They can be seen either as the embodiment of democratic political traditions that have not been allowed to flourish because the legal nation has not recognized them for what they are, or as the incarnation of autochthonous political traditions of a profoundly authoritarian nature. In *La campaña* Fuentes presents both perspectives simultaneously. This is clear from the role of Miguel Lanza in the novel: on the one hand, Lanza offers Baltasar a lesson on the importance of linking freedom with equality, and on the other hand, he seems intent on creating a mini-state where absolute allegiance is expected from everyone. Baltasar absorbs the lesson about equality, then leaves for more congenial surroundings.

This ambivalent perspective on the real nation goes hand in hand with a more complex appraisal of the legal nation. In his response to the law against nomadism issued by the Buenos Aires government, Baltasar had seemed harsh and naive. In declaring the freedom of the Indians of upper Peru, Baltasar appears deluded, but noble. For surely the mockery aimed by the narrative at Baltasar's high-handedness cannot be taken to imply that the principles he enunciates are themselves objectionable. The law freeing the Indians of their servitude simply cannot be judged in the same way as the law depriving the gauchos of their freedom of movement. By alluding to the *mita*, the system of forced labor imposed on the Andean Indians by the Creole elite, the narrative clearly shifts the terms of the conflict. In the chapter on the pampa, traditional Creole authority is embodied in the figure of Baltasar's father, who is described as a firm, but gentle patriarch whose power serves as a necessary brake on the anarchic impulses of the local population (58/50–51). But there is no such justification for the *mita*, which father Ildefonso describes as "the great reality and the great curse of this land" (84–85/75). Indeed, in the context of a social and economic order governed by the *mita*, the problem with the law must be redefined. The criticism aimed at the legal nation now appears to be not so much that its codes and conventions are remote from reality, as that it fails to enforce the principles for which it stands. When Simón Rodríguez complains that the Buenos Aires government makes promises it does not keep, his criticism targets not the promise itself, but the failure to fulfill it. When Baltasar acknowledges the sad truth that "the Creole republic was going to turn its back on the slavery issue; it was going to reform it only on paper" (65/57), the problem is not that the legal nation refuses to take account of the real state of affairs in Spanish America, but that it declines to make a genuine effort to change that state of affairs.

Fuentes hesitates between two different prescriptions: sometimes he seems to suggest that the legal nation must reform itself; at other times, it is the real nation that must be reformed. He bridges the contradiction with the help of father Julián Ríos, Baltasar's Jesuit preceptor who pops up in Lima, the next stop on Baltasar's pilgrimage. Father Ríos wishes to convince Baltasar that however abominable Spanish America's past may appear to him, without that past the continent will never make the transition to modernity: "Would the South American patriots ever understand that without that past they would never be what they so desired: paradigms of modernity?" (144/134). Father Ríos does not reject the legal nation's goal of modernization. He simply believes he has a better idea of how to achieve modernity: "a past renewed is the only guarantee of modernity" (144/135). It is, of course, significant that

Fuentes places this message in the mouth of a priest. For Fuentes sees Catholicism as an essential ingredient of the Spanish American tradition that must be preserved and revitalized in order to prevent the road to modernity from becoming a road to alienation. The seriousness with which Fuentes takes this argument is clear from the fact that the last stop on Baltasar's journey through Spanish America is Mexico, and his last reality-instructor is a priest, albeit an excommunicated one.

When Baltasar disembarks in Veracruz, the first thing he sees is a firing-squad of the Spanish Army executing an effigy of the Virgin of Guadalupe. He quickly concludes that he has arrived in "the strangest land in the Americas" (209/197). But there is a lesson in this strangeness. The Mexican movement for independence has a social and religious content (missing from the movements elsewhere in Spanish America) that suggests a unique way of bridging the divide between the real nation and the legal nation. The first Mexican revolutionaries did not rally around slogans imported from abroad, but around a native symbol, the Virgin of Guadalupe.[24] The earliest leaders of the independence movement in Mexico were two priests: Miguel Hidalgo and José María Morelos. It is in order to highlight the role of religion in the Mexican war of independence that Fuentes creates the character of Anselmo Quintana, a defrocked priest who spells out the lessons of the Mexican experience to Baltasar. But Quintana is not only "the heir of Hidalgo and Morelos" (212/200); he is also "the last defender . . . of an egalitarian revolution in North America" (213/200). The Mexican priests led what the narrator describes as "the only peasant and Indian uprising" (210/197). They fought for a genuine social revolution, rather than for largely cosmetic changes in the law. The egalitarianism and traditionalism of the Mexican revolutionaries suggested solutions to dilemmas that the modernizing, cosmopolitan elites of Spanish America barely got around to thinking about.

But Fuentes does not use the Mexican experience merely in order to disparage the modernizing project of the legal nation. Quintana is a highly complex character. In fact, one of his messages to Baltasar is: "always be a problem" (242/229). When Baltasar

arrives at Quintana's encampment in Orizaba, he finds himself surrounded by a mountain of documents—the archives of the revolution. This huge paper trail is the work of the innumerable scribes
and lawyers who fill the encampment—"theologians of the law"
(215/202) who believe that only what is written is real. Quintana
expresses considerable disdain for what he calls "these constipated
lawyers who fill my head with projects and laws" (223/210). But
soon after, we see Quintana manifesting his respect for these
learned men who risk their lives for the sake of "an honorable place
in history" (227/214). The lawyers may not know how to fight a
battle, yet Quintana declares that "Never in the history of Mexico
has there been, nor will there ever be in the future, a band of men
more patriotic and honorable" than they (228/214–15).

Quintana's recognition of the interdependence of arms and letters reflects a broader inclination on his part to search for a reconciliation of opposites. Quintana notes that for Baltasar "there can be
no freedom with religion, independence with a church, or reason
with faith" (230/217). Quintana insists on joining what Baltasar
wishes to keep separate: "my political rebellion is inseparable from
my spiritual rebellion" (230/216). His vision of a free nation, without slavery, hunger, or ignorance, would not have been possible for
Quintana without his faith in God (242/229). Quintana reminds
Baltasar that Spanish America is a continent "marked by the symbols, values, follies, the crimes and the dreams of Christianity in the
New World" (243/230). Young intellectuals like Baltasar want to
shed the past. They long to be "European, modern" (243/230).
Quintana argues that this kind of leap out of one's past is neither
possible nor desirable. The people of Spanish America must pre-
serve the multiple dimensions of their culture: "What I'm asking
you is that we not sacrifice anything, son, not the magic of the
Indians, not the theology of the Christians, not the reason of our
European contemporaries" (243/230).

Quintana's speech to Baltasar is perhaps the culminating
moment of the novel. His simultaneous affirmation of the different
components of Mexico's multileveled cultural heritage can be seen
as a strategy for bridging the divide between the real nation and the

legal nation. Quintana appears to offer a solution to the problem that has been plaguing Baltasar since the beginning of his journey. Yet it would be a mistake to suggest that Quintana provides a final answer to the dilemmas explored in *La campaña*. On one level, the novel expresses Fuentes's hope that Spanish America will find a way of harmonizing the fragments of which its culture is composed. On another level, *La campaña* manifests a deep skepticism with regard to the very possibility of a unified culture. Insofar as *La campaña* is a novel about the beginnings of modernity in Spanish America, it is important to recall that Fuentes has frequently put forward the thesis that modernity commences with the rupture of the unified world-view of the Middle Ages. In a recent text, Fuentes offers a very precise date for this event: "For me, the modern world begins when don Quixote leaves his village and discovers that the world does not resemble the books he has read."[25] Don Quixote leads us into "an open field in which there is a constant divorce between writing and life."[26] But once modernity is defined in this way, the split between the real nation and the legal nation, which Fuentes has often depicted as a typically Spanish American problem, must be viewed in an entirely different light. Octavio Paz has recently argued that "the Modern Age, from the Renaissance onwards, has been the age of rupture: for over five hundred years we have been living the discord between ideas and beliefs, philosophy and tradition, science and faith."[27]

Does this mean that Spanish America is a quintessentially modern culture? I will not try to answer such a broad question here. But the definition of modernity offered by Paz and Fuentes does help in reading *La campaña*. For Baltasar, like don Quixote, is a character on the threshold of modernity. Baltasar repeats don Quixote's discovery of the divorce between text and reality. But he makes this discovery in a work that proposes that this divorce is an inexpungeable feature of our era. *La campaña*, then, presents us with the image of an unresolved conflict in Fuentes's outlook. On the one hand, the novel reflects his desire to suggest solutions to what he regards as the fundamental problem of the split between the real nation and the legal nation in Latin America. On the other hand, the novel proposes that text and reality, the real nation and the legal nation, can in fact never be reconciled with each other.

Whither the Latin American Intellectual?

In a recent newspaper article, Fuentes reveals a surprising source for the distinction between the real nation and the legal nation. In a discussion of a book by Julieta Campos, *¿Qué hacemos con los pobres?*, Fuentes alludes to Charles Maurras as the author of the opposition between "the legal nation, embodied in laws, projects and models, and the real nation, embodied in work, family, and home."[28] The reference to Maurras appears in the context of a sharp critique of neoliberalism, which Fuentes views as the current version of the modernizing model which the legal nation in Mexico has consistently sought to impose on the real nation. Fuentes insists that the neoliberal economic policies pursued during the administration of President Carlos Salinas, and continued by his successor, Ernesto Zedillo, have failed to solve Mexico's most serious problem, which, as Julieta Campos points out in her book, is the problem of poverty. They have, in fact, only made the problem worse. Fuentes argues that the fundamental aim of economic policy in Mexico should be to overcome "the constant divorce between the modern and traditional sectors of society."[29] And he goes on to offer some prescriptions for achieving this goal, such as a reform of the tax code, more emphasis on education, and, above all, a policy of "providing training, incentives and assistance in order to stimulate the productive activities" of the poorer sectors of society.[30]

Fuentes's reference to Maurras appears, then, in the context of an argument for a more equitable distribution of economic power in Mexico. It is an argument that reflects the progressive and social democratic nature of Fuentes's political orientation. But why, then, allude to Maurras—a royalist and ultra-Catholic, a man who revered order and hierarchy, and who detested modern democracy?[31] On an explicit level, Fuentes introduces Maurras in his discussion in order to rebuke Mexico's conservatives, whom Fuentes taxes with a lack of concern with the problem of social and national integration. Maurras's "rejection of national schizophrenias" makes him an exemplary conservative,[32] and very different from Mexico's conservatives, who with their sympathy for modernizing projects imported from abroad have aggravated the divisions within the Mexican nation. Implicitly, then, it is clear that Fuentes shares with Maurras a basic nationalism of outlook. Maurras's political views were characterized by his furious opposition to the three forces of Romanticism, Revolution, and Protestantism, all of which he regarded as foreign imports profoundly alien to France's authentic character. Fuentes has similarly been a consistent critic of foreign influence over his country. Yet underneath the shared concern with national interests there is a great deal that separates Fuentes from Maurras.

It is important not to make the mistake of thinking that Fuentes's reference to Maurras means that there is a rightist element to his thought, or to the theme of the real nation and the legal nation. In France itself, the left as well as the right has made use of this opposition in its polemics.[33] Moreover, the nationalist perspective which underpins the conceptual opposition Fuentes shares with Maurras has been, as Jorge Castañeda points out, a consistent feature of leftist political thought in Latin America.[34] Yet what most clearly distinguishes Fuentes from Maurras is that Fuentes invokes the opposition between the real nation and the legal nation in the context of an argument for social change. Fuentes shares the fundamentally modern and progressive belief in the human capacity to modify reality. Hence, for example, his insistence on the importance of education—the preferred tool for bringing about social change of a long list of Latin American modernizers.[35] Now, Maurras was a peculiar type of conservative, for alongside the predictable emphasis on limits, and on the givenness of human existence, there is in his thought a voluntaristic view of the political process that seems to owe a considerable debt to the very revolutionary tradition he professed to despise. At the same time, Fuentes is a peculiar type of progressive, for he combines a belief in social and political transformation with a deep concern for the preservation of social and cultural traditions. Yet while Maurras advocated the use of modern political techniques in order to restore a premodern social order, Fuentes defends tradition so that Mexico can participate more fully in modernity. It is this orientation toward modernity that explains why Fuentes never wholly condemns the legal nation, even when his main purpose seems to be to unmask its failings.

The question of Fuentes's relation to modernity is addressed by Carlos Alonso in a recent article on *La campaña* and Gabriel García Márquez's *El general en su laberinto*. Alonso argues that these two novels represent a succesful overcoming of the rhetoric of modernity, in particular of the utopianism which has dominated this rhetoric in Spanish American cultural discourse since Independence. Alonso describes *La campaña* and *El general en su laberinto* as "decidedly not the latest installment in that long-standing gesture that has sought to diagnose the ills of Spanish America in order to then argue for impossible or draconian solutions."[36] The analysis I undertook earlier in this chapter of *La campaña* revealed a profound uncertainty on Fuentes's part with regard to the challenge of modernity. But the fact that Fuentes continues to grapple with this challenge indicates that he has not yet put the problem of modernity behind him. For to refuse to argue for impossible solutions is not the same as giving up on the search for realistic solutions. Fuentes does not offer an unambiguous prescription for how to deal with the deep divisions of Spanish American culture.[37] But he does offer a critical perspective on the problem of the real nation and the legal nation in Spanish America, a perspective that indicates that Fuentes does not simply surrender "rhetorical or interpretive authority," as Alonso claims.[38] Moreover, any description of Fuentes's relationship to the rhetoric of modernity remains incomplete unless it takes his political writings into account. After all, Fuentes has always regarded his journalism as the appropriate site for diagnosing the ills of his country and continent, and for offering recommendations for their improvement. It is clear that Fuentes's interventions in current political debates are no longer informed by the belief that a fundamental transformation of society is just around the corner. In a recent newspaper article, Fuentes speaks of how a meeting with ex-president Raúl Alfonsín of Argentina helped him strengthen his faith "not in the instant democracies dreamed of by our nineteenth-century liberators, but in the patient democracy we can build for the twenty-first century."[39] And he goes on to speculate that perhaps the time has come for "a modest politics, on a human scale, a politics that is in harmony with the nation and its culture."[40] In speaking of a modest and patient politics, Fuentes appears to be turning away from the much grander visions of many of his precursors in the Spanish American cultural tradition, as well as from some of his own earlier positions. Yet Fuentes does not give up on a better future — however slowly constructed. In fact, Fuentes employs in the article on Alfonsín certain terms — such as nation, culture, and democracy — that are clearly meant to provide the conceptual basis for any discussion of Mexico's future. His valorization of these terms indicates that Fuentes is not searching in his current work for access to the "de-centered, transnational and multidimensional happening of contemporary cultural life," as Alonso puts it.[41] What he is doing, rather, is to continue to think about ways of bringing about a reconciliation between the wealth and weight of tradition — hence the references to nation and culture — with the best of the promises of modernity — hence the emphasis on democracy, not only in the article on Alfonsín, but in all of Fuentes's recent political statements.

CHAPTER VIII

Carlos Fuentes in the 1990s

With eight books published in the period 1990–1995, as well as innumerable contributions to newspapers and magazines to his name, it is clear that as he approaches his seventieth birthday Carlos Fuentes continues to be an astonishingly productive writer. It is also clear that the question of Mexico's place in the world continues to be one of his leading concerns.

In the 1950s, in the days of the *Revista Mexicana de Literatura*, Fuentes sought to lift Mexican culture out of its traditional isolation. By the 1990s, many of the barriers separating Mexico from the outside world had broken down—a new situation producing a new set of challenges. These challenges have provoked in Fuentes a turn to a more nationalist position, something that is particularly clear from his commentaries on political and economic developments, but also emerges from some aspects of his literary endeavors.

Fuentes acknowledges the inevitability of the current process of globalization. A recent essay on the problems Mexico faces as it approaches the millennium opens with the declaration, "We are in the world."[1] Fuentes realizes moreover that the impact of globalization is experienced in the first place at the level of the economy. Since 1988, the year in which Carlos Salinas became president, the economic policies of the Mexican government have been based on the assumption that economic globalization is not only inevitable, but also potentially beneficial for Mexico. Hence the efforts to open the Mexican economy to the outside world, efforts that culminated in the creation of a free-trade zone linking Mexico with Canada and the United States. In his commentaries on Salinas's economic policies, Fuentes has consistently indicated his agreement with their underlying premise. In March 1994, he referred to the "successes owed to the economic reforms of President Carlos Salinas de Gortari," the principal of these reforms being the opening up of Mexico's "closed and over-protected economy" to current processes of "global integration."[2]

In 1995, after the collapse of the Mexican economy in the very first month of the administration of Salinas's hand-picked successor, Ernesto Zedillo, had brought the weaknesses of Salinas's economic program into sharp focus, Fuentes did not revise his views on the need to reduce the role of the Mexican state in the economy. In January 1995, in a piece subsequently included in *Nuevo tiempo mexicano*, he described "the inevitable opening to the world" as one of "the good ideas of the recent past" (240). By the end of the year, as the proliferating scandals surrounding Salinas were resulting in a drastic and widespread reevaluation of his regime, Fuentes was still insisting that Salinas deserved credit for having taken "the necessary step to Mexico's presence in the globalizing economy."[3]

Yet all of these nods of approval in the direction of Salinas's goal of accelerating the process of Mexico's integration into the global economy are framed by a set of serious reservations concerning some of the consequences of this process. The problem that most exercises Fuentes is the threat economic globalization poses to Mexico's sovereignty. Several of the essays collected in *Nuevo tiempo mexicano* provide an overview of Fuentes's positions on this topic. In a piece he wrote prior to the passage of the North American Free Trade Agreement (NAFTA), Fuentes draws attention to the risks attached to the project of integrating Mexico with the U.S. economy, risks that have to do in the first place with the fact that Mexico must sacrifice some of its nationalist positions even while the United States is becoming the most nationalist country in the world, as evidenced by the Panama invasion and the Gulf War (89). In a later piece, in which he expresses his approval of the decision to join NAFTA, Fuentes simultaneously insists on the need for Mexico to defend its sovereignty (107–8). After the collapse of the peso in late 1994 had forced the Mexican government to turn to the United States for a large loan, Fuentes deplored what he called the "rapid erosion of our sovereignty" (235) and called on the country to "find solutions within ourselves, our tradition, our culture" (239). In late 1995, Fuentes lamented the current absence of "great figures in power" in Latin America (though he makes an exception for President Cardoso of Brazil). This absence is a particularly serious matter in Mexico, inasmuch as the president of Mexico has the greatest responsibility of all: "Here, in Tijuana, in Ciudad Juárez, in Matamoros, all of Latin America begins. That is, whether we like it or not, the burden if you wish, the luck if you prefer, of Mexico: to be the very face of an identity, the shield of our independence."[4] The reference to the cities on Mexico's border with the United States evokes the idea of a threat from the north, a threat to Latin America's political, economic and cultural independence, which Mexico, because of its location, is the first to experience, and must be the first to resist. Mexican nationalism, then, is a necessary defense against the expansive nationalism of its powerful neighbor. In a world characterized by huge imbalances in the distribution of power, it is important to recall that "true interdependence can develop only among independent nations."[5]

In recent years, Mexico has faced not only external, but also internal challenges. Of these, the Zapatista uprising in Chiapas is perhaps the most noteworthy. Fuentes's response to the conflict in Chiapas once again reveals his tendency to argue in political matters from the point of view of the nation. Fuentes sees in the Zapatistas a relationship to the past, as well as a project for the future, but in both cases his interpretation is framed by a vision of Mexico as a whole. When Fuentes expresses his gratitude in a piece from *Nuevo tiempo mexicano* to the Zapatistas for "having reminded us of all that we had forgotten" (174), he is referring to the fact that the Zapatistas have recalled Mexico to a sense of its indigenous roots. And when he commends the Zapatistas for recognizing that "the goals of your communities can only be achieved by democratic means" (175), Fuentes turns them into allies in his struggle to convince his fellow Mexicans that democracy is the best tool for achieving the political integration of Mexico. There is no doubt, of course, that Fuentes wishes to see solutions to the specific problems of the Indians of Chiapas. But the Zapatista rebellion acts for Fuentes in the first place as a spur to rethink the problems of Mexico as a nation.

In Fuentes's literary and cultural work of the last few years, there is a similar tension between nationalist and globalist perspectives. In the title essay of *Geografía de la novela*, Fuentes suggests that Goethe's notion of *Weltliteratur* is finally achieving its true realization in our era. In Goethe's time, Europe was taken to be the world. As a result, the universalist vision encoded in Goethe's concept of a "world literature" masked something much narrower. But, Fuentes argues, the old Eurocentric view of the world is now giving way to a truly "polycentric" perspective. Under these circumstances, "Goethe's 'world literature' is finally taking on its true meaning: the literature of difference, the narration of diversity" (167). Elsewhere in the same volume, Fuentes defines fiction as "an expression of humankind's cultural, personal and spiritual diversity" and "a herald of the multipolar and multicultural world of the near future" (161). One of the writers who in Fuentes's eyes best reflects this dimension of contemporary fiction is Salman Rushdie, whose work he describes in an article in *La Jornada* as "a vast history of *mestizajes*"[6] and praises in *Geografía de la novela* for announcing "the great reality, the great drama" of the future: "The encounter with the other, with the man or woman of a different creed, a different race, a different culture, the man or woman who is not like you or me" (164). The novel, Fuentes argues, will have a key role to fulfill in our era, for more than any other mode of expression or communication it offers a kind of training in how to live in an increasingly diverse world.

Yet in a paradoxical manner a world where we are more aware of differences is also a world where we are more aware of identities. In *Geografía de la novela* Fuentes speaks of mixture and exchange, of diversity and multiplicity, yet he also describes a literary world in which each writer is firmly linked to a specific place. In speaking of the literature of the Caribbean, for example, Fuentes mentions "Alejo Carpentier in Havana, Jean Rhys in Dominica, Luis Rafael Sánchez in San Juan de Puerto Rico, Arturo Uslar Pietri in Caracas, Jacques Roumain in Port-au-Prince" (168). The geography of the novel in English includes, according to Fuentes, Chinua Achebe writing from Nigeria, Nadine Gordimer from South Africa, Anita Desai from India, Salman Rushdie from Pakistan, and so on (167). The United States constitutes the one exception to this pattern, perhaps because, as Gertrude Stein once said of Oakland, "there is no there there." In Fuentes's description, writers from the United States are linked not to a place, but to an ethnic group: "There would be no novel of the United States without the Chinese American narratives of Amy Tan, the Mexican American narratives of Sandra Cisneros, or the Cuban American narratives of Cristina Garcia" (168–69). In a literary world organized around the principle of diversity, it appears that a writer's position is tied to her cultural identity. Instead of structuring the literary field around the opposition between realists and experimentalists, or traditionalists and vanguardists, as he had done in *La nueva novela hispanoamericana*, Fuentes now perceives it as a kind of United Nations where every writer represents a specific culture.

The point that the meeting between different cultures may produce not only processes of exchange but also gestures of self-affirmation is illustrated in Fuentes's most recent work of fiction, *La frontera de cristal* (1995), a collection of linked narratives dealing with the relationship between Mexico and the United States. In making the encounter between Mexico and the United States the principal theme of his new collection, Fuentes is merely exemplifying his observation in the essay on Rushdie in *Geografía de la novela* that the encounter with the other is the great drama of our time and of the time to come. But if the implication in the essay on Rushdie seemed to be that the encounter with the other was going to open the way to a new syncretistic world, in *La frontera de cristal* the meeting between Mexico and the United States seems for now at least to promise a far less heartening outcome. Even though Fuentes takes care not to make his tale of two nations into too much of a black-and-white affair, what lingers in the reader's memory after closing the book is the mordant satire of the American way of life combined with the almost amorous evocation of certain aspects of Mexican culture. In this case, the encounter with the other results in a more intense consciousness of one's own identity. Thus *La frontera de cristal* is ambiguously located between the will to transcend cultural boundaries, and the desire to safeguard them. In placing the issue of migration at the center of the text, Fuentes develops a picture of the new multicultural world of mixtures and crossings in which we must now all live. Yet in turning *La frontera de cristal* into an affirmation of Mexican culture at the limit where it is potentially most vulnerable—the border with the United States—Fuentes also offers a strong plea for the preservation of a specific and distinctive cultural tradition.

Notes
Bibliography
Index

Notes

Chapter I

1. See Annick Lempérière, *Intellectuels, état et société au Mexique: Les clercs de la nation, 1910–1968* (Paris: L'Harmattan, 1992), 189–237.

2. Fuentes recalls that when "Los Presentes" was launched, he and many others began to write feverishly for the new publishing house. See Luis Harss, "Carlos Fuentes, o la nueva herejía," in *Los Nuestros* (Buenos Aires: Sudamericana, 1966), 343.

3. Lempérière, 223.

4. Lempérière, 220–25.

5. Héctor Aguilar Camín writes, "More than anyone else, more than Octavio Paz or Juan Rulfo, Alfonso Reyes or José Revueltas, Carlos Fuentes was the true embodiment of the professional writer." See "Algo sobre Carlos Fuentes y *La muerte de Artemio Cruz*," in Georgina García Gutiérrez, ed., *Carlos Fuentes. Relectura de su obra: "Los días enmascarados" y "Cantar de ciegos"* (Guanajuato: Universidad de Guanajuato, 1995), 165.

6. Quoted in Alberto Ruy Sánchez, *Una introducción a Octavio Paz* (Mexico City: Joaquín Mortiz, 1990), 79.

7. Carlos Blanco Aguinaga, "Realidad y estilo de Juan Rulfo," *Revista Mexicana de Literatura* 1 (September–October 1955): 59–86.

8. Jorge Portilla, "Crítica de la crítica," *Revista Mexicana de Literatura* 1 (September–October 1955): 48–58.

9. Talón de Aquiles [Carlos Fuentes], "Nacionalismo camellero," *Revista Mexicana de Literatura* 1 (September–October 1955): 90–91.

10. Talón de Aquiles, "Apuesta," *Revista Mexicana de Literatura* 1 (September–October 1955): 91.

11. Talón de Aquiles, "La burra al trigo," *Revista Mexicana de Literatura* 1 (September–October 1955): 93–94.

12. Rafael Gutiérrez Girardot, "Notas sobre la imagen de América en Alfonso Reyes," *Revista Mexicana de Literatura* 2 (November–December 1955): 116.

13. Emmanuel Carballo, "Me importa madre y otros textos," *Revista Mexicana de Literatura* 4 (March–April 1956): 386.

14. Jaime Torres Bodet, "Sobre la responsabilidad del escritor," *Revista Mexicana de Literatura* 5 (May–June 1956): 520.

15. Talón de Aquiles, "La crítica iletrada," *Revista Mexicana de Literatura* 2 (November–December 1955): 190.

16. Harss, 343.

17. José Donoso, *Historia personal del 'boom'*, rev. ed. (Buenos Aires: Sudamericana, 1984), 44–45.

18. Donoso, 48.

19. Elena Poniatowska, "Carlos Fuentes ¡Si tuviera cuatro vidas, cuatro vidas serían para tí!" in *¡Ay vida, no me mereces!* (Mexico City: Joaquín Mortiz, 1985), 3.

20. Poniatowska, 36.

21. Harss, 356.

22. Poniatowska, 13.

23. Donoso, 47.

24. Talón de Aquiles, "Diálogo," *Revista Mexicana de Literatura* 3 (January–February 1956): 530.

25. Talón de Aquiles, "Y crítica fáustica," *Revista Mexicana de Literatura* 5 (May–June 1956): 530.

26. An excellent discussion of this tension in the early part of Fuentes's career can be found in Georgina García Gutiérrez's introduction to her edition of *La región más transparente* (Madrid: Cátedra, 1991), 9–61.

27. See, for example, Carlos Fuentes, *The Buried Mirror: Reflections on Spain and the New World* (Boston: Houghton Mifflin, 1992).

28. Fuentes was a strong critic of the U.S. role in the *contra* war in Nicaragua during the 1980s, and of the invasion of Panama in 1989. In recent years, he has taken up the cause of Mexican immigrants in the United States. For a brief statement of his position on Nicaragua, see "A Harvard Commencement," in *Myself With Others* (New York: Farrar, Straus & Giroux, 1988), 211. On the Panama invasion, see "Las lecciones de Panamá," *El País* (December 24, 1989): 13–14. On the treatment of Mexican immigrants in the United States, see *Nuevo tiempo mexicano*, 2nd ed. (Mexico City: Aguilar, 1995), 108–13.

29. See the essays in *Geografía de la novela* (Mexico City: Fondo de Cultura Económica, 1993).

30. Liah Greenfeld claims that the England "that emerged from the civic and religious trials of the mid-seventeenth century" was the first nation in the world. And she argues that "English national consciousness was first and foremost a consciousness of one's dignity as an individual. It implied and pushed toward . . . the principles of individual liberty and

political equality." The idea of the nation represented a break with the old society of orders, and so amounted to "the first major breakthrough toward democracy." See Liah Greenfeld, *Nationalism: Five Roads to Modernity* (Cambridge, Mass.: Harvard University Press, 1992), 86. She also describes the idea of the nation as "the constitutive element of modernity" (18).

31. Eric Hobsbawm argues that nationalism satisfies the need for a sense of collective belonging during times of rapid social change. See *Nations and Nationalism Since 1780: Programme, Myth, Reality* (New York: Cambridge University Press, 1990), 109. See also the essays in *The Invention of Tradition,* ed. Eric Hobsbawm and Terence Ranger (New York: Cambridge University Press, 1983).

Chapter II

1. For a description of this process, see José Joaquín Brunner, "Experiencias de la modernidad," in *América Latina: cultura y modernidad* (Mexico City: Grijalbo, 1992), 78.

2. Although Gide is not strictly speaking part of the existentialist movement, there are a number of important affinities between his work and the work of Sartre and Camus. They share, for example, an interest in the motif of the *acte gratuit*, a motif they use in order to articulate a common set of ideas about temporality and individual freedom. Sartre himself suggested an overall link between Gide and existentialism when, in an essay he wrote upon Gide's death, he described Gide's literary and intellectual project in terms that could very well be applied to his own work: "The most valuable thing Gide offered us was his decision to live to the full the agony and the death of God." See "Gide vivant," in *Situations, IV* (Paris: Gallimard, 1964), 88.

3. One of Fuentes's first published pieces was an article on existentialism, entitled "La autopsia del existencialismo." Fuentes's mocking attitude toward existentialist philosophy, which he sees as yet another tired fad to reach Mexico from Europe, and which, as the title suggests, he clearly regards as being entirely passé, does not foreshadow his also critical but far more subtle treatment of existentialist ideas in *La región*. The article does serve, however, to demonstrate Fuentes's familiarity with existentialist thought in the 1950s. See "La autopsia del existencialismo," *Hoy* (December 24, 1949): 29–30. In spite of this, only two critics, Michael W. Moody and Catherine M. Allen, have discussed Fuentes's relationship to existentialism. Both Moody and Allen focus exclusively on *La muerte de*

Artemio Cruz (1962), and both read this novel as a straightforward illustration of existentialist ideas rather than as a critical and conflictive exploration of the implications of these ideas. See Catherine M. Allen, "La correlación entre la filosofía de Jean-Paul Sartre y *La muerte de Artemio Cruz* de Carlos Fuentes," in Helmy Giacoman, ed., *Homenaje a Carlos Fuentes* (New York: Las Américas, 1971), 399–442; and Michael W. Moody, "Existentialism, Mexico and Artemio Cruz," *Romance Notes* 10 (1968): 27–31.

4. In a 1964 interview with Emmanuel Carballo, Fuentes discusses Lawrence's impact on his early work. He praises Lawrence as "a writer who knew how to reach certain dark dimensions, certain nights of the soul, certain of man's muddy deposits." See Emmanuel Carballo, *Diecinueve protagonistas de la literatura mexicana del siglo XX* (Mexico City: Empresas Editoriales, 1965), 434. For a discussion of the modern fascination with the primitive, see Marianna Torgovnick, *Gone Primitive: Savage Intellects, Modern Lives* (Chicago: University of Chicago Press, 1990).

5. Carlos Fuentes, *La región más transparente*, 2nd ed. (Mexico City: Fondo de Cultura Económica, 1972); English version, *Where the Air Is Clear*, trans. Sam Hileman (New York: Farrar, Straus & Giroux, 1989). Quotations will be followed by parenthetical page references to the Spanish original and the corresponding place in the English text, respectively. The translations, however, are my own.

6. Carlos Fuentes, "Situación del escritor en América Latina," interviewed by Emir Rodríguez Monegal, *Mundo Nuevo* 1 (July 1966): 7.

7. The allusion to the cantina as a characteristic site of violence in Mexico may also remind us of the scene of the Consul's death in Malcolm Lowry's *Under the Volcano*.

8. André Gide, *Les caves du Vatican* (Paris: Gallimard, 1922), 188.

9. Gide, 194.

10. Gide, 187.

11. Albert Camus, *L'homme révolté* (Paris: Gallimard, 1951), 124.

12. Carlos Fuentes, *Las buenas conciencias* (Mexico City: Fondo de Cultura Económica, 1959); English version, *The Good Conscience*, trans. Sam Hileman (New York: Farrar, Straus & Giroux, 1989). Quotations will be followed by parenthetical page references to the Spanish original and the corresponding place in the English text, respectively. The translations, however, are my own.

13. Steven Boldy reads *Las buenas conciencias* as a family romance that develops on two different levels: Jaime's need to overcome "the dependent status of the son" parallels Fuentes's need to overcome "his precursors in

European literary realism." Boldy sees the trajectory that leads Jaime to become "the father of both his father figures" as part of a necessary forging of an independent identity, and he reads Jaime's renunciation of his rebellion against the conventional social order as part of a mature recognition on the young man's part that he can only make a claim to authentic selfhood if he also "enters into a dialogue with the values of his community." Yet Boldy also states that Jaime's actions are "compromised by bad faith." See "Family Tradition and the Individual Talent in Carlos Fuentes' *Las buenas conciencias*," *Bulletin of Hispanic Studies* 71 (1994): 359–80.

14. The line is from Nerval's sonnet "Artémis." One possible reading of this poem is that it expresses a vision of time as eternal recurrence. It is worth noting that Octavio Paz uses the quatrain from "Artémis" which includes this line as the epigraph to "Piedra de sol," a poem published the year before *La región*. "Piedra de sol," a long poem that opens and closes with the exact same six verses, constitutes a classic expression of the notion of cyclical time. For both Spanish and English versions of "Piedra de sol," see *The Collected Poems of Octavio Paz, 1957–1987*, ed. and trans. Eliot Weinberger (New York: New Directions, 1987), 2–35. Given Paz's impact on the young Fuentes, it is very likely that the reference to Nerval in *La región* is at the same time a reference to Paz. In fact, Enrique Krauze has pointed out that the figure of Zamacona is based on Paz. See "La comedia mexicana de Carlos Fuentes," *Vuelta* 139 (June 1988): 17. English version, "The Guerilla Dandy," *The New Republic* (June 27, 1988): 29. Yet in the line Zamacona recites to himself just before his death the allusion to cyclical time is countered by an opposite vision of time as a series of discontinuous, isolated moments. Nerval's preoccupation with the idea of the death of God—especially vivid in "Le Christ aux Oliviers"—reinforces this aspect, and confirms the link with existentialism. In effect, the line from Nerval seems to hover between two diametrically opposed readings, in a manner that reflects the ambiguity of the entire scene of Zamacona's death. Both "Artémis" and "Le Christ aux Oliviers" are included in *Les chimères* (Paris: José Corti, 1941).

15. Jean-Paul Sartre, "Explication de *L'étranger*," in *Situations, I* (Paris: Gallimard, 1947), 108.

16. Sartre, 117.

17. Sartre held a variety of views on the nature of temporality. Although he often expresses a concept of time as a series of isolated instants, Sartre also evolves a quite different view in some of his writings, according to which consciousness is defined by its orientation toward the future. In his essay on *The Sound and the Fury*, for example, Sartre criticizes

Faulkner for creating characters who are wholly determined by the past. This, Sartre argues, is a falsification of human experience: "The nature of consciousness implies on the contrary that it leaps ahead of itself into the future; one can only understand what consciousness is by understanding what it will be." See "A propos de *La bruit et la fureur*. La temporalité chez Faulkner," in *Situations, I*, 79. In *L'être et le néant*, Sartre defines the for-itself ("pour-soi") as an entity that is "originally a project, which is to say that it is defined by its goal." See *L'être et le néant* (Paris: Gallimard, 1943), 530. From his observations in "La autopsia del existencialismo" and his comments in the interview with Rodríguez Monegal, however, it is clear that Fuentes regarded Sartre as a proponent of time as pure present. In "La autopsia," for example, Fuentes offers the following summary of Sartre's position: "All that matters is to live in the present. . . . Only this moment exists, and I, for myself" (29).

18. Enrique Krauze suggests that the chapter on Mexican death in Octavio Paz's *El laberinto de la soledad* provided the inspiration for the scene of Zamacona's death. See "La comedia mexicana de Carlos Fuentes," 17. Indeed, in "Todos santos día de muertos," Paz describes two contrasting views of death that parallel the two possible interpretations of the manner in which Zamacona dies. On the one hand, Paz speaks of how ancient Mexican and Christian cultures share a conception of death as a mode of transcendence. On the other hand, Paz describes modern death as a meaningless fact among other facts. The specifically Mexican version of this modern view of death is composed of mockery, indifference, and fascination. See Octavio Paz, *El laberinto de la soledad* (Madrid: Cátedra, 1993), 182–201. Fuentes appears to echo this combination of harking back to an earlier experience of death as something deeply meaningful while confronting the modern sense of death as fundamentally lacking in significance.

19. The argument I am setting forth here touches on the much-discussed issue of the relationship between myth and history in Fuentes's work. It is too often assumed that Fuentes succeeds in creating a tidy sense of unity out of the meeting of these opposed forces. Luis Leal's comment on *La región* to the effect that "history and myth balance each other to give the novel equilibrium" exemplifies this approach. See "History and Myth in the Narrative of Carlos Fuentes," in Robert Brody and Charles Rossman, eds., *Carlos Fuentes: A Critical View* (Austin: University of Texas Press, 1982), 7. My reading aims to restore a sense of the problematic nature of this relationship in Fuentes's first novel.

20. See *L'existentialisme est un humanisme* (Paris: Nagel, 1966).

21. Albert Camus, *L'homme révolté*, 36.

22. Jean-Paul Sartre, *La nausée* (Paris: Gallimard, 1938), 33–36.

23. Sartre, *La nausée*, 177.

24. See Sartre's "La liberté cartésienne," in *Situations, I*, 314–35, for the idea that human freedom is analogous to the freedom attributed to God in theistic readings of the universe.

25. Francisco Javier Ordiz suggests that underneath the "'social narrative' in the realist mode" (Rodrigo's world) there exists a "complicated web of mythical and mythological references" (Ixca's realm). He argues that the mythical references constitute "the true key to the interpretation of the novel." See *El mito en la obra narrativa de Carlos Fuentes* (León: Universidad de León, 1987), 41. My own view is that *La región* develops its meaning not by leading the reader from the realist surface to the mythical depths of the text, but rather by sustaining the tension between the two levels.

26. See Wendy Faris, "The Return of the Past: Chiasmus in the Texts of Carlos Fuentes," *World Literature Today* 57 (Autumn 1983): 578–84.

27. Octavio Paz, *El arco y la lira*, 3rd ed. (Mexico City: Fondo de Cultura Económica, 1972), 25.

28. See Joseph Frank, "Spatial Form in Modern Literature," *The Widening Gyre* (New Brunswick, N.J.: Rutgers University Press, 1963), 3–62. In a recent essay, Fuentes refers to Joseph Frank's work on the transformation of space in modern literature. See "Tiempo y espacio de la novela," in *Valiente mundo nuevo: Épica, utopía y mito en la novela hispanoamericana* (Mexico City: Fondo de Cultura Económica, 1990), 213.

29. For Fuentes's relationship to modernist writing, see Wendy Faris, "*Ulysses* in Mexico: Carlos Fuentes," *Comparative Literature Studies* 19 (1982): 236–53; and Morton P. Levitt, "Joyce and Fuentes: Not Influence but Aura," *Comparative Literature Studies* 19 (1982): 254–71.

30. For the development of the debate on spatial form, see Joseph Frank, "Spatial Form: An Answer to Critics," *Critical Inquiry* 4 (1977): 231–52; Joseph Frank, "Spatial Form: Some Further Reflections," *Critical Inquiry* 5 (1978):275–90; Frank Kermode, "A Reply to Joseph Frank," *Critical Inquiry* 4 (1978): 579–88; W. J. T. Mitchell, "Spatial Form in Literature: Toward a General Theory," *Critical Inquiry* 6 (1980): 539–67; and Jeffrey R. Smitten and Ann Daghistany, eds., *Spatial Form in Narrative* (Ithaca, N.Y.: Cornell University Press, 1981).

31. Frank, *The Widening Gyre*, 60.

32. Octavio Paz, *Los hijos del limo: Del romanticismo a la vanguardia*, 3rd ed. (Barcelona: Seix Barral, 1987), 182.

33. Carlos Fuentes, "Kierkegaard en la Zona Rosa," in *Tiempo mexicano* (Mexico City: Joaquín Mortiz, 1971), 11.

34. Fuentes, "Kierkegaard en la Zona Rosa," 9–10.

35. Fuentes, "Kierkegaard en la Zona Rosa," 10.

36. Fuentes, "Kierkegaard en la Zona Rosa," 11.

37. Paz, *El laberinto de la soledad*, 292.

38. See Paz's essay "Revuelta, revolución, rebelión" in *Corriente alterna* (Mexico City: Siglo XXI, 1967), 147–52, for a more detailed account of the different meanings of the word "revolution."

39. See Wendy Faris, "Desire and Power, Love and Revolution: Carlos Fuentes and Milan Kundera," *The Review of Contemporary Fiction* 8, no. 2 (Summer 1988): 273–84, for a useful account of this aspect of Fuentes's work.

40. Carlos Fuentes, "A Harvard Commencement," in *Myself With Others*, 200.

41. Fuentes, "A Harvard Commencement," 200–201.

42. Carlos Fuentes, "History Out of Chaos," review of *Revolutionary Mexico: The Coming and Process of the Mexican Revolution*, by John Mason Hart, *The New York Times Book Review* (March 13, 1988): 13.

43. Fuentes, *The Buried Mirror*, 308.

44. Carlos Fuentes, *Cristóbal Nonato* (Mexico City: Fondo de Cultura Económica, 1987); English version, *Christopher Unborn*, trans. Alfred MacAdam and the author (New York: Farrar, Straus & Giroux, 1989). Quotations from the novel will be followed by parenthetical page references to the Spanish original and the English translation, respectively.

45. Enrique Krauze attacks Fuentes for presenting the Mexican Revolution, and, in fact, all revolutions as sacred, universal, and inevitable events. See "La comedia mexicana de Carlos Fuentes," 25. Krauze is right to draw attention to this strain of mystification in Fuentes's view of the Revolution, but the case of *Cristóbal Nonato* indicates that there is in Fuentes also an alternative, demystifying perspective on the nation's past.

46. Faris, "Desire and Power," 282.

47. Carlos Fuentes, "El prisionero de Las Lomas," in *Constancia y otras novelas para vírgenes* (Mexico City: Fondo de Cultura Económica, 1990), 175; English version, "The Prisoner of Las Lomas," in *Constancia and Other Stories for Virgins*, trans. Thomas Christensen (New York: Farrar, Straus & Giroux, 1990), 155. I have slightly altered Christensen's translation.

48. José Francisco Conde Ortega, "Carlos Fuentes: 40 años de congruencia," in José Francisco Conde Ortega and Arturo Trejo Villafuerte,

eds., *Carlos Fuentes: 40 años de escritor* (Mexico City: Universidad Metropolitana Azcapotzalco, 1993), 13.

49. Conde Ortega, 14.

50. Carlos Fuentes, "El 94: Diario de un año peligroso," in *Nuevo tiempo mexicano*, 174.

51. Fuentes, "El 94," 174.

Chapter III

1. Octavio Paz, *Tiempo nublado* (Barcelona: Seix Barral, 1986), 119.

2. See Domingo F. Sarmiento, *Facundo: Civilización y barbarie* (Madrid: Cátedra, 1990).

3. See, for example, Octavio Paz, *Posdata* (Mexico City: Siglo XXI, 1970).

4. Fuentes refers to Voltaire's "negation of the past" and Condorcet's "enthronement of the future" as characteristic instances of Enlightenment thought. See *Valiente mundo nuevo*, 44. Further references will appear in parentheses in the text.

5. This is evident from several recent critical treatments of Fuentes's work. Julio Ortega opens a long essay on Fuentes with the statement that "Few Latin American writers have succeeded like him in making plurality the very character of their identity." He describes Fuentes as the novelist of "the true New History of Spanish America, the history of its hybrid modernization, at once decentering and eccentric," and praises Fuentes for being "one of the first Mexican writers to put into question the idea of identity as something identical, stable and fixed. From his first stories onward, he has explored identity in terms of indeterminacy, process and difference." See *Retrato de Carlos Fuentes* (Barcelona: Círculo de Lectores, 1995), 27, 29, 51. Georgina García Gutiérrez speaks of "the intertextual, multicultural and multilinguistic richness" of Fuentes's work, and refers to the importance to Fuentes of "the criteria of rupture, critique of the real, transformation of genre, dialogism and polyphony." See "Dos libros a conmemorar," in Georgina García Gutiérrez, ed., *Carlos Fuentes. Relectura de su obra: "Los días enmascarados" y "Cantar de ciegos"*, 16, 27. The guiding thread in Kristine Ibsen's discussion of Fuentes is the notion that his novels are "polysemic" and "multivocal," and that they produce a vision of reality as "pluridimensional" and "changeable." See *Author, Text and Reader in the Novels of Carlos Fuentes* (New York: Peter Lang, 1993), 5, 137.

6. The shift was clear to Emmanuel Carballo, who, writing in 1965, noted that in politics Fuentes had gone from "abstention to participation," from "the timid left to the frank left." See *Diecinueve protagonistas*, 427.

7. See Carlos Fuentes and Emmanuel Carballo, "Tercera fuerza y primera posición," *Revista Mexicana de Literatura* 4 (March–April 1956): 419–22.

8. See Talón de Aquiles, "Camus, el escritor y la política," *Revista Mexicana de Literatura* 3 (January–February 1956): 289–91.

9. See, for example, Talón de Aquiles, "Los peligros del realismo socialista," *Revista Mexicana de Literatura* 1 (September–October 1955): 94.

10. Carlos Fuentes, "Carne y cartón de Stalín," *Política* (November 15, 1961): 16.

11. Fuentes, "Carne y cartón de Stalín," 16.

12. Carlos Fuentes, "El argumento de América Latina: Palabras a los norteamericanos," *Siempre!* (April 25, 1962): 22.

13. Carlos Fuentes, "Cárdenas en su sitio," *Política* (March 1, 1961): 17.

14. Carlos Fuentes, "EEUU: Notas para un análisis," *Ciencias políticas y sociales* 6 (April–June 1960): 270.

15. Carlos Fuentes, "Nueve años: 1953–1962," *Siempre!* (August 8, 1962): ii.

16. Fuentes, "Nueve años," ii.

17. Carlos Fuentes, "Latinoamérica: Tierra nuestra," *Siempre!* (March 28, 1962): iv.

18. Carlos Fuentes, "América Latina surge a la escena," *Siempre!* (April 4, 1962): 29.

19. Carlos Fuentes, "Doctrina Estrada para Perú," *Siempre!* (August 8, 1962): 23.

20. Fuentes, "América Latina surge a la escena," 28.

21. Carlos Fuentes, "Notas de un novelista: La revolución cubana," *Novedades* (February 2, 1959): 5.

22. Carlos Fuentes, "Las horas de Cuba," *Novedades* (August 9, 1959): 3.

23. Fuentes, "Las horas de Cuba," 3.

24. Fuentes, "Las horas de Cuba," 3. In his first piece on the Cuban Revolution, Fuentes had already claimed that "what is new about Castro is that he speaks to the people in a language they understand; he speaks the language of truth." See "Notas de un novelista," 5.

25. Fuentes, "Las horas de Cuba," 11.

26. Carlos Fuentes, "La hora de la definición: con el fascismo o con el pueblo," *Política* (May 1, 1961): 10.

27. Fuentes, "La hora de la definición," 11.

28. Fuentes, "La hora de la definición," 11.

29. Carlos Fuentes, "De Bandung a Belgrado," *Política* (September 15, 1962): 16.

30. Carlos Fuentes, "La hora de la definición," 10.

31. The statement is quoted by Robert E. Quirk in *Fidel Castro* (New York: Norton, 1993), 400. My account of the Punta del Este meeting is drawn from Quirk, 397–400, and from Hugh Thomas, *Cuba: The Pursuit of Freedom* (New York: Harper & Row, 1971), 1375.

32. Carlos Fuentes, "Coexistencia o fascismo," *Política* (February 15, 1962): 27.

33. Carlos Fuentes, "López Mateos, Goulart y la izquierda," *Siempre!* (May 23, 1962): 24–25.

34. Fuentes, "López Mateos," 24.

35. Anonymous, "¿A qué vino Kennedy?" *Política* (July 1, 1962).

36. Carlos Fuentes, "¿Qué hará López Mateos con su fuerza?" *Siempre!* (August 1, 1962): 22.

37. Carlos Fuentes, "A.L.M. fija rutas a su sucesor," *Siempre!* (March 13, 1963): 70.

38. Carlos Fuentes, "América Latina y EEUU: Notas para un panorama," *Universidad de México* 13 (March 1959): 11.

39. Fuentes, "América Latina y EEUU," 11.

40. See Carlos Fuentes, "La prensa, el PRI y la conferencia latinoamericana," *Política* (March 15, 1961): 12–13; and "Amos y esclavos," *Política* (November 1, 1961): 20–21.

41. Carlos Fuentes, "Vietnam," *Siempre!* (July 6, 1966): ii.

42. Fuentes, "Vietnam," ii.

43. Alejo Carpentier et al., "Carta abierta a Pablo Neruda," *Casa de las Américas* 6 (September–October 1966): 131–35.

44. Roberto Fernández Retamar, Lisandro Otero, Edmundo Desnoes, and Ambrosio Fornet, "Sobre la penetración intelectual del imperialismo yanqui en América Latina," *Casa de las Américas* 6 (November–December 1966): 133–39.

45. Carpentier et al., "Carta abierta a Pablo Neruda," 134.

46. Carlos Fuentes, "El P.E.N.: Entierro de la guerra fría en la literatura," *Life en español* (August 1, 1966): 54–61.

47. Fernández Retamar et al., "Sobre la penetración intelectual," 135.

48. Carlos Fuentes to Fernando Benítez, Paris, February 26, 1967, Carlos Fuentes Papers, Special Collections, Princeton University Library.

49. Carlos Fuentes, "Cronología personal," in Julio Ortega, *Retrato de Carlos Fuentes*, 108.

50. Carlos Fuentes, *La muerte de Artemio Cruz* (Mexico City: Fondo de Cultura Económica, 1962); English version, *The Death of Artemio Cruz*, trans. Alfred MacAdam (New York: Farrar, Straus & Giroux, 1991). Quotations from the novel will be followed by parenthetical page references to the Spanish original and English translation, respectively. I have made some changes in MacAdam's translation.

51. Raymond L. Williams uses *Artemio Cruz* to support his claim that Latin American modernists "unlike many of their Anglo-American counterparts . . . generally refused to lose a sense of history." See "Truth Claims, Postmodernism, and the Latin American Novel," *Profession* 92 (1992): 8.

52. Georg Lukács, *The Theory of the Novel*, trans. Anna Bostock (Cambridge: MIT Press, 1971), 121.

53. Gerald Martin, *Journeys Through the Labyrinth: Latin American Fiction in the Twentieth Century* (London: Verso, 1989), 211–12.

54. In a fascinating account of the changes that have occurred over the years in his views of *Artemio Cruz*, Héctor Aguilar Camín recalls that in the early 1960s, when he first read the novel, he felt that Fuentes had not been severe enough in his condemnation of Artemio: "Fuentes had in my view made an unacceptable concession to Artemio Cruz in granting him the story of Regina. . . . Irascible young man that I was, I believed that a wretch like Cruz did not deserve this mouthful of fresh water in his life." But Aguilar Camín has now come to agree with a friend of his who back in the 1960s already argued that the story of Regina ought to be seen as "an act of generosity of the novelist toward his character" and as "a way of balancing the dark and critical perspective that governs almost the entire work." My reading of the novel will show in the first place that Fuentes makes more concessions to Artemio than Aguilar Camín recognizes: above all, the memory of his childhood and the moments of happiness shared with his son Lorenzo. In the second place, I will demonstrate that such concessions serve not only to make Artemio a more rounded character, but also to provide a more vivid sense of the extent and depth of Fuentes's condemnation of him, for the passages in question are to be seen as evocations of all that Artemio has lost as a result of what Aguilar Camín calls Artemio's "moral wretchedness." See "Algo sobre Carlos Fuentes y *La muerte de Artemio Cruz*," in Georgina García Gutiérrez, ed., *Carlos Fuentes: Relectura de su obra: "Los días enmascarados" y "Cantar de ciegos"*, 173.

55. Jonathan Tittler uses words such as "disintegration," "splintering," "dispersal," "destabilization," and "multiplication" to describe the state of Artemio Cruz's psyche. See "*The Death of Artemio Cruz*: Anatomy of a Self,"

in *Narrative Irony in the Contemporary Spanish-American Novel* (Ithaca, N.Y.: Cornell University Press, 1984), 31–57. Djelal Kadir speaks of Artemio Cruz's "shattered consciousness" and his "dismembered identity." He reads Fuentes's novel as an example of Gothic romance, a genre Kadir argues is centrally concerned with the "disintegration of the individual and his world." See *Questing Fictions: Latin America's Family Romance* (Minneapolis: University of Minnesota Press, 1986), 79–80. Raymond L. Williams draws attention to the "subversion of individual identity" in *Artemio Cruz*, and, setting the novel in the context of the broader development of Fuentes's career, sees it as laying the groundwork for "a much more elaborate and complex fragmentation of the individual subject in *Terra Nostra*." See *The Writings of Carlos Fuentes* (Austin: University of Texas Press, 1996), 123.

56. Steven Boldy writes that "the deep impulse behind all the works of Fuentes is the millennium, an Arcadia in the past projected onto a utopia in the future." See "Fathers and Sons in Fuentes' *La muerte de Artemio Cruz*," *Bulletin of Hispanic Studies* 61 (1984): 32. At the end of this chapter, I will argue that Fuentes's more recent work puts forward a more qualified view of the possibility of utopia.

57. Carlos Fuentes, "La novela como reconocimiento: Jane Austen," "La novela como símbolo: Herman Melville," and "La novela como trage-dia: William Faulkner," in *Casa con dos puertas* (Mexico City: Joaquín Mortiz, 1970), 13–78. Further references to these three essays will appear in parentheses in the text.

58. See Octavio Paz, *El arco y la lira*, 226–27. Roberto González Echevarría suggests that Paz took his definition of the novel from Georg Lukács's *The Theory of the Novel*. See "*Terra Nostra*: Theory and Practice," in *The Voice of the Masters: Writing and Authority in Modern Latin American Literature* (Austin: University of Texas Press, 1985), 90.

59. In his translation of Paz, Lysander Kemp leaves the word "chingón" and its cognates in Spanish. See Octavio Paz, *The Labyrinth of Solitude*, trans. Lysander Kemp (New York: Grove, 1985). Alfred MacAdam translates "chingón" as "motherfucker" and "chingada" as "the fucked mother." I have decided to follow Kemp's example in quoting from *Artemio Cruz*.

60. See Paz, *El laberinto de la soledad*, 211–27.

61. Steven Boldy situates the relationship between Artemio and Lorenzo within "an archetypal structure of father, legitimate son and ille-gitimate son or symbolic heir which occurs three times in the novel. The first instance of this pattern is the relationship between Ireneo Menchaca and his two sons Atanasio and Pedro; the second is the relationship

between Gamaliel Bernal, his son Gonzalo and his son-in-law Artemio; the third is the relationship between Artemio, Lorenzo and Jaime Ceballos." See "Fathers and Sons in Fuentes's *La muerte de Artemio Cruz*," 31.

62. Doris Sommer, "Irresistible Romance: The Foundational Fictions of Latin America," in Homi K. Bhabha, ed., *Nation and Narration* (London: Routledge, 1990), 91.

63. Doris Sommer, *Foundational Fictions: The National Romances of Latin America* (Berkeley: University of California Press, 1991), 29.

64. Roberto Fernández Retamar, "Carlos Fuentes y la otra novela de la revolución mexicana," *Casa de las Américas* 4 (October–November 1964): 126.

65. Gerald Martin, *Journeys Through the Labyrinth*, 212. María Stoopen voices a similar criticism, noting that the Lorenzo chapter "renews hope in the Revolution and faith in humanity," but then complaining that the episode, "in being displaced to a foreign setting, is devalued from the perspective of the actual history of the nation." Stoopen concludes that Fuentes has a one-dimensional view of Mexican history: "He sees no hope of salvation for our country." See *"La muerte de Artemio Cruz": Una novela de denuncia y traición* (Mexico City: UNAM, 1982), 131–32.

66. Fernando Moreno offers a striking description of the effect of Fuentes's use of repetition, as with the phrase "We crossed the river on horseback." It is, he says, "as if the ephemeral wished to make itself eternal." Moreno suggests that the river crossing allows Artemio and his son to accede to "another domain, in this case the domain of authenticity, of total communion." Moreno sees Artemio as a person defined by the experience of loss, by "an agonized consciousness of all that might have been." See *Carlos Fuentes. "La mort d'Artemio Cruz": entre le mythe et l'histoire* (Paris: Editions Caribéenes, 1989), 66, 133, 141.

67. Carlos Fuentes, *"El ángel exterminador*: nadie encontrará una respuesta dogmática," *Siempre!* (June 13, 1962): xix.

68. There have been many discussions of the significance of Artemio Cruz's name. Bernard Fouques wonders whether the name "Cruz" might not be "the 'x' which for Alfonso Reyes encoded the very enigma of Mexico?" See "El Espacio Órfico de la Novela en *La muerte de Artemio Cruz*," *Revista iberoamericana* 91 (April–June 1975): 237. Paul Dixon argues that Artemio's last name alludes to the novel's vision of Mexican culture as a "cross" of two races and two cultures. See "Simetría y centralidad en *La muerte de Artemio Cruz*," in Ana María Hernández de López, ed., *La obra de Carlos Fuentes: Una visión múltiple* (Madrid: Pliegos, 1988), 98. Robin

Fiddian suggests that Artemio's surname refers to the "cara o cruz" of "a coin flipped to decide who wins and who loses a contest," and concludes that Artemio is "a faceless man who has fulfilled only half of his potential [and who] might also be described as 'cruz sin cara.'" See "Carlos Fuentes: *The Death of Artemio Cruz*," in Philip Swanson, ed., *Landmarks of Modern Latin American Fiction* (London: Routledge, 1990), 103.

69. Fuentes, *The Buried Mirror*, 268.

70. See Roberto González Echevarría, *Alejo Carpentier: The Pilgrim at Home* (Austin: University of Texas Press, 1990), 155–89.

71. Carlos Fuentes, prologue to *Ariel*, by José Enrique Rodó, trans. Margaret Sayers Peden (Austin: University of Texas Press, 1988), 23.

72. Fuentes, "Prologue," 24.

73. Fuentes, "Prologue," 25.

74. Carlos Fuentes, "Land of Jekyll and Hyde," *The Nation* (March 22, 1986): 337.

75. Carlos Fuentes, "Hail to the Chief, and Never Mind the Truth," *Los Angeles Times* (August 2, 1987): sec. v, p. 2.

76. Fuentes, "Prologue," 26–27.

77. Fuentes, "Hail to the Chief," 2.

78. Fuentes, "Prologue," 27.

79. See Carlos Fuentes, "Argentina: A Prayer for Democracy," *Los Angeles Times* (May 31, 1987): sec. v, p. 1 ff.; and "A New Society Tests Mexico's Old Politics of Unity," *Los Angeles Times* (September 27, 1987): sec. v, p. 2.

80. Carlos Fuentes, "Uncle Sam, Stay Home," *Harper's Magazine* (January 1989): 14–17.

81. Carlos Fuentes, "Discurso de Carlos Fuentes en la entrega del Premio Cervantes 1987," in *Carlos Fuentes: Premio de Literatura en Lengua Castellana "Miguel de Cervantes" 1987* (Barcelona: Anthropos, 1988), 80.

82. Fuentes, "Prologue," 26.

83. Fuentes, "Prologue," 19–20.

84. Carlos Fuentes, *La campaña* (Mexico City: Fondo de Cultura Económica, 1990); English version, *The Campaign*, trans. Alfred MacAdam (New York: Farrar, Straus & Giroux, 1991). Quotations from the novel will be followed by parenthetical page references to the Spanish original and English translation, respectively. I have made some changes in MacAdam's translation.

85. Roberto González Echevarría, "Passion's Progress," review of *The Campaign*, by Carlos Fuentes, *The New York Times Book Review* (October 6, 1991): 25.

86. For further evidence of Fuentes's interest in Diderot, see "Two Centuries of Diderot," in *Myself With Others*, 72–88.

87. In the novel's last chapter, Varela speaks of "a life of the liberator Simón Bolívar, a manuscript stained with rain and tied with tricolor ribbons, which the author, who called himself Aureliano García, had sent to me, as best he could, from Barranquilla." He complains that this chronicle is "too sad" and declines to publish it (251–52/238). The name Aureliano García alludes to Colonel Aureliano Buendía, a character in Gabriel García Márquez's *Cien años de soledad* (1967), as well as to García Márquez himself. The manuscript Varela decides not to publish resembles García Márquez's *El general en su laberinto*, which appeared the year before *La campaña*.

Chapter IV

1. Carlos Fuentes, interviewed by Herman P. Doezema, *Modern Fiction Studies* 18 (Winter 1972–1973): 493. Further references will appear in parentheses in the text.

2. Carlos Fuentes, *Cambio de piel* (Mexico City: Joaquín Mortiz, 1967); English version, *A Change of Skin*, trans. Sam Hileman (London: Jonathan Cape, 1968). Quotations will be followed by parenthetical page references to the Spanish original and the corresponding place in the English text, respectively. However, I have provided my own translations of the passages I quote from Fuentes's novel.

3. In a 1980 interview with Jorge Anadón, Fuentes was already claiming that his work should be viewed as a unified whole: "I think I have written a single novel, with different chapters, a little like a Mexican comedy, in the manner of Balzac." See Carlos Fuentes, interviewed by Jorge Anadón, *Revista Iberoamericana* 123–124 (April–September 1983): 630.

4. In the interview with Doezema, Fuentes describes *Cambio de piel* as the expression of a "*will* . . . to plunge into the crisis [of the novel] and drown in it if necessary, to be crushed and killed" (493).

5. Carlos Fuentes, "Situación del escritor en América Latina," interviewed by Emir Rodríguez Monegal, 19. Further references will appear in parentheses in the text.

6. He writes that "the development of the mass media and social sciences effectively led to the annexation of the traditional novel's themes and procedures." See Carlos Fuentes, *La nueva novela hispanoamericana* (Mexico City: Joaquín Mortiz, 1969), 22. Further references will appear in parentheses in the text.

7. Carlos Fuentes, "¿Ha muerto la novela?" in *Geografía de la novela*, 9. Further references will appear in parentheses in the text.

8. See Daniel Bell, *The End of Ideology*, rev. ed. (New York: Free Press, 1967).

9. Drawing on an existentialist thematics, Paz claimed that it was through the universal human experience of solitude that Mexicans had become "contemporaries of all humankind." See *El laberinto de la soledad*, 340.

10. Jean Franco criticizes Fuentes for succumbing to the attractions of what she calls the "universalism of the stars" of the society of the spectacle (a phrase she borrows from Guy Debord). See "Narrador, Autor, Superestrella: La Narrativa Latinoamericana en la Época de la Cultura de Masas," in *La Cultura Moderna de América Latina* (Mexico City: Grijalbo, 1983), 329. Jorge Ruiz Basto describes Fuentes as a "leading protagonist of the moment in time in Latin America when the literary work comes to be viewed once and for all as a commodity." He suggests that Fuentes understood the need to make himself into a "glamorous figure" because "like all commodities, in order to circulate successfully in the market, the literary work needs a charismatic figure who with his prestige and personal qualities can make the commodity more attractive to the consumer." See *De la modernidad y otras creencias (en torno a "Cambio de piel" de Carlos Fuentes)* (Mexico City: UNAM, 1992), 12.

11. In her history of the Mexican novel, Sara Sefchovich notes that beginning around 1965 there emerges in Mexico a body of work that is profoundly hermetic and self-reflexive in nature. For Sefchovich, this constitutes a significant—and temporary—departure from the main tradition of the Mexican novel, which, she argues, is fundamentally realist and didactic in orientation. For the first time, she writes, "novels were written that had no ideas . . . no themes, no history, but dealt instead with the act of writing novels." Sefchovich ties this development to the rise of the mass media: "The more mass culture demanded passivity from its audience . . . the more these novels forced the reader to participate, to be present and active." See *México: país de ideas, país de novelas: Una sociología de la literatura mexicana* (Mexico City: Grijalbo, 1987), 210, 208.

12. Fuentes's somewhat cavalier assertion of the indistinguishability of an Amazon Indian and an avant-garde European novelist was symptomatic of an antihistorical perspective that made him highly vulnerable to attacks from the left. Carlos Blanco Aguinaga produced a biting critique of Fuentes's use of the categories of myth, language, and structure, arguing that they serve only to project a vision of social and political immobility.

See "Sobre la idea de la novela en Carlos Fuentes," in *De mitólogos y novelistas* (Madrid: Turner, n.d.), 73–108. Roberto Fernández Retamar saw reflected in Fuentes's theory of the novel a "vogue for linguistics" which Retamar regarded as symptomatic of "the attempt at ahistorization peculiar to a dying class." Fuentes's refusal to engage in an "understanding and evaluation" of the vision of history presented in the Latin American novel, his resort to "mere linguistic speculations," led Retamar to charge Fuentes with occupying a "shrewd rightist viewpoint within our countries." See "Caliban," in *Caliban and Other Essays*, trans. Edward Baker (Minneapolis: University of Minnesota Press, 1989), 31–33.

13. The picture of Nietzsche appears to be a reproduction of an 1899 drawing by Hans Olde. It shows him at the end of his life—both physically and mentally incapacitated—sunk in the contemplation of a sunset. The choice of this particular image of Nietzsche serves to draw attention to the possible madness of the narrator of *Cambio de piel*. Hans Olde's drawing appears in Joachim Köhler, *Zarathustras Geheimnis: Friedrich Nietzsche und seine verschlüsselte Botschaft* (Nördlingen: Greno, 1989).

14. The photograph was originally part of a report on the destruction of the Jewish quarter of Warsaw by the SS in 1943. The report, which reveals the Nazi obsession with documentation, consists of both written and photographic documents. It came to be known as the Stroop Report after the SS officer who commanded the operation in Warsaw, and who, after the liquidation of the Ghetto, submitted the report to SS chief Heinrich Himmler. The Stroop Report was first published in a facsimile edition in Germany in 1960. For the English edition, see Sybil Milton, ed., *The Stroop Report: The Jewish Quarter of Warsaw Is No More!* (New York: Pantheon, 1979).

15. In the interview with Doezema, Fuentes explains that "Freddy Lambert is actually a character composed of two names, the name of Nietzsche and the name of Louis Lambert, the character from the Balzac novel" (497). In the same interview, he explains the link with *The Cabinet of Dr. Caligari* when he says that at the end of *Cambio de piel* the reader is "left with nothing but a sort of Doctor Caligari who is in a madhouse, who doesn't know very well why he is there, who is probably the narrator" (497).

16. Jean Franco, "Memoria, Narración y Repetición: La Narrativa Hispanoamericana en la Época de la Cultura de Masas," in David Viñas et al., *Más Allá del Boom: Literatura y Mercado* (Mexico City: Marcha, 1981), 127.

17. Carlos Fuentes, "Tener sólo historia sagrada es vivir fuera de la

historia," *Siempre!* (March 30, 1966): ii. All quotations from this article are taken from this page.

18. Susan Sontag, "Notes on Camp," in *Against Interpretation* (New York: Dell, 1966), 289. Further references will appear in parentheses in the text.

19. Andrew Ross points out that "in liberating the objects and discourses of the past from disdain and neglect, camp generates its own kind of economy. Camp, in this respect, is the *re-creation of surplus value from forgotten forms of labor.*" But he also calls attention to the fact that the ability to engage in this kind of re-creative operation is reserved for a select group: "What is being threatened in an age of mass culture is precisely the power of tastemaking intellectuals to influence the canons of taste, and . . . the significance of the 'new sensibility' of camp in the 60s is that it presents a means of salvaging that privilege." See "Uses of Camp," in *No Respect: Intellectuals and Popular Culture* (New York: Routledge, 1989), 151, 145.

20. Perhaps the single theorist most responsible for the excitement surrounding the possibilities created by the rise of the electronic media in these years was Marshall McLuhan. See especially *The Gutenberg Galaxy* (Toronto: University of Toronto Press, 1962); *Understanding Media* (New York: McGraw-Hill, 1965); and *The Medium is the Massage* (New York: Bantam, 1967). One of McLuhan's principal theses was that the electronic media were beginning to draw the entire globe into a single community, a notion that was captured in the term "global village." The concept of the global village clearly resonated with Fuentes's idea of Latin America's contemporaneity with the rest of the world. Fuentes alludes to McLuhan in the interview with Rodríguez Monegal.

21. There is a similar slippage in the interview with Rodríguez Monegal. At one point, Fuentes responds to an observation by Rodríguez Monegal about the Latin American taste for camp by talking about surrealism: "In our countries, and especially in Mexico, there has always existed a kind of radical intuition. You remember that Breton called Mexico the promised land of surrealism" (7).

22. Patricia Waugh, *Metafiction: The Theory and Practice of Self-Conscious Fiction* (London: Methuen, 1984), 2.

23. In his 1964 interview with Emmanuel Carballo, Fuentes describes Robbe-Grillet's novels as the self-consuming kind that "exist only for themselves," and indicated that such novels were not the type he was interested in writing. See Carballo, *Diecinueve protagonistas*, 430.

24. Such an argument is a common strategy for reaffirming the relevance to reality of apparently narcissistic fiction. Patricia Waugh offers a

succinct expression of this position: "Metafictional deconstruction has not only provided novelists and their readers with a better understanding of the fundamental structure of narrative; it has also offered extremely accurate models for understanding the contemporary experience of the world as a construction, an artifice, a web of interdependent semiotic systems." See *Metafiction*, 9.

25. David Gallagher, "Mexico's Stifled Tiger," review of *A Change of Skin*, by Carlos Fuentes, *The New York Times Book Review* (February 4, 1968): 41.

26. Steven Boldy has developed the most sustained and thought-provoking critical reading of *Cambio de piel*. In several articles, Boldy argues that the pervasive unreliability and uncertainty of *Cambio de piel* —the virtual impossibility of reconstructing a stable representational world from the text—is part of a deliberate strategy to oppose every tendency to fix meaning, to sublimate a threatening otherness, to establish hierarchies, to recuperate strangeness. All these techniques of control Boldy defines as elements in the rationalist project of modernity. See Steven Boldy, "Carlos Fuentes," in John King, ed., *On Modern Latin American Fiction* (New York: Farrar, Straus & Giroux, 1989), 155–72; "*Cambio de piel*: Literature and Evil," *Bulletin of Hispanic Studies* 66 (1989): 55–72; and, "*Cambio de piel*, de Carlos Fuentes: El poder de la contradicción," *Revista Canadiense de Estudios Hispánicos* 19 (Winter 1995): 401–6.

27. I discuss the role of ancient Greece in *Cambio de piel* in "The Banquets of Civilization: The Idea of Ancient Greece in Rodó, Reyes and Fuentes," *Annals of Scholarship* 7 (1990): 313–18.

28. Terry Eagleton, "Capitalism, Modernism and Postmodernism," *New Left Review* 152 (1985): 60–72.

29. In *La nueva novela*, Fuentes gives the title "Cortázar: La caja de Pandora" to his discussion of *Rayuela*. Fuentes centers his reading on the notion of "impossibility"—in particular the impossibility of representing certain experiences in language: "the passion of love cannot be named: one can only apprehend it in smells, kisses, touching, penetration, dreams. A dream, like love, is a unity without words. . . . But a dream cannot be represented in a state of waking" (77). Some further relevant details: Javier's first book is titled *El sueño*; *El sueño* was the original title of *Cambio de piel*; Fuentes dedicated *Cambio de piel* to Julio Cortázar and his wife Aurora.

30. Steven Boldy, "*Cambio de piel*: Literature and Evil," 64.

31. Matei Calinescu, *Five Faces of Modernity* (Durham: Duke University Press, 1987), 275–76.

32. Linda Hutcheon, *A Poetics of Postmodernism: History, Theory, Fiction* (New York: Routledge, 1988), 88.

33. Fredric Jameson, *Postmodernism, or, The Cultural Logic of Late Capitalism* (Durham: Duke University Press, 1993), 18.

34. Jameson, 6.

35. Jameson, 25.

Chapter V

1. Aníbal González argues that journalism has often served as an instrument with which Latin American writers have sought to promote the modernization of their societies. See *Journalism and the Development of Spanish American Narrative* (New York: Cambridge University Press, 1993), especially chapter 1, "Journalism, modernity, and narrative fiction in Spanish America," 1–20.

2. Carlos Fuentes, interviewed by Lee Baxandall, *Studies on the Left* 3, no. 1 (1962): 49–50.

3. Carlos Fuentes, interviewed by Jason Weiss, in Jason Weiss, *Writing at Risk: Interviews in Paris with Uncommon Writers* (Iowa City: University of Iowa Press, 1991), 117–18.

4. Carlos Fuentes to Fernando Benítez, Paris, February 26, 1967, Carlos Fuentes Papers, Special Collections, Princeton University Library.

5. Fuentes to Benítez, Paris, May 16, 1966; and Fuentes to Benítez, London, March 7, 1968.

6. Fuentes to Benítez, London, May 3, 1968.

7. Fuentes to José Donoso, Paris, November 1, 1968, José Donoso Papers, Special Collections, Princeton University Library.

8. Carlos Fuentes, "Cronología personal," in Julio Ortega, *Retrato de Carlos Fuentes*, 109.

9. In *Diana, o la cazadora solitaria*, Fuentes describes a writer named Carlos in whom the events of 1968 provoke a severe crisis of conscience. Carlos condemns himself for his failure to participate more directly in "that parting of the waters in modern Mexican life that was 1968." He deplores his writing's lack of engagement with the world around him: "Tlatelolco was for me a terrible sign . . . of the separation between the vital content of things and their literary expression in my work." See *Diana, o la cazadora solitaria* (Mexico City: Alfaguara, 1994), 64, 67; English version, *Diana: The Goddess Who Hunts Alone*, trans. Alfred MacAdam (New York: Farrar, Straus & Giroux, 1995), 57, 60.

10. The massacre took place on the afternoon of June 10, 1971. It is generally referred to as *el Jueves de Corpus*, because it occurred on the day of Corpus Christi. Alan Riding believes Echeverría was responsible for the massacre: he points out that while Echeverría fired the mayor and the

police chief of Mexico City, thus implicitly blaming them for the event, both men returned to powerful posts in the government within a few years. See Alan Riding, *Distant Neighbors: A Portrait of the Mexicans* (New York: Vintage, 1985), 62, 78.

11. Carlos Fuentes, "La disyuntiva mexicana," in *Tiempo mexicano*, 147–93. Further references will appear in parentheses in the text.

12. Carlos Fuentes, "Opciones críticas en el verano de nuestro descontento," *Plural* 11 (August 1972): 3–9. Further references will appear in parentheses in the text.

13. See "La historia como toma de poderes," in *Tiempo mexicano*, 137. Further references will appear in parentheses in the text. An earlier version of this essay—in the form of a review of John Womack's *Zapata and the Mexican Revolution*—appeared in *The New York Review of Books*. See "Viva Zapata," *The New York Review of Books* (March 13, 1969), 5–6, 8, 10, 12.

14. James R. Fortson, *Perspectivas mexicanas desde París: Un diálogo con Carlos Fuentes* (Mexico City: Corporación Editorial, 1973), 115. Further references will appear in parentheses in the text.

15. Fuentes to Benítez, Paris, September 15, 1973.

16. Gabriel Zaid, "Carta a Carlos Fuentes," *Plural* 12 (September 1972): 53.

17. Carlos Fuentes, statement in "México 1972: Los escritores y la política," *Plural* 13 (October 1972): 27. In "La disyuntiva mexicana" Fuentes had developed an analogous argument in his criticism of those who hoped that a spontaneous uprising of the masses would bring about the desired changes in Mexican society. Fuentes places such thinkers in the tradition of Georges Sorel, whom he describes as "the prophet of spontaneous catastrophe and radical abstention." He notes that on the theoretical level Lenin provided the arguments against the spontaneist position, and that on a practical level history had proven the weakness of Sorel's "catastrophic expectations," for they had led only to a different catastrophe, that is, to the rise of fascism. See "La disyuntiva mexicana," 180–84.

18. Carlos Fuentes, statement in "México 1972," 28.

19. Only a few years earlier, Fuentes had written a long essay on the May '68 uprising in Paris, in which he described the French students who had taken to the streets as "the children of Marx and Rimbaud," and celebrated their way of mixing poetry and politics. In later years, critics who felt that Fuentes was in some way not a truly Mexican writer sometimes supported their contention by noting that in 1968, when Mexico was going through tremendous upheavals culminating in the Tlatelolco massacre of October of that year, Fuentes was in Paris rather than in his home

country. Perhaps it was in anticipation of such criticisms that Fuentes wrote in his essay on May 1968: "Through France we can understand and be understood." This was meant to indicate that his interest in France derived from a prior desire to understand his own country. Clearly, the experience of May 1968 left a mark on *Terra Nostra*, both in the choice of setting for the opening chapter, and in the favorable treatment of the revolutionary millenarian movements, which in Fuentes's version acquire a distinctly sixties-like flavor. See *París: La revolución de mayo* (Mexico City: Era, 1968), 10, 32.

20. Fuentes to Benítez, Paris, July 5, 1976.

21. Fuentes to Benítez, Paris, July 5, 1976.

22. Gastón García Cantú, "El desafío y la marea," *Plural* 57 (June 1976): 51.

23. The first speech was titled "Los Diez Desafíos que Debe Superar México." It was published in *El Sol de México* (December 1, 1975): 1, 14. A note preceding the text of Fuentes's speech explains that it was presented at a national convention on the mining industry presided over by López Portillo. The second speech was presented at a meeting of the IEPES (an organ of the PRI) on nationalism and international solidarity held in Mazatlán in May 1976. A report in *Excélsior* notes that because Fuentes was unable to attend the meeting in person, somebody else read his speech for him. The *Excélsior* article quotes a number of sentences from Fuentes's text. See Roberto Vizcaino, "El Embajador Flores Olea, Ante JLP: Permanente Intervención Imperialista en América Latina, Para Crear 'una Falange de Dictaduras,'" *Excélsior* (May 15, 1976): 19A.

24. Fuentes, "Los Diez Desafíos que Debe Superar México," 14.

25. Vizcaino, "El Embajador Flores Olea, Ante JLP," 19A.

26. Carlos Fuentes, *Terra Nostra* (Barcelona: Seix Barral, 1975); English version, *Terra Nostra*, trans. Margaret Sayers Peden (New York: Farrar, Straus & Giroux, 1976). Quotations will be followed by parenthetical page references to the Spanish original and the English translation, respectively.

27. Fuentes mentions Cohn's book in the "Reconocimientos" with which he prefaces *Terra Nostra* (these acknowledgements were not included in the English translation of the novel). The fullest discussion of the immense range of sources Fuentes used in writing *Terra Nostra* is provided by Luz Rodríguez Carranza in *Un teatro de la memoria: Análisis de "Terra Nostra" de Carlos Fuentes* (Leuven/Buenos Aires: Leuven University Press/Danilo Albero Vergara, 1990), 105–249. Rodríguez Carranza points out that Fuentes's other major source of information, besides Cohn's book,

is Jean Marquès-Rivière's *Histoire des Doctrines Esotériques* (Paris: Payot, 1971).

28. Norman Cohn, *The Pursuit of the Millennium: Revolutionary Millenarians and Mystical Anarchists of the Middle Ages* (New York: Oxford University Press, 1970), 285–86. Further references will appear in parentheses in the text.

29. Carlos Fuentes, *Cervantes o la crítica de la lectura* (Mexico City: Joaquín Mortiz, 1976), 36. Further references will appear in parentheses in the text.

30. Fuentes's principal source for this reading is José Antonio Maravall's *Las comunidades de Castilla* (1963), which Fuentes describes in *Cervantes* as the definitive work on the rebellion of the *comuneros* (56).

31. Fuentes, *The Buried Mirror*, 153–55. Further references will appear in parentheses in the text.

32. José Antonio Maravall, *Las comunidades de Castilla: Una primera revolución moderna*, 2nd ed. (Madrid: Revista de Occidente, 1970).

33. Maravall, 234–36.

34. Maravall, 267.

35. See Rodríguez Carranza, 189.

36. Lois Parkinson Zamora provides the fullest discussion of the interlinked themes of utopia and apocalypse in *Terra Nostra*. Zamora's assessment of the role of the millenarian groups in Fuentes's novel parallels my own: she argues that Fuentes uses them "to signal the irruption of the modern, multivalent world of relative values into Felipe's Spain." She also notes that "in the heresy of the Free Spirit, with its deification of human beings, Fuentes locates a radical intersection of humanistic politics and erotic idealism such as that which characterizes *Terra Nostra* itself." But Zamora frames these claims within an overall argument that presents *Terra Nostra* as an anti-utopian and anti-apocalyptic novel. Zamora distinguishes between a utopianism that has as its goal "earthly transformations," on the one hand, and an apocalypticism moved by "otherworldly visions," on the other. The latter Fuentes rejects; the former "proposes exactly the engagement with history that *Terra Nostra* confirms." Yet it would appear that the vision of earthly transformation held by the revolutionary millenarians is fueled by a distinctly otherworldly mind-set. See *Writing the Apocalypse: Historical Vision in Contemporary U.S. and Latin American Fiction* (New York: Cambridge University Press, 1989), 162–65.

37. Rodríguez Carranza has established that Fuentes in fact mixes references to various different heretical doctrines in these passages. See *Un teatro de la memoria*, 122–23.

38. For a discussion of the role of eroticism in Fuentes's work, see Wendy Faris, "'Without Sin, and with Pleasure': The Erotic Dimensions of Fuentes' Fiction," *Novel* 20 (Fall 1986): 62–77. Faris coins the term "sexual Zapatism" (63) to describe Fuentes's exalted view of the erotic dimension of life.

39. Allen Josephs, in a detailed discussion of the several layers of intertextual references that compose the ending of *Terra Nostra*, argues that Fuentes draws on the literary, philosophical, and religious notion of the two halves of the soul which need each other in order to become whole. See "The End of *Terra Nostra*," *World Literature Today* 57 (Autumn 1983): 563–67. Catherine Swietlicki draws on the work of Mircea Eliade to suggest that the androgynous being of the conclusion of *Terra Nostra* is "a mythological expression of the primordial state of creative wholeness and tranquility which existed before the beginning of time, according to the belief systems of archaic peoples." See "Doubling, Reincarnation, and Cosmic Order in *Terra Nostra*," *Hispanófila* 79 (September 1983): 101.

40. I owe this insight to Alberto Ruy Sánchez.

41. José Joaquín Blanco offers a very sharp description of the paradox of Fuentes's work when he says that "the reader of *Cambio de piel* detests the author of utterings such as the one about the 'historical crime' of not supporting the state, while the audience that admires such statements detests the elitism of *Cumpleaños*." See "Fuentes: de la pasión por los mitos al polyforum de las mitologías," in *La paja en el ojo* (Puebla: Universidad Autónoma de Puebla, 1980), 267.

42. Brian McHale, *Postmodernist Fiction* (New York: Methuen, 1987), 16.

43. Fuentes, *La nueva novela hispanoamericana*, 88.

44. See Roderic Camp, *Intellectuals and the State in Twentieth-Century Mexico* (Austin: University of Texas Press, 1985).

45. McHale, *Postmodernist Fiction*, 10.

46. McHale, 13.

47. Raymond L. Williams offers the fullest discussion of *Terra Nostra* from the point of view of a postmodernist poetics in *The Writings of Carlos Fuentes*, 95–104. Williams describes *Terra Nostra* both as a "fundamentally . . . postmodern text" and as a "transitional text that is both modern and postmodern" (103). *Terra Nostra* is modern because it is "an ambitious grand narrative, a totalizing and utopian project" (96), while it is postmodern because it "questions, undermines, and subverts Western historical truth" (104).

48. Fuentes, "Situación del escritor en América Latina," 17.

49. Carlos Fuentes, "Travails with Time," interviewed by Debra A. Castillo, *The Review of Contemporary Fiction* 8, no. 2 (Summer 1988): 159.

50. See Carlos Fuentes, "Las dos orillas," in *El naranjo o los círculos del tiempo* (Mexico City: Alfaguara, 1993), 9–60. See also my review of the English translation of this collection in *Review: Latin American Literature and Arts* 52 (Spring 1996): 100–102.

51. The reference is to Jean-François Lyotard, *The Postmodern Condition: A Report on Knowledge* (Minneapolis: University of Minnesota Press, 1984).

52. Martín Hopenhayn, "Postmodernism and Neoliberalism in Latin America," *boundary 2* 20, no. 3 (1993): 96–97. Further references will appear in parentheses in the text.

53. It should be noted that Hopenhayn is very alert to the "service" postmodern discourse lends to "the political-cultural offensive of the market economy." Hopenhayn draws attention to the convergence between the postmodernist exaltation of diversity and the neoliberal celebration of the market "considered as the only social institution that orders without coercion, guaranteeing a diversity of tastes, projects, languages, and strategies." In the neoliberal argument, the rise of the market implies an assault on the state: "Only by expanding the reach of the market can the interventionist and globalizing excesses of the state be avoided" (98–99). Nevertheless, Hopenhayn believes it is possible to pursue a postmodern thematics without becoming captive to the ideology of neoliberalism.

54. Norbert Lechner makes a similar point when he observes (echoing Habermas) that what is involved in postmodernism is a "critique that is interior to an incomplete project of modernity." See Norbert Lechner, "A Disenchantment Called Postmodernism," *boundary 2* 20, no. 3 (1993): 123.

55. Carlos Fuentes, "Después de la guerra fría: los problemas del nuevo orden mundial," in *Tres discursos para dos aldeas* (Buenos Aires: Fondo de Cultura Económica, 1993), 99.

56. I note that one of the sections in *The Buried Mirror* on contemporary Spain is entitled "Rescued by Culture." See *The Buried Mirror*, 338–39.

57. Zamora, *Writing the Apocalypse*, 172.

58. Margaret Sayers Peden, "A Reader's Guide to *Terra Nostra*," *Review* 31 (January/April 1982): 42.

59. Djelal Kadir, "Fuentes and the Profane Sublime," in *The Other Writing: Postcolonial Essays in Latin America's Writing Culture* (West Lafayette, Ind.: Purdue University Press, 1993), 86.

60. Carl Gutiérrez, "Provisional Historicity: Reading through *Terra Nostra*," *The Review of Contemporary Fiction* 8, no. 2 (Summer 1988): 257–58.

61. Rodríguez Carranza, 254.

62. Blanco, 68.

63. Roberto González Echevarría, "*Terra Nostra*: Theory and Practice," in *The Voice of the Masters*, 96.

64. González Echevarría, 96.

Chapter VI

1. Eric Hobsbawm, *Nations and Nationalism Since 1780: Programme, Myth, Reality* (New York: Cambridge University Press, 1990), 92.

2. Carlos Fuentes, *Agua quemada* (Mexico City: Fondo de Cultura Económica, 1981); English version, *Burnt Water*, trans. Margaret Sayers Peden (New York: Farrar, Straus & Giroux, 1980). *Burnt Water* includes stories from *Los días enmascarados* and *Cantar de ciegos* (1964), as well as from *Agua quemada*. Quotations will be followed by parenthetical page references to the Spanish original and the English translation, respectively. I have made some changes in Peden's translations.

3. Benedict Anderson, *Imagined Communities: Reflections on the Origin and Spread of Nationalism*, rev. ed. (New York: Verso, 1991), 25.

4. Anderson, 25.

5. Octavio Paz, *Corriente alterna* (Mexico City: Siglo XXI, 1967), 132.

6. Sigmund Freud, "Contributions to the Psychology of Love. A Special Type of Object Choice Made by Men," trans. Joan Riviere, *Collected Papers*, Vol. 4 (New York: Basic Books, 1959), 201.

7. René Girard, *Deceit, Desire, and the Novel: Self and Other in Literary Structure*, trans. Yvonne Freccero (Baltimore: The Johns Hopkins University Press, 1965), 1.

8. Girard, *Deceit*, 13.

9. René Girard, *Violence and the Sacred*, trans. Patrick Gregory (Baltimore: The Johns Hopkins University Press, 1977), 170.

10. Girard, *Violence*, 175.

11. Girard, *Violence*, 174.

12. Becky Boling, "Parricide and Revolution: Fuentes's 'El día de las madres' and *Gringo viejo*," *Hispanófila* 96 (May 1989): 77.

13. Carlos Fuentes, *Una familia lejana* (Mexico City: Era, 1980); English version, *Distant Relations*, trans. Margaret Sayers Peden (New York: Farrar, Straus & Giroux, 1982). Quotations from the novel will be followed by parenthetical page references to the Spanish original and English translation, respectively. I have made some changes in Peden's translation.

14. James V. Romano, reading *Una familia lejana* from the perspective of dependency theory, interprets Fuentes's invention of an alternative (French) identity for himself as a sign of Fuentes's alienation from national historical experience and of his alignment with the interests of transnational capital. See "Authorial Identity and National Disintegration in Latin America," *Ideologies and Literature* 4 (Spring 1989): 167–98. My own reading is closer to the one developed by Margo Glantz, who views the oscillation between France and Spanish America in *Una familia lejana* as the expression of "an acceptance of transculturation and the constant coming and going of the caravels: the inhabitants of the Indies are hybrid beings, never fully identified with themselves." See "Fantasmas y jardines: Una familia lejana," *Revista iberoamericana* 118–119 (January–June 1982): 397–402.

15. Perry Anderson, "Nation-States and National Identity," review of *The Identity of France*, Vol. II, *People and Production*, by Fernand Braudel, *London Review of Books* (May 9, 1991): 6.

16. See Samuel Ramos, *Perfil del hombre y la cultura en México* (Mexico City: SEP, 1987).

17. Paz, *El laberinto de la soledad*, 154.

18. Paz, *El laberinto de la soledad*, 217.

19. See Martin Stabb, *América Latina en busca de una identidad: modelos del ensayo ideológico hispanoamericano 1890–1960* (Caracas: Monte Ávila, 1969).

20. Octavio Paz, *Posdata* (Mexico City: Siglo XXI, 1970), 134.

21. Roger Bartra, *La jaula de la melancolía: Identidad y metamorfosis del mexicano* (Mexico City: Grijalbo, 1987), 205.

22. Bartra, 238.

23. For Michel Foucault's argument concerning the link between the production of subjects and techniques of subjection, see *Discipline and Punish: The Birth of the Prison*, trans. Alan Sheridan (New York: Vintage, 1979).

24. Fuentes, *The Buried Mirror*, 308.

Chapter VII

1. Simón Bolívar, "Discurso de Angostura (1819)," in *Escritos políticos*, ed. Graciela Soriano (Madrid: Alianza, 1990), 101.

2. Bolívar, 101.

3. Bolívar, 107.

4. Domingo Faustino Sarmiento, *Facundo: Civilización y barbarie* (Madrid: Cátedra, 1990), 173–75.

5. Sarmiento, 174.

6. Sarmiento, 176.

7. José Martí, "Nuestra América," in *Sus mejores páginas*, ed. Raimundo Lazo (Mexico City: Porrúa, 1985), 88.

8. José Carlos Mariátegui, *Siete ensayos de interpretación de la realidad peruana* (Mexico City: Era, 1988), 193.

9. Paz, *El laberinto de la soledad*, 265.

10. See Paz, *El laberinto de la soledad*, 273–78.

11. Octavio Paz, "El espejo indiscreto," in *El ogro filantrópico: Historia y política 1971–1978* (Mexico City: Joaquín Mortiz, 1979), 57.

12. Paz, "El espejo indiscreto," 57.

13. The topic of the real nation and the legal nation is debated not only in the tradition of the political and cultural essay in Latin America, but also in several modern academic disciplines. I will give two examples. The anthropologist Guillermo Bonfil Batalla proposes an opposition between a "deep" Mexico rooted in the indigenous past and an "imaginary" Mexico linked to Europe. This opposition is analogous to the opposition between the real and the legal, as is clear from Bonfil's description of the goal pursued by the "imaginary" Mexico: "The country wants to be modern right away, by virtue of the law, and if reality follows a different path, then it must be a mistaken and illegal reality." See *México profundo: Una civilización negada* (Mexico City: Grijalbo, 1994), 107. The literary and cultural critic Roberto Schwarz offers an interpretation of nineteenth-century Brazilian culture that centers on the dissonance between the ideas and institutions copied from European bourgeois civilization and the real persistence of forms of economic exploitation, such as slavery, inherited from colonial times. See *Misplaced Ideas: Essays on Brazilian Culture*, ed. John Gledson (London: Verso, 1992), especially 1–40.

14. Fuentes, *The Buried Mirror*, 257.

15. Fuentes, *Valiente mundo nuevo*, 112. Further references will appear in parentheses in the text.

16. Carlos Fuentes, "The Lessons of Latin America," keynote speech, "Dialogue of the Americas" Conference, Rutgers University, New Jersey, November 7, 1996.

17. In 1971, in the concluding essay of *Tiempo mexicano*, Fuentes was already arguing that civil society, a concept he defined with the help of Antonio Gramsci, ought to be viewed as the principal agent of social change in Mexico. As I showed in an earlier chapter, this enthusiasm for civil society was complicated and even undermined in the 1970s by Fuentes's support for President Echeverría. By the late 1970s, however,

Fuentes had once again assumed a more distant stance with regard to the Mexican state. Throughout the 1980s and '90s, Fuentes has been a consistent advocate of a stronger civil society. For a discussion of the relationship in Latin America between intellectuals and civil society, see George Yúdice, "Intellectuals and Civil Society," *Annals of Scholarship* 11 (1996): 157–74.

18. The chapter that includes this passage was left out of the English translation.

19. See George Pendle, *A History of Latin America* (New York: Penguin, 1973), 86–88, for a statement of this thesis. A dissenting note comes from John Lynch, who argues that "the greatest threat to the Spanish Empire came from American interests rather than European ideas. To suppose that the thought of the Enlightenment made revolutionaries of Spanish Americans is to confuse cause and effect. Some were already dissenters; for this reason they sought in the new philosophy further inspiration for their own ideals, intellectual justification for the revolution to come. While the Enlightenment had an important role in Spanish America, therefore, this role was not primarily a 'cause' of independence." See *The Spanish American Revolutions, 1808–1826*, 2nd ed. (New York: Norton, 1986), 28.

20. For a brief account of this episode in Spanish American history, see Fuentes, *The Buried Mirror*, 235–37.

21. The paradox is related to a broad opposition at the heart of the twentieth-century reception of the Enlightenment. On the one hand, there is a powerful current of thought, associated with thinkers ranging from Adorno and Horkheimer to Jean-François Lyotard, which believes that the Enlightenment adherence to concepts such as "reason" and "progress" produces an abstract, coercive, and homogenizing ideology that neglects and suppresses the multiplicity of the real. On the other hand, there is a tradition that maintains that Enlightenment philosophy proposes an experimental, practical, and unprejudiced approach to reality. For expressions of the second point of view, see the essays in Arthur P. Whitaker, ed., *Latin America and the Enlightenment*, 2nd ed. (Ithaca, N.Y.: Cornell University Press, 1961). Fuentes sees this duality as a feature of the Enlightenment itself: in *Valiente mundo nuevo* he contrasts Voltaire's negation of everything that does not fit his abstract principles with Diderot's openness to the flux and variety of reality (45).

22. In *The Buried Mirror*, Fuentes describes how "the fiery and fanatical Buenos Aires Jacobin Juan José Castelli spread the ideas of the French Enlightenment in upper Peru, spreading the gospel of Rousseau and Voltaire to the Quechua and Aymará Indians while forcibly suppressing

tributes, distributing land, building schools, and promoting equality" (261). But Fuentes expresses serious reservations about the historical role of the intellectuals in the Spanish American revolutions: "This democracy, stated in law and proclaimed from above, disregarded the multiple realities that had to be changed if democracy was to be more than an intention, or freedom more than a declaration like Castelli's to the Indians" (262). It is clear that Baltasar Bustos is to some extent based on Castelli.

23. See, for example, *Valiente mundo nuevo*, 16.

24. On the specific features of Mexican nationalism, see David Brading, *Los orígenes del nacionalismo mexicano*, 2nd ed. (Mexico City: Era, 1988), and *The First America: The Spanish Monarchy, Creole Patriots, and the Liberal State 1492–1867* (New York: Cambridge University Press, 1991).

25. Carlos Fuentes, "Nota del autor," in *Tres discursos para dos aldeas* (Buenos Aires: Fondo de Cultura Económica, 1993), 21–22.

26. Fuentes, "Nota del autor," 22.

27. Octavio Paz, *Itinerario* (Mexico City: Fondo de Cultura Económica, 1993), 43.

28. Carlos Fuentes, "Imaginación y cambio," *El País* (November 23, 1995): 13.

29. Fuentes, "Imaginación y cambio," 13.

30. Fuentes, "Imaginación y cambio," 13.

31. On Charles Maurras I have found it useful to consult Yves Chiron, *La vie de Maurras* (Paris: Perrin, 1991); Michael Sutton, *Nationalism, Positivism and Catholicism: The Politics of Charles Maurras and French Catholics 1890–1914* (Cambridge: Cambridge University Press, 1982); Pol Vandromme, *Maurras: entre le légiste et le contestataire* (Paris: Téqui, 1991); and Maurice Weyembergh, *Charles Maurras et la Révolution française* (Paris: J. Vrin, 1992).

32. Fuentes, "Imaginación y cambio," 13.

33. Tony Judt writes that "Sartre . . . paid indirect homage to Maurras by adopting the latter's categories of *pays réel* and *pays légal*, with the interests of the proletariat . . . standing in for the *pays réel* of Maurras's royalist imaginings." See *Past Imperfect: French Intellectuals, 1944–1956* (Berkeley: University of California Press 1992), 298.

34. See Jorge Castañeda, *Utopia Unarmed: The Latin American Left After the Cold War* (New York: Knopf, 1993), 267–97.

35. For Fuentes's views on the importance of education for the future of Mexico, see "Hacia el milenio," in Carlos Fuentes et al., *Los compromisos con la nación* (Mexico City: Plaza & Janés, 1996), 35–36.

36. Carlos Alonso, "The Mourning After: García Márquez, Fuentes

and the Meaning of Postmodernity," *MLN* 109 (March 1994): 265. For a broader exposition of Alonso's argument about Spanish American modernity, see *The Spanish American Regional Novel: Modernity and Authochthony* (New York: Cambridge University Press, 1990), 1–37.

37. Seymour Menton argues that the "primary goal of the novel is . . . to show the disastrous results of a passionate adherence to any ideology, not only in the early nineteenth century but also in the late twentieth century." See *Latin America's New Historical Novel* (Austin: University of Texas Press, 1993), 184.

38. Alonso, "The Mourning After," 265.

39. Carlos Fuentes, "Meditación del poder," *El País* (December 16, 1995): 18.

40. Fuentes, "Meditación del poder," 18.

41. Alonso, "The Mourning After," 260.

Chapter VIII

1. Fuentes, "Hacia el milenio," 9.

2. Carlos Fuentes, *Nuevo tiempo mexicano* 2nd ed. (Mexico City: Aguilar, 1995), 128. Further references will appear in parentheses in the text.

3. Carlos Fuentes, "En medio del desplome, la injuria de los crímenes y la corrupción," *Proceso* (December 11, 1995): 9.

4. Fuentes, "En medio del desplome," 8.

5. Fuentes, "Hacia el milenio," 9.

6. Carlos Fuentes, "Los tres Rushdies," *La Jornada* (January 14, 1996): 12.

Bibliography

Books by Fuentes

Books in Spanish

Los días enmascarados. Mexico City: Los Presentes, 1954.

La región más transparente. Mexico City: Fondo de Cultura Económica, 1958 (2nd ed. 1972).

Las buenas conciencias. Mexico City: Fondo de Cultura Económica, 1959.

Aura. Mexico City: Era, 1962.

La muerte de Artemio Cruz. Mexico City: Fondo de Cultura Económica, 1962.

Cantar de ciegos. Mexico City: Joaquín Mortiz, 1964.

Zona sagrada. Mexico City: Siglo XXI, 1967.

Cambio de piel. Mexico City: Joaquín Mortiz, 1967.

París: La revolución de mayo. Mexico City: Era, 1968.

La nueva novela hispanoamericana. Mexico City: Joaquín Mortiz, 1969.

Cumpleaños. Mexico City: Joaquín Mortiz, 1969.

Casa con dos puertas. Mexico City: Joaquín Mortiz, 1970.

Tiempo mexicano. Mexico City: Joaquín Mortiz, 1971.

Terra Nostra. Barcelona: Seix Barral, 1975.

Cervantes, o la crítica de la lectura. Mexico City: Joaquín Mortiz, 1976.

La cabeza de la hidra. Mexico City: Joaquín Mortiz, 1978.

Una familia lejana. Mexico City: Era, 1980.

Agua quemada. Mexico City: Fondo de Cultura Económica, 1981.

Gringo viejo. Mexico City: Fondo de Cultura Económica, 1985.

Cristóbal Nonato. Mexico City: Fondo de Cultura Económica, 1987.

Constancia y otras novelas para vírgenes. Mexico City: Fondo de Cultura Económica, 1990.

La campaña. Mexico City: Fondo de Cultura Económica, 1990.

Valiente mundo nuevo: Épica, utopía y mito en la novela hispanoamericana. Mexico City: Fondo de Cultura Económica, 1990.

El espejo enterrado. Mexico City: Fondo de Cultura Económica, 1992.

Geografía de la novela. Mexico City: Fondo de Cultura Económica, 1993.

El naranjo o los círculos del tiempo. Mexico City: Alfaguara, 1993.

Tres discursos para dos aldeas. Buenos Aires: Fondo de Cultura Económica, 1993.

Diana, o la cazadora solitaria. Mexico City: Alfaguara, 1994.

La frontera de cristal. Mexico City: Alfaguara, 1995.
Nuevo tiempo mexicano. Mexico City: Aguilar, 1995.

Books in English

Where the Air Is Clear. Trans. Sam Hileman. New York: Farrar, Straus & Giroux, 1989.
The Good Conscience. Trans. Sam Hileman. New York: Farrar, Straus & Giroux, 1961.
Aura. Trans. Lysander Kemp. New York: Farrar, Straus & Giroux, 1968.
The Death of Artemio Cruz. Trans. Alfred MacAdam. New York: Farrar, Straus & Giroux, 1991.
A Change of Skin. Trans. Sam Hileman. London: Jonathan Cape, 1968.
Terra Nostra. Trans. Margaret Sayers Peden. New York: Farrar, Straus & Giroux, 1976.
The Hydra Head. Trans. Margaret Sayers Peden. New York: Farrar, Straus & Giroux, 1978.
Burnt Water. Trans. Margaret Sayers Peden. New York: Farrar, Straus & Giroux, 1980.
Distant Relations. Trans. Margaret Sayers Peden. New York: Farrar, Straus & Giroux, 1982.
The Old Gringo. Trans. Margaret Sayers Peden. New York: Farrar, Straus & Giroux, 1985.
Myself With Others. New York: Farrar, Straus & Giroux, 1988.
Christopher Unborn. Trans. Alfred MacAdam and Carlos Fuentes. New York: Farrar, Straus & Giroux, 1989.
Constancia and Other Stories for Virgins. Trans. Thomas Christensen. New York: Farrar, Straus & Giroux, 1990.
The Campaign. Trans. Alfred MacAdam. New York: Farrar, Straus & Giroux, 1991.
The Buried Mirror: Reflections on Spain and the New World. Boston: Houghton Mifflin, 1992.
The Orange Tree. Trans. Alfred MacAdam. New York: Farrar, Straus & Giroux, 1994.
Diana: The Goddess Who Hunts Alone. Trans. Alfred MacAdam. New York: Farrar, Straus & Giroux, 1995.

Other Works by Fuentes

"La autopsia del existencialismo." *Hoy* (December 24, 1949): 29–30.
Entries under the heading "Talón de Aquiles." *Revista Mexicana de Literatura* 1–12 (September–October 1955—July–August 1957).

"América Latina y EEUU: Notas para un panorama." *Universidad de México* 13 (March 1959): 11–15.

"Notas de un novelista: la revolución cubana." *Novedades* (February 2, 1959): 5.

"Las horas de Cuba." In "México en la Cultura." Supplement of *Novedades* (August 9, 1959): 3, 11.

"EEUU: Notas para un análisis." *Ciencias políticas y sociales* 6 (April–June 1960): 251–71.

"Cárdenas en su sitio." *Política* (March 1, 1961): 17.

"La prensa, el PRI y la conferencia latinoamericana." *Política* (March 15, 1961): 12–13.

"La hora de la definición: Con el fascismo o con el pueblo." *Política* (May 1, 1961): 10–11.

"Amos y esclavos." *Política* (March 15, 1961): 20–21.

"Carne y cartón de Stalín." *Política* (November 15, 1961): 16–17.

"Coexistencia o fascismo." *Política* (February 15, 1962): 26–27.

"Latinoamérica: Tierra Nuestra." In "La Cultura en México." Supplement of *Siempre!* (March 28, 1962): ii–iv.

"América Latina surge a la escena." *Siempre!* (April 4, 1962): 28–29, 70.

"El argumento de América Latina: Palabras a los norteamericanos." *Siempre!* (April 25, 1962): 20–23.

"López Mateos, Goulart y la izquierda." *Siempre!* (May 23, 1962): 24–25.

"*El ángel exterminador*: nadie encontrará una respuesta dogmática." In "La Cultura en México." Supplement of *Siempre!* (June 13, 1962): xix.

"¿Qué hará López Mateos con su fuerza?" *Siempre!* (August 1, 1962): 22–23.

"Doctrina Estrada para Perú." *Siempre!* (August 8, 1962): 22–23.

"Nueve años: 1953–1962." In "La Cultura en México." Supplement of *Siempre!* (August 8, 1962): ii–iii.

"De Bandung a Belgrado." *Política* (September 15, 1962): 16–19.

"A.L.M. fija rutas a su sucesor." *Siempre!* (March 13, 1963): 15, 70.

"Tener sólo historia sagrada es vivir fuera de la historia." In "La Cultura en México." Supplement of *Siempre!* (March 30, 1966): ii.

"Vietnam." In "La Cultura en México." Supplement of *Siempre!* (July 6, 1966): i–ii.

"El P.E.N.: Entierro de la guerra fría en la literatura." *Life en español* (August 1, 1966): 54–61.

"Viva Zapata." *The New York Review of Books* (March 13, 1969): 5–6, 8, 10, 12.

"Opciones críticas en el verano de nuestro descontento." *Plural* 11 (August 1972): 3–9.

"México 1972: Los escritores y la política." *Plural* 12 (October 1972): 27–28.

"Los Diez Desafíos que Debe Superar México." *El Sol de México* (December 1, 1975): 1, 14.

"Land of Jekyll and Hyde." *The Nation* (March 22, 1986): 334 ff.

"Hail to the Chief, and Never Mind the Truth." *Los Angeles Times* (August 2, 1987): sec v, p. 2.

"Argentina: A Prayer for Democracy." *Los Angeles Times* (31 May 1987): sec. v, p. 1 ff.

"A New Society Tests Mexico's Old Politics of Unity." *Los Angeles Times* (September 27, 1987): sec. v., p. 2.

"Discurso de Carlos Fuentes en la entrega del Premio Cervantes 1987." In *Carlos Fuentes: Premio de Literatura en Lengua Castellana "Miguel de Cervantes" 1987*, 69–80. Barcelona: Antropos, 1988.

"Prologue." In José Enrique Rodó, *Ariel*, 13–25. Trans. Margaret Sayers Peden. Austin: University of Texas Press, 1988.

"History Out of Chaos." Review of *Revolutionary Mexico: The Coming and Process of the Mexican Revolution*, by John Mason Hart. *The New York Times Book Review* (March 13, 1988): 12–13.

"Uncle Sam Stay Home." *Harper's Magazine* (January 1989): 14–17.

"Las lecciones de Panamá." *El País* (December 24, 1989): 13–14.

"Imaginación y cambio." *El País* (November 23, 1995): 13.

"En medio del desplome, la injuria de los crímenes y la corrupción." *Proceso* (December 11, 1995): 6–9.

"Meditación del poder." *El País* (December 16, 1995): 18.

"Cronología personal." In Julio Ortega, ed., *Retrato de Carlos Fuentes*, 104–15. Barcelona: Círculo de Lectores, 1995.

"Los tres Rushdies." *La Jornada* (January 14, 1996): 12–13.

"Hacia el milenio." In Carlos Fuentes et al., *Los compromisos con la Nación*, 9–37. Mexico City: Plaza & Janés, 1996.

"The Lessons of Latin America." Lecture at Rutgers University, November 7, 1996.

Correspondence with Fernando Benítez and José Donoso, Princeton University Library.

Works on Fuentes

Aguilar Camín, Héctor. "Algo sobre Carlos Fuentes y *La muerte de Artemio Cruz*." In Georgina García Gutiérrez, ed., *Carlos Fuentes: Relectura de su obra: "Los días enmascarados" y "Cantar de ciegos,"* 165–82. Guanajuato: Universidad de Guanajuato, 1995.

Allen, Catherine. "La correlación entre la filosofía de Jean-Paul Sartre y *La muerte de Artemio Cruz* de Carlos Fuentes." In Helmy Giacoman, ed., *Homenaje a Carlos Fuentes*, 399–442. New York: Las Américas, 1971.

Alonso, Carlos. "The Mourning After: García Márquez, Fuentes and the Meaning of Postmodernity." *MLN* 109 (March 1994): 252–67.

Anadón, Jorge. "Entrevista a Carlos Fuentes (1980)." *Revista Iberoamericana* 123–124 (April–September 1983): 621–30.

Baxandall, Lee. "An Interview with Carlos Fuentes." *Studies on the Left* 3, no.1 (1962): 48–56.

Blanco, José Joaquín. "Fuentes: de la pasión por los mitos al polyforum de las mitologías." In *La paja en el ojo*, 243–70. Puebla: Universidad Autónoma de Puebla, 1980.

Blanco Aguinaga, Carlos. "Sobre la idea de la novela en Carlos Fuentes." In *De mitólogos y novelistas*, 73–108. Madrid: Turner, n.d.

Boldy, Steven. "Fathers and Sons in Fuentes' *La muerte de Artemio Cruz*." *Bulletin of Hispanic Studies* 61 (1984): 31–40.

———. "*Cambio de piel*: Literature and Evil." *Bulletin of Hispanic Studies* 66 (1989): 55–72.

———. "Carlos Fuentes." In John King, ed., *On Modern Latin American Fiction*, 155–72. New York: Farrar, Straus & Giroux, 1989.

———. "*Cambio de piel*, de Carlos Fuentes: El poder de la contradicción." *Revista Canadiense de Estudios Hispánicos* 19 (Winter 1995): 401–6.

———. "Family Tradition and the Individual Talent in Carlos Fuentes' *Las buenas conciencias*." *Bulletin of Hispanic Studies* 71 (1994): 359–80.

Boling, Becky. "Parricide and Revolution: Fuentes' 'El día de las madres' and *Gringo viejo*." *Hispanófila* 96 (May 1989): 73–81.

Carballo, Emmanuel. "Carlos Fuentes." In *Diecinueve protagonistas de la literatura mexicana del siglo XX*, 425–48. Mexico City: Empresas Editoriales, 1965.

Castillo, Debra. "Travails with Time: An Interview with Carlos Fuentes." *The Review of Contemporary Fiction* 8, no. 2 (Summer 1988): 153–67.

Conde Ortega, José Francisco, and Arturo Trejo Villafuerte, eds. *Carlos Fuentes: 40 años de escritor*. Mexico City: Universidad Metropolitana Azcapotzalco, 1993.

Dixon, Paul. "Simetría y centralidad en *La muerte de Artemio Cruz*." In Ana María Hernández de López, ed., *La obra de Carlos Fuentes: Una visión múltiple*, 95–104. Madrid: Pliegos, 1990.

Doezema, Herman. "Interview with Carlos Fuentes." *Modern Fiction Studies* 18 (Winter 1972–1973): 491–503.

Faris, Wendy. "*Ulysses* in Mexico: Carlos Fuentes." *Comparative Literature Studies* 19 (1982): 236–53.

————. "The Return of the Past: Chiasmus in the Texts of Carlos Fuentes." *World Literature Today* 57 (Autumn 1983): 578–84.

————. "'Without Sin, and with Pleasure': The Erotic Dimensions of Fuentes' Fiction." *Novel* 20 (Fall 1986): 62–77.

————. "Desire and Power, Love and Revolution: Carlos Fuentes and Milan Kundera." *The Review of Contemporary Fiction* 8, no. 2 (Summer 1988): 273–84.

Fernández Retamar, Roberto. "Carlos Fuentes y la otra novela de la revolución mexicana." *Casa de las Américas* 4 (October–November 1964): 123–28.

Fiddian, Robin. "Carlos Fuentes: *The Death of Artemio Cruz.*" In Philip Swanson, ed., *Landmarks of Modern Latin American Fiction*, 96–117. London: Routledge, 1990.

Fortson, James R. *Perspectivas mexicanas desde París: Un diálogo con Carlos Fuentes.* Mexico City: Corporación Editorial, 1973.

Fouques, Bernard. "El Espacio Órfico de la Novela en *La muerte de Artemio Cruz.*" *Revista iberoamericana* 91 (April–June 1975): 237–48.

Gallagher, David. "Mexico's Stifled Tiger." Review of *A Change of Skin*, by Carlos Fuentes. *The New York Times Book Review* (February 4, 1968): 5, 40–41.

García Cantú, Gastón. "El desafío y la marea." *Plural* 57 (June 1976): 51–53.

García Gutiérrez, Georgina. "Introduction." In Carlos Fuentes, *La región más transparente*, 9–61. Madrid: Cátedra, 1991

————. "Dos libros a conmemorar." In Georgina García Gutierrez, ed., *Carlos Fuentes. Relectura de su obra: "Los días enmascarados" y "Cantar de ciegos,"* 9–32. Guanajuato: Universidad de Guanajuato, 1995.

————, ed. *Carlos Fuentes. Relectura de su obra: "Los días enmascarados" y "Cantar de ciegos."* Guanajuato: Universidad de Guanajuato, 1995.

Giacoman, Helmy, ed. *Homenaje a Carlos Fuentes.* New York: Las Américas, 1971.

Glantz, Margo. "Fantasmas y jardines: Una familia lejana." *Revista iberoamericana* 118–119 (January–June 1982): 397–402.

González Echevarría, Roberto. "*Terra Nostra*: Theory and Practice." In *The Voice of the Masters: Writing and Authority in Modern Latin American Literature*, 86–97. Austin: University of Texas Press, 1985.

————. "Passion's Progress." Review of *The Campaign*, by Carlos Fuentes. *The New York Times Book Review* (October 6, 1991): 3, 24–26.

Gutiérrez, Carl. "Provisional Historicity: Reading through *Terra Nostra.*" *The Review of Contemporary Fiction* 8, no. 2 (Summer 1988): 257–65.

Harss, Luis. "Carlos Fuentes, o la nueva herejía." In *Los Nuestros*, 338–80. Buenos Aires: Sudamericana, 1966.

Ibsen, Kristine. *Author, Text and Reader in the Novels of Carlos Fuentes*. New York: Peter Lang, 1993.

Josephs, Allen. "The End of *Terra Nostra*." *World Literature Today* 57 (Autumn 1983): 563–67.

Kadir, Djelal. "Fuentes and the Profane Sublime." In *The Other Writing: Postcolonial Essays in Latin America's Writing Culture*, 73–110. West Lafayette, Ind.: Purdue University Press, 1993.

Krauze, Enrique. "La comedia mexicana de Carlos Fuentes." *Vuelta* 139 (June 1988): 15–27.

Leal, Luis. "History and Myth in the Narrative of Carlos Fuentes." In Robert Brody and Charles Rossman, eds., *Carlos Fuentes: A Critical View*, 3–17. Austin: University of Texas Press, 1982.

Levitt, Morton P. "Joyce and Fuentes: Not Influence but Aura." *Comparative Literature Studies* 19 (1982): 254–71.

Moody, Michael W. "Existentialism, Mexico and Artemio Cruz." *Romance Notes* 10 (1968): 27–31.

Moreno, Fernando. *Carlos Fuentes. "La mort d'Artemio Cruz": entre le mythe et l'histoire*. Paris: Editions Caribéenes, 1989.

Ordiz, Francisco Javier. *El mito en la obra narrativa de Carlos Fuentes*. León: Universidad de León, 1987.

Ortega, Julio. *Retrato de Carlos Fuentes*. Barcelona: Círculo de Lectores, 1995.

Peden, Margaret Sayers. "A Reader's Guide to *Terra Nostra*." *Review: Latin American Literature and Arts* 31 (January–April 1982): 42–48.

Poniatowska, Elena. "Carlos Fuentes ¡Si tuviera cuatro vidas, cuatro vidas serían para tí!" In *¡Ay vida, no me mereces!*, 3–41. Mexico City: Joaquín Mortiz, 1985.

Rodríguez Carranza, Luz. *Un teatro de la memoria: Análisis de "Terra Nostra" de Carlos Fuentes*. Leuven/Buenos Aires: Leuven University Press/Danilo Albero Vergara, 1990.

Rodríguez Monegal, Emir. "Situación del escritor en América Latina." *Mundo Nuevo* 1 (July 1966): 5–21.

Romano, James V. "Authorial Identity and National Disintegration in Latin America." *Ideologies and Literature* 4 (Spring 1989): 167–98.

Ruiz Basto, Jorge. *De la modernidad y otras creencias (en torno a "Cambio de piel" de Carlos Fuentes)*. Mexico City: UNAM, 1992.

Stoopen, María. *"La muerte de Artemio Cruz." Una novela de denuncia y traición*. Mexico City: UNAM, 1982.

Swietlicki, Catherine. "Doubling, Reincarnation, and Cosmic Order in *Terra Nostra.*" *Hispanófila* 79 (September 1983): 93–104.

Tittler, Jonathan. "*The Death of Artemio Cruz*: Anatomy of a Self." In *Narrative Irony in the Contemporary Spanish-American Novel,* 31–57. Ithaca, N. Y.: Cornell University Press, 1984.

Van Delden, Maarten. "The Banquets of Civilization: The Idea of Ancient Greece in Rodó, Reyes, and Fuentes." *Annals of Scholarship* 7 (1990): 303–21.

———. Review of *The Orange Tree,* by Carlos Fuentes. *Review: Latin American Literature and Arts* 52 (Spring 1996): 100–102.

Vizcaino, Roberto. "El Embajador Flores Olea, Ante JLP: Permanente Intervención Imperialista en América Latina, Para Crear 'una Falange de Dictaduras.'" *Excélsior* (May 15, 1976): 19A.

Weiss, Jason. "Carlos Fuentes." In *Writing at Risk: Interviews in Paris with Uncommon Writers,* 108–24. Iowa City: University of Iowa Press, 1991.

Williams, Raymond Leslie. *The Writings of Carlos Fuentes.* Austin: University of Texas Press, 1996.

Zaid, Gabriel. "Carta a Carlos Fuentes." *Plural* 12 (September 1972): 52–53.

Zamora, Lois Parkinson. "Beyond Apocalypse: Carlos Fuentes' *Terra Nostra.*" In *Writing the Apocalypse: Historical Vision in Contemporary U.S. and Latin American Fiction,* 148–75. New York: Cambridge University Press, 1989.

Other Works Cited

Anderson, Benedict. *Imagined Communities: Reflections on the Origin and Spread of Nationalism.* Rev. ed. New York: Verso, 1991.

Anderson, Perry. "Nation-States and National Identity." Review of Fernand Braudel, *The Identity of France. Vol. II: People and Production. London Review of Books* (May 9, 1991): 3, 5–6.

Anonymous. "¿A qué vino Kennedy?" *Política* (July 1, 1962): n.p.

Bartra, Roger. *La jaula de la melancolía: Identidad y metamorfosis del mexicano.* Mexico City: Grijalbo, 1987.

Blanco Aguinaga, Carlos. "Realidad y estilo de Juan Rulfo." *Revista Mexicana de Literatura* 1 (September–October 1955): 59–86.

Bolívar, Simón. *Escritos políticos.* Ed. Graciela Soriano. Madrid: Alianza, 1990.

Bonfil Batalla, Guillermo. *México profundo: Una civilización negada.* Mexico City: Grijalbo, 1994.

Brading, David. *Los orígenes del nacionalismo mexicano*. 2nd ed. Mexico City: Era, 1988.

————. *The First America: The Spanish Monarchy, Creole Patriots, and the Liberal State, 1492–1867*. New York: Cambridge University Press, 1991.

Brunner, José Joaquín. *América Latina: cultura y modernidad*. Mexico City: Grijalbo, 1992.

Calinescu, Matei. *Five Faces of Modernity*. Durham: Duke University Press, 1987.

Camp, Roderic. *Intellectuals and the State in Twentieth-Century Mexico*. Austin: University of Texas Press, 1985.

Camus, Albert. *L'étranger*. Paris: Gallimard, 1942.

————. *L'homme révolté*. Paris: Gallimard, 1951.

Carballo, Emmanuel. "Me importa madre y otros textos." *Revista Mexicana de Literatura* 4 (March–April 1956): 378–87.

Carpentier, Alejo, et al. "Carta abierta a Pablo Neruda." *Casa de las Américas* 6 (September–October 1966): 131–35.

Chiron, Yves. *La vie de Maurras*. Paris: Perrin, 1991.

Cohn, Norman. *The Pursuit of the Millennium: Revolutionary Millenarians and Mystical Anarchists of the Middle Ages*. New York: Oxford University Press, 1970.

Donoso, José. *Historia personal del 'boom'*. Rev. ed. Buenos Aires: Sudamericana, 1984.

Dos Passos, John. *Manhattan Transfer*. Boston: Houghton Mifflin, 1950.

Eagleton, Terry. "Capitalism, Modernism and Postmodernism." *New Left Review* 152 (1985): 60–72.

Fernández Retamar, Roberto, Lisandro Otero, Edmundo Desnoes, and Ambrosio Fornet. "Sobre la penetración intelectual del imperialismo yanqui en América Latina." *Casa de las Américas* 6 (November–December 1966): 133–39.

Fernández Retamar, Roberto. *Caliban and Other Essays*. Trans. Edward Baker. Minneapolis: University of Minnesota Press, 1989.

Foucault, Michel. *Discipline and Punish: The Birth of the Prison*. Trans. Alan Sheridan. New York: Vintage, 1979.

Franco, Jean. *La Cultura Moderna de América Latina*. Mexico City: Grijalbo, 1983.

————. "Memoria, Narración, y Repetición: La Narrativa Hispanoamericana en la Época de la Cultura de Masas." In David Viñas et al., eds., *Más Allá del Boom: Literatura y Mercado*, 111–29. Mexico City: Marcha, 1981.

Frank, Joseph. "Spatial Form in Modern Literature." In *The Widening Gyre*, 3–62. New Brunswick, N.J.: Rutgers University Press, 1963.

———. "Spatial Form: An Answer to Critics." *Critical Inquiry* 4 (1977): 231–52.

———. "Spatial Form: Some Further Reflections." *Critical Inquiry* 5 (1978): 275–90.

Freud, Sigmund. "Contributions to the Psychology of Love. A Special Type of Object Choice Made by Men." Trans. Joan Riviere. *Collected Papers* 4: 192–202. New York: Basic Books, 1959.

Gide, André. *Les caves du Vatican*. Paris: Gallimard, 1922.

Girard, René. *Deceit, Desire, and the Novel: Self and Other in Literary Structure*. Trans. Yvonne Freccero. Baltimore: Johns Hopkins University Press, 1965.

———. *Violence and the Sacred*. Trans. Patrick Gregory. Baltimore: Johns Hopkins University Press, 1977.

González, Aníbal. *Journalism and the Development of Spanish American Narrative*. New York: Cambridge University Press, 1993.

González Echevarría, Roberto. *Alejo Carpentier: The Pilgrim at Home*. Austin: University of Texas Press, 1990.

Greenfeld, Liah. *Nationalism: Five Roads to Modernity*. Cambridge, Mass.: Harvard University Press, 1992.

Gutiérrez Girardot, Rafael. "Notas sobre la imagen de América en Alfonso Reyes." *Revista Mexicana de Literatura* 2 (November–December 1955): 112–21.

Hobsbawm, Eric. *Nations and Nationalism Since 1780: Programme, Myth, Reality*. New York: Cambridge University Press, 1990.

Hobsbawm, Eric, and Terence Ranger, eds. *The Invention of Tradition*. New York: Cambridge University Press, 1983.

Hopenhayn, Martín. "Postmodernism and Neoliberalism in Latin America." *boundary 2* 20, no. 3 (1993): 93–109.

Hutcheon, Linda. *A Poetics of Postmodernism: History, Theory, Fiction*. New York: Routledge, 1988.

Jameson, Frederic. *Postmodernism, or, The Cultural Logic of Late Capitalism*. Durham, N.C.: Duke University Press, 1993.

Joyce, James. *Ulysses*. New York: Random House, 1986.

Judt, Tony. *Past Imperfect: French Intellectuals, 1944–1956*. Berkeley: University of California Press, 1992.

Kadir, Djelal. *Questing Fictions: Latin America's Family Romance*. Minneapolis: University of Minnesota Press, 1986.

Kermode, Frank. "A Reply to Joseph Frank." *Critical Inquiry* 4 (1978): 579–88.

Köhler, Joachim. *Zarathustras Geheimnis: Friedrich Nietzsche und seine verschlüsselte Botschaft*. Nördlingen: Greno, 1989.

Lechner, Norbert. "A Disenchantment Called Postmodernism." *boundary 2* 20, no. 3 (1993): 122–39.

Lempérière, Annick. *Intellectuels, état et société au Mexique: Les clercs de la nation, 1910–1968*. Paris: L'Harmattan, 1992.

Lowry, Malcolm. *Under the Volcano*. New York: Penguin, 1971.

Lukács, Georg. *The Theory of the Novel*. Trans. Anna Bostock. Cambridge, Mass.: MIT Press, 1971.

Lynch, John. *The Spanish American Revolutions, 1808–1826*. 2nd ed. New York: Norton, 1986.

Lyotard, Jean-François. *The Postmodern Condition: A Report on Knowledge*. Minneapolis: University of Minnesota Press, 1984.

Maravall, José Antonio. *Las comunidades de Castilla: Una primera revolución moderna*. 2nd ed. Madrid: Revista de Occidente, 1970.

Mariátegui, José Carlos. *Siete ensayos de interpretación de la realidad peruana*. Mexico City: Era, 1988.

Marquès-Rivière, Jean. *Histoire des Doctrines Esotériques*. Paris: Payot, 1971.

Martí, José. "Nuestra América." In *Sus mejores páginas*, ed. Raimundo Lazo, 89–93. Mexico City: Porrúa, 1988.

Martin, Gerald. *Journeys Through the Labyrinth: Latin American Fiction in the Twentieth Century*. London: Verso, 1989.

McHale, Brian. *Postmodernist Fiction*. New York: Methuen, 1987.

McLuhan, Marshall. *The Gutenberg Galaxy*. Toronto: University of Toronto Press, 1962.

———. *Understanding Media*. New York: McGraw-Hill, 1965.

———. *The Medium is the Massage*. New York: Bantam, 1967.

Menton, Seymour. *Latin America's New Historical Novel*. Austin: University of Texas Press, 1993.

Milton, Sybil, ed. *The Stroop Report: The Jewish Quarter of Warsaw is No More!* New York: Pantheon, 1979.

Mitchell, W. J. T. "Spatial Form in Literature: Toward a General Theory." *Critical Inquiry* 6 (1980): 539–67.

Nerval, Gérard de. *Les chimères*. Paris: José Corti, 1942.

Paz, Octavio. *El laberinto de la soledad*. Ed. Enrico Mario Santí. Madrid: Cátedra, 1993.

———. *Itinerario*. Mexico City: Fondo de Cultura Económica, 1993.

———. *Los hijos del limo: Del romanticismo a la vanguardia*. 3rd. ed. Barcelona: Seix Barral, 1987.

———. *Tiempo nublado*. Barcelona: Seix Barral, 1986.

———. *Collected Poems of Octavio Paz, 1957–1987*. Ed. and trans. Eliot Weinberger. New York: New Directions, 1987.

———. *El ogro filantrópico: Historia y política 1971–1978.* Mexico City: Joaquín Mortiz, 1979.

———. *El arco y la lira.* 3rd ed. Mexico City: Fondo de Cultura Económica, 1972.

———. *Posdata.* Mexico City: Siglo XXI, 1970.

———. *Corriente Alterna.* Mexico City: Siglo XXI, 1967.

Pendle, George. *A History of Latin America.* New York: Penguin, 1973.

Portilla, Jorge. "Crítica de la crítica." *Revista Mexicana de Literatura* 1 (September–October 1955): 48–58.

Quirk, Robert E. *Fidel Castro.* New York: Norton, 1993.

Ramos, Samuel. *Perfil del hombre y la cultura en México.* Mexico City: SEP, 1987.

Riding, Alan. *Distant Neighbors: A Portrait of the Mexicans.* New York: Vintage, 1985.

Ross, Andrew. *No Respect: Intellectuals and Popular Culture.* New York: Routledge, 1989.

Ruy Sánchez, Alberto. *Una introducción a Octavio Paz.* Mexico City: Joaquín Mortiz, 1990.

Sarmiento, Domingo F. *Facundo. Civilización y barbarie.* Ed. Roberto Yahni. Madrid: Cátedra, 1990.

Sartre, Jean-Paul. *La nausée.* Paris: Gallimard, 1938.

———. *L'être et le néant.* Paris: Gallimard, 1943.

———. "A propos de *La bruit et la fureur.* La temporalité chez Faulkner." In *Situations, I,* 70–81. Paris: Gallimard, 1947.

———. "Explication de *L'étranger.*" In *Situations, I,* 99–121. Paris: Gallimard, 1947.

———. "La liberté cartésienne." In *Situations, I,* 314–35. Paris: Gallimard, 1947.

———. "Gide vivant." In *Situations, IV,* 85–89. Paris: Gallimard, 1964.

———. *L'existentialisme est un humanisme.* Paris: Nagel, 1966.

Schwarz, Roberto. *Misplaced Ideas: Essays on Brazilian Culture.* Ed. John Gledson. London: Verso, 1992.

Sefchovich, Sara. *México: país de ideas, país de novelas: Una sociología de la literatura mexicana.* Mexico City: Grijalbo, 1987.

Smitten, Jeffrey R., and Ann Daghistany, eds. *Spatial Form in Narrative.* Ithaca, N.Y.: Cornell University Press, 1981.

Sommer, Doris. "Irresistible Romance: the Foundational Fictions of Latin America." In Homi K. Bhabha, ed., *Nation and Narration,* 71–98. London: Routledge, 1990.

————. *Foundational Fictions: The National Romances of Latin America*. Berkeley: University of California Press, 1991.

Sontag, Susan. *Against Interpretation*. New York: Dell, 1966.

Stabb, Martin. *América Latina en busca de una identidad: Modelos del ensayo ideológico hispanoamericano 1890–1960*. Caracas: Monte Ávila, 1969.

Sutton, Michael. *Nationalism, Positivism and Catholicism: The Politics of Charles Maurras, 1890–1914*. Cambridge: Cambridge University Press, 1982.

Thomas, Hugh. *Cuba: The Pursuit of Freedom*. New York: Harper and Row, 1971.

Torgovnick, Marianna. *Gone Primitive: Savage Intellects, Modern Lives*. Chicago: University of Chicago Press, 1990.

Torres Bodet, Jaime. "Sobre la responsabilidad del escritor." *Revista Mexicana de Literatura* 5 (May–June 1956): 518–20.

Vandromme, Pol. *Maurras: entre le légiste et le contestataire*. Paris: Téqui, 1991.

Waugh, Patricia. *Metafiction: The Theory and Practice of Self-Conscious Fiction*. London: Methuen, 1984.

Weyembergh, Maurice. *Charles Maurras et la Révolution française*. Paris: J. Vrin, 1992.

Whitaker, Arthur P., ed. *Latin America and the Enlightenment*. 2nd ed. Ithaca, N.Y.: Cornell University Press, 1961.

Williams, Raymond Leslie. "Truth Claims, Postmodernism, and the Latin American Novel." *Profession* 92 (1992): 6–9.

Yúdice, George. "Intellectuals and Civil Society." *Annals of Scholarship* 11 (1996): 157–74.

Index

MAARTEN VAN DELDEN is associate professor of
Latin American Literature at Rice University.